BLISS IN TRIPLE RHYTHM— A TOOLBOX FOR POETS

BLISS IN TRIPLE RHYTHM— A TOOLBOX FOR POETS: NINE WAYS TO SHAPE A WORD SONG

Shown in 291 Original Poems

by Martin Bidney

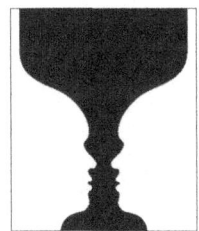

Dialogic
Poetry
Press

Copyright © 2018 by Martin Bidney
Dialogic Poetry Press
Vestal, New York

All Rights Reserved

ISBN 13: 978–1987402568
ISBN 10: 1987402561

Printed in the United States of America

Available from Amazon at
http://www.amazon.com/dp/1987402561

Contents

Prefatory Poem: Four Amphibrachic Word Songs	21
Introduction	**25**
I Amphibrach	27
II Anapest	30
III Dactyl	35
Triple and Duple Meters Combined	38
IV Third Asclepiadic	38
V Fourth Asclepiadic	43
VI Stichic Strophes: Fifth Asclepiadic and Hendecasyllabic	47
VII Alcaic	56
VIII Sapphic, Lesser and Greater	62
IX Experimental Rhythms with Duplets and Triplets	67
PART ONE: Three Kinds of Triple Rhythms	**77**
I Amphibrach	77
1. Weather Retort	78
2. Hail, Holy Light	79

3. Within	80
4. The Jinns Are Winning	81
5. March, April, May	82
6. Ludus Tonalis	83
7. Twin Within	84
8. Explanatory Amphibrachs	85
9. March (An Imperative)	87
10. Infinities	88
11. Nameless	89
12. Instruction	90
13. Solace Will Call Us	91
14. Zabur	92
15. A Thank-you on Awaking	93
16. Sticktoitiveness and Stiffneckitude	94
17. Freedom of Threedom	95
18. Sermonette	96
19. Gentleman-in-Waiting	97
20. Conjuror	98
21. Opening Adore	99
22. Morning Paper	100
23. Anchorite? Not Quite Right	101
24. Bliss of Triplicity	102
25. Prolegomenon	103
26. On a Phrase of Larry Lockridge	104
27. Spent years of my youth reading Pushkin and Goethe	105
28. But why include wording in Russian and German?	106

29. Peccate Audaciter	*107*
30. His Burden is Lite	*108*
31. Hymn of Thanksgiving	*109*
32. Insistent the world in besieging, besetting	*110*
33. When Shakespeare and I wrote our sonnets for pleasure	*112*
34. Inconclusion	*113*
35. So Plato was right when he claimed that the poet could not	*114*
36. Amphibrachic Reply to Annie Finch	*115*
37. Song for Paul Jordan	*116*
38. Song for Johanna Masters	*117*
39. Birthday Limericks for Larissa Shmailo	*118*
40. Lecture on the Limerick	*119*
41. Limericks for Richard	*121*
42. Lives of the Poets	*122*
43. An Upbeat, Three Triplets, and Ringingly	*123*
II Anapest	*125*
44. Lim(b)ericks	*126*
45. James Joyce	*129*
46. Invitation to the Dance	*130*
47. Three Lermontovian Seekers	*131*
48. Pharaoh Accepts Allah	*132*
49. Asiyah Accepts Allah	*133*
50. Asiya Welcomes Moses	*134*
51. Midnight Hymn	*135*
52. Reading Miles Tittle on William Morris	*136*
53. Reading Helsinger on Hegel	*137*

54. A Thought from Lao-Tse — *138*
55. A Stray Bird from Tagore — *139*
56. Wave — *140*
57. Hippo — *141*
58. Beard — *142*
59. Cor Ma(t)ris — *143*
60. Haydn's De Angustiis *and Fauré's* Requiem — *144*
61. Life in Color — *145*
62. Indef(l)ectible — *146*
63. Staying Power — *147*
64. Thanksgiving Wreath — *148*
65. I Sing, Therefore I Am — *149*
66. Song on a Saying — *150*
67. Chant — *151*
68. Style — *152*
69. Torch and Bucket — *153*
70. The Cats of Istanbul — *154*
71. Preoccupied Mind — *156*
72. An Apostle Epistle — *157*
73. I'm beginning to write, and again as before — *158*
74. Should the time and the clime and sky be exciting — *159*
75. I've with pleasure described the contentment of cats — *160*
76. Deep the breath you inhale while you're waiting for thought — *161*
77. Excerpt from "To Saul Levin, a Letter in Sonnets" — *163*
78. Glossolaliology — *164*

III Dactyl   165

- 79. Why should we write in the form of dactylic Ovidian distich?   *166*
- 80. Rhymes or blank verse for my couplet? Well, no one will offer an answer   *167*
- 81. Being two people at once may lend energy perfect requital   *168*
- 82. Long have I wanted to see in the mind as a painting the prophet   *170*
- 83. Parable of the Squirrel   *172*
- 84. Why do religions live on? In the brain we've an organ for oneness   *174*
- 85. Seeking a melody fittingly handsome I need to be hearsome   *175*
- 86. Cold makes the birds a bit quieter: why should my words follow after?   *176*
- 87. Here's how the hours of the therapy went. Though the dream would be altered   *177*
- 88. Nature Preserve   *179*
- 89. Helpful Counsel: Versifying a Letter from Anni Johnson   *180*
- 90. Colors of the Day: Versifying a Letter from Anni Johnson   *181*
- 91. Watching Anni Make a Table Centerpiece   *183*
- 92. Sonnet of Classical Distichs for Louise Fairfax   *185*
- 93. Making Jeff's Party the Epic It Is   *187*
- 94. Newsletter to Friends   *188*
- 95. Homage to Bach   *190*

96. Andrei Guruianu's "Text Page Three" Versified with Reply	191
97. Video-Sonnet	192
98. Letter to Johanna Masters	193
99. Letter to Johann Wolfgang von Goethe	194
100. A Sunflower	196
101. A Month in Germany	197
102. A Thought for Singers of Handel	201
103. Summoned for Jury Duty	203
104. "Maggie Brown's Favorite": Irish Folk Jig Sonnet	204
105. Mem'ry engendering music machine!	205
PART TWO: Triple and Duple Meters Combined	**207**
IV Third Asclepiadic	207
106. Praise the gift of the hymn, found ere the seeker try	208
107. Kept the sugar count low— favor bestowed a sigh	209
108. "Here's a lyric event, Thursday, it's four to five"	210
109. What? My lines aren't profound? Well, they're at least pro-funned	211
110. Take a look at the sky. Light that we view in stars	212
111. Lunch today with a friend. Topics would greatly range	213
112. Blest, I'm seventy-four. Cup runneth over, Lord	214
113. Venevitinov wrote, He whom the deities	215

114. *Raise the shell to your ear. Why's there
    an ocean tone?*   *216*
115. *Twofold elegy sent, lately, a friend to me*   *217*
116. *Loud the bird in the height, crying!
    A strength intense*   *218*
117. *Not a mystery why ancient asclepiads*   *219*
118. *Lo! arose in the land one whom the
    surf-rush trees*   *220*
119. *Move me, lunary height, orrery for a bard*   *221*
120. *What is meant by a crown? Simple,
    enwreathing leaves*   *222*
121. *Three-year classical ode colloquy I review*   *223*
122. *Morning portrait: a cat, placed for the
    painter-brush*   *224*
123. *Color patches and then delicate brush
    you need*   *225*
124. *Gone the wrongful rebuke, damning
    Narcissal doom*   *226*
125. *Once had hymns to a boy told of a thing
    to be*   *227*
126. *Keep the rhythm in mind. That is the key
    to life*   *228*
127. *"Make the phrase like a fish, gliding, with
    central swell"*   *229*
128. *Breathe what meter you will, body's
    attentive grown*   *230*
129. *Drinking coffee today, pondering themes,
    I heard*   *231*
130. *Mind won't stop, and the view, bright,
    on the saver screen*   *232*

131. Gabrieli's "Jubilate Deo": Metric Modulation	233
V Fourth Asclepiadic	235
132. Be reborn in the random shell	236
133. There's a gospel, a marvel, called	237
134. Harbor harvest the Lord had lent	239
135. Comes the cardinal: threes and fours	241
136. Weather Theater comes to us	242
137. Who's my teacher of olden tunes?	243
138. You of life can a bible write	244
139. Here is one of the finer things	245
140. Biggest underground tomb in Greece	246
141. Holy mage of the healing arts	247
142. Bony snout, and with hollow rings	248
143. Keep it simple, the bird outside	249
144. Waked at last from the longest dream	250
145. Rilke, heading for Venice where	251
146. You've survived from the ancient time	252
147. Meter, mood, even pitch compete	253
148. Shaman-named is a showman known	255
149. Finish packing and then relax	256
150. Boldly sang my Berlin-spring friend	257
151. "Speak to me of the sculptured ILM"	258
152. "Don't grow up—it's a trap!" A sign	259
153. When he goes on a pray'r retreat	260
154. Endless time of a night deprived	261
155. Three I laud, of Qur'anic fame	262
156. "Unicorn" she would "rather be"?	263
157. Tones arise when the man arrives	264
158. New York/Pennsylvania Disaster	265

159. Bluish mauve in the sky tonight	266
160. Ancient Snake Worship	267
VI Stichic Strophes: Fifth Asclepiadic and Hendecasyllabic	269
161. Strength and vigor we love: thus when we look, charmed, at a waterfall	270
162. Hi there! Learning to use metrical forms history left behind?	272
163. Truth I've newly acquired: this I would like, here, to impart to you	274
164. Breathing in, we can feel mouth-tongue-and-throat cooled by the evening air	276
165. Goddess entered the room, baby asleep, silent the night and calm	278
166. Please, don't ask—'tis a thing wretched to know, either for me or you	280
167. Cruel weapons, I fear, Venus can wield, so you will soon find out	282
168. Don't be planting a tree, Varus I pray, soft in the Tibur ground	284
169. Fifth asclepiad themes—adding them up helps me to comprehend	286
170. Swift Wind of Welcome	288
171. February	289
172. Plato and the Flute-Girl	290
173. Listen, Lesbia, let us live in loving	291
174. Young, who bothers to read obituaries?	292
175. Who, I wonder, would like this new-made booklet?	293
176. While Septimius held his lover Acme	294

177. You, of Romulus' line most gifted speaker 296
178. Triple miracle rose for me awoken 297
179. Dining well is a guarantee, Fabellus 298
180. Paradox from the game of life emerges 299
181. If Mary Had Borne Twins 300
182. "The Poet Nothing Affirmeth" 302
183. Hendecasyllabic Sonnet on a Ted Kooser Poetry Workshop, with Dodecasyllabic Response 3/22/06 303
184. While the boughs of the arching willow tower 305
185. What bad mind, little Ravidus the Wretched 306
186. Ah, Licinius—what a day! what pleasure! 307
187. Done with shopping, and heading for the exit 309
188. How in heart of my heart I want to wander! 310

VII Alcaic 311
189. Al-Jábir worked in front of his home one day 312
190. The lady pastor told me she'd liked my talk 313
191. Consider what a motherly heart can do 314
192. My friend was paid a fee to contribute help 315
193. My friend likes giving flowery compliments 316
194. I have to say, my Fat Little Wireless Book 317
195. A movie should be made of the varied styles 318
196. Conduct while looking down and around you now 319
197. A virtuoso lives in the twofold rule 320
198. If we the plan of Rilke would here fulfil 321
199. Third Symphony: if no one had told of war 322

200. Concerto—string quartet with orchestral friend	323
201. Four Telemann cantatas— I felt an ease	324
202. Max Reger—solo cello, a triple suite	325
203. Works two and thirty Henry the Eighth composed	326
204. In every bagatelle of the Bartók set	327
205. In 3 + 3 + 2 we've a way to change	328
206. A silent white, as here on the page I face	329
207. Yes, "man was ever hasty": the sermon-quote	330
208. What's therapeutic? Therapon had in Greek	331
209. The nineteen-nine concerto for cello proves	332
210. I'm fourteen years of age and today I face	334
211. With "Alles jauchzet, lacht" I arise to write	336
212. A gray and drippy morning of early June	338
213. King Solomon's great Canticle I revive	340
214. Roused by Rossi	341
215. Proofreading Plus	343
216. Scorpion Venom	344
VIII Sapphic, Lesser and Greater	345
217. Buxtehude's Passion you well might call it	346
218. In Mendelssohn's Elijah we find (scene five—	348
219. Schütz the Little Sacred Concertos tranquil	350
220. I, melodic memories lauding nightly	351
221. Rare is the greater sapphic	352
222. What would happen, Chanter, if pen attempted	353

223. Moses, David's son had they named him.
(Angel — 354
224. Songs you hear are not like the ones
you sing — 355
225. Bach has brought (Sinfonia 9, F Minor) — 356
226. Eighth of the odes of Horace — 357
227. Béla Bartók, double delight revealing — 358
228. Unexpected bird in the breath-held dusk — 359
229. How to vanquish claims of the vast
and many — 361
230. Hear my lyric lines for the long-haired Ella — 363
231. Friend Chagall, be blest, for the Dead Man's
living — 364
232. Elegy for Margaux Fragoso — 366
233. Simple, real—the joy of a second childhood — 367
234. June concludes—my mood is attuned,
letitial — 369
235. Glorious cat, you're brindled — 370
236. Thoughts on Things Greek — 371
237. Vegetarian Values — 372
238. Sapphic Rewrite of Christine's Anni Poem — 373
239. The Standout — 374
240. Sapphic Sonnet — 375
241. Choral works of Schütz and of Gabrieli — 376
242. "The Coming Storm" — 378

IX Experimental Rhythms with Duplets
and Triplets — 379

243. Barbaric Yawp: A Dactyl-Compromise — 380
244. Étude on a Phrase by Avideh Shashaani — 381
245. Choriambic Sonnet: Ruskin — 382

246. Triplets Triply Considered	383
247. Trochee Begins and Lends a Triplet-Twist	384
248. My head is awhirl with competing demands	386
249. A marvelous poet I'm copying here	387
250. Invigorate, breeze—while we bathe in the air	388
251. The poets who either by chance or by fate	389
252. Since no one had thought of a Trumpery win	390
253. Adam and Eve would snatch a fruit	391
254. Building on Scriptural Rhythms	392
255. My sleeping-waking cycle disarranged	393
256. The influence, the inflow, penetrated slowly	394
257. Getting a Haircut	396
258. Daring, Will You Dance with Me Awhile?	397
259. The Nature of the Sonnet	398
260. Encountering Horace	399
261. Spoken by a Matriot	400
262. Overheard	401
263. Tremendum	402
264. Blowing your nose, more of the cough, what a routine!	403
265. Half Asleep, and Later Answered	404
266. Latter-Day Cinderella; or, Do You Myth Me?	406
267. Portrait of a Lady	408
268. Passport	410
269. Jinx	412
270. Idyll	414
271. Two Attractions	416

272. Today I Am a Man   418
273. Holiday   420
274. Train Whistle   422
275. Fairy Tale Mood   424
276. Getting Ready to Fight   426
277. Reply to Kind Acknowledgments   427
278. Rolando's Diner   428
279. Detroit Airport   429
280. Two Sonnets   430
281. Sonnet in a Meter of George Herbert   432
282. On Reading a Memoir Essay
     by Andrei Guruianu   433
283. Minuet of the Will-o'-the-Wisps   434
284. Why Did I Laugh?   435
285. Introduction to Poetry   436
286. Thoughts on "A Mystical Ballad"
     by James Russell Lowell   437
287. A New Song Rhythm   439
288. First Wind of Morning   440
289. Sonnet in Alternating Iambic Threes and
     Fours with a Few Initial Trochees for Triplet
     Effect   442
290. Drunk on Lilac   443
291. Scribal Error?   444

Appendix A: Trisyllable Poems by Mikhail Lermontov 445
    (1) Angel   445
    (2) Desire   446
    (3) Mermaid   447

Appendix B: Three Poems Written Between First
and Second Proofs   449
   (1) A Valentine   *449*
   (2) Reply to a Friend   *450*
   (3) Anapestic Improvisation   *451*

Prefatory Poem: Four Amphibrachic Word Songs

(1)

Thanksgiving—November—the chill twenty-second—
    And here is a cardinal perched on a place
For stopping and thinking and resting. He reckoned,
    Considering best how the season to face.

And now comes a doe! In the time I've been writing
    She, wanting some breakfast, had pensively wandered.
The blossoms are dry, but the ground looks inviting ...
    The cardinal, watching, had quietly pondered.

Enough is the wetness of leaves that are falling,
    The doe is content—she'll remain for a snack.
The bird felt that destiny elsewhere was calling
    And left and is probably not coming back.

I know he was liking the branches that, bouncy,
    Had rocked while he thought. He appeared a bit fat:
He's big, and his redness intense, and with jouncy

    Resolve he'd keep shifting from where he had
       sat.

At eight in the morning the time was long gone for
       The summons prophetic of dawn to be rising.
More faint was the chirping: he'd have to move on, for
       The warming gave hints of a wider devising.

He offered enough, though, of morningtime bird song
       To power me up for some lines of my own.
A preface they'll be for the banquet of word song
       I plan for the reader. We're never alone.

(2)

Two bundles of ardor in fieriest hue
Had stopped on a twig to enkindle the view,
Add warmth to the mind with their fluffied-up flame,
And teach me: "Though silent, we're speaking to
    you!"

Black netting on snow in the place where they came,
Wand, twig, trunk and bough in a niveous frame—
The color's all gone from the black-and-white still.
Yet cardinals, parted, are here, all the same.

You creatures are emblems; you've taught the tired
    will:
"Re-energied, blood with your goal-motion fill!
We've travelers all, through the worldscape who fly:
From heart overbrimming our hymns overspill.

Who space overtraipse in the favoring sky,
Surveying the places in quiet that lie,

Can frame, for survival, imaginings true:
Explore what's before, and your neume-life renew."

(3)

Beginning with springtime activity, squirrel,
    You're comical, plump, as when seeking a seed
Or bud of a leftover leaf, no demurral
    You take till you find what you think you
        might need.

The flexible twigs where you search won't support
  your
    Lithe body for long, so you twist and you leap
To gain a sure footing. 'Tis humor, not torture—
    Your rubbery form an apt balance will keep.

You sniff at a willow-root: provender hiding?
    Minutely observing, uncovering sticks,
You spy little bugs, tiny grass-blades abiding:
    Aromas attention are helping to fix.

Your gray-and-brown fur with the rootage is blended;
    You scamper with sculptural tail-wave, then
        stand.
As if you suspected I'm there, long-extended
    The time you are moveless—then—motion
        command!

(4)

The spirit each curious creature will see,
Observing *e pluribus* features that he

Will graciously favor as they in their Station
Of Being achieved may occasion elation.

As I on a rabbit or squirrel might gaze
Or bird, though hibernal, discern in the haze,
Espy will his eye a perceptible trembling,
A quiver of thrill in a feather resembling.

He knows how the blood speeding up will prepare,
Expectant, the fingers to soar through the air
And light on the keyboard as bird on a twig,
A squirrel on rock, or a rabbit on sprig.

The hands on the letters refreshment will seek
Renewing the strength I'm surrendering meek.
The digits are leaping, excited about
Thought sleeping they'll seek and require to come
    out.

The spirit-nepheliad, smiling with pleasure,
Delighted abides for he science will treasure:
The cells, hundred billion, in writerly brain
A ganglion ardor will spryly attain.

The feet are astir of the creature he's viewing,
The music-allure all the body enduing
With gratitude, avid, for that which today
Kind Nature had granted in labor-and-play.

Introduction

This book of word songs in unexpected melodic patterns will surprise you by its equally unusual liveliness. I'm so eager to begin singing for you that, as you noticed, I've already written a prefatory poem in one of the varied kinds of triple rhythm units I'll be illustrating (*la LA la; weak STRONG weak; one TWO three; x/x*). The strangest thing I'll be doing in my collection is to bring about a resurrection of *ancient* stanza patterns embodying the musical structures I love. The uncustomary triple-rhythm stanza forms richly displayed will acquire a real if unlikely novelty by presenting tools so extremely old. Treasured discoveries by the Greeks and Romans (though briefly and brilliantly revived in Germany during the age of Goethe [1749–1832] and Hölderlin [1770–1843]) have so long lain dead and buried in most writers' mentalities that the verse forms will laugh and shout hallelujah when I re-awake them. The result will be an illustrated creative writing course for today's poets, featuring guidelines not readily available elsewhere. I offer you a book of renewable tools.

What are "triple rhythms" in "word songs"? They are verse forms involving three-syllable structure units helping to create in a poem a rhythmic verbal song in any mood, on any topic. I'll show you three forms that each highlight one of the syllable-units. These triple-syllable "feet" or rhythm-building tools, though slighted for centuries in English literature, can still be heard today—but, for the most part, only in limited realms of writing.

Sadly, as the titanic gods and spirits of classical myth were shrunk into little fairies and elves or kobolds and gnomes, so the arousing three-syllable feet so popular and standard for the Greeks and Romans are mainly available today only in nursery rhymes and lyrics for children. It's easy to show examples. (1) The *anapest*, made up of two weak syllables followed by a strong one (one two THREE, one two THREE), is remembered from "'Twas the NIGHT before CHRISTmas, when ALL through the HOUSE. ..." (2) The *dactyl*, which consists of one strong syllable followed by two weak ones (ONE two three, ONE two three) appears in a poem from Robert Louis Stevenson's *A Child's Garden of Verses*: "HOW do you LIKE go UP in a SWING, / UP in the AIR so BLUE? / OH, I do THINK it the PLEASantest THING / E-ver a CHILD can DO!" (3) And the *amphibrach* (used in my prefatory poem), a strong syllable flanked by two weak ones (one TWO three, one TWO three) may take us to Dr. Seuss' *The Cat in the Hat*: "I SAT there with SAL-ly. / We SAT there, we TWO."

Did it have to happen—the confinement of these three triple-syllable feet mainly to childhood rhymes and reading primers or bedtime stories in English-language poetry? Not by any means. In poems 39–40 I pay tribute to three gloriously memorable trisyllabic-foot poems by Russian poet Mikhail Lermontov (1814–1841), who in "Angel," "Desire," and "Raven" (see "Appendix A" below) taught me to love what I'm now calling "bliss in triple rhythm."

In Part One I'll be showing the three elementary forms I've mentioned: the amphibrach (la-LA-la), the anapest (la-la-LA), and the dactyl (LA-la-la). I'll offer examples of each. The main thing to be noticed is the flair, the swing and verve, that every lyrical excerpt conveys. These rhythms are *fun to write!* Later you'll see the variety of themes, moods, anecdotes, narratives, and reflections that a three-syllable foot structure will enable you to present. If you read each of the sections straight through, you'll be powered forward by the rhythm-will through a changing thematic landscape—as when traveling in a car or a rapid train or on horseback. Rhythms with a three-syllable foot-structure inherently bear the speed of their own self-powering. The beat-scheme itself acts as a mantra to stimulate awareness of your own latent song-drive.

I Amphibrach

The first poem in the section ushers in the mood and main focus. And the first four-liner, or quatrain stanza, ties in with what I did while teaching literature for 35 years, often concentrating on the legacy of the Romantic poets (late 18th and early 19th centuries):

1. Weather Retort

amphibrachic tetrameter
x/x x/x x/x x/x
x/x x/x x/x x/x
   x/x x/x x/x x/
   x/x x/x x/x x/

Snowed in by the drift of the outer environs,
My spirit I lift with a vigor like Byron's
   Who, pacing the shoreline, the wrinkles marine
   Called free of all aging in glory pristine.

I go for a walk, and the passage comes to mind where Lord Byron tells the ocean: "Time writes no wrinkle on thine azure brow: / Such as Creation's dawn beheld, thou rollest now" (*Childe Harold,* canto IV, stanza 182). Unlike people who worry about wrinkled skin and aging, the sea is ever-wrinkled yet a fountain of youth. That's the keynote of my own "weather retort," or brisk reply to anybody's weather report:

The river of time in your mind that is flowing,
Compliant, will feel that your spirit, bestowing
    The tempo, direction, and speed of the piece,
    Can grant from dull slowing a freedom-release.

Byron's energetic sea-surge gets the time-river going more rapidly as you read. Who's in charge here, after all? A speedy music-making tempo gives you control of the horse-reins and spur, or sets in motion the train, the auto, the boat, even the airplane of your mind. Your mental time is a friendly rival to the example of physical time:

I'll cover more space and more time in a minute
Should life to a triumph pay tribute within it
    And generate luck where no lack will be known
    If glory outpoured to the heaven be shown.

The responsive glory, the emotional energy and force outpoured in the heart-mind, again rivaling the precedent and example of the physical world, turns lack to luck while speeding up space-time for you.

Philosophy, Helmsman, you aid in preparing
The ventures that Poetry soon will be daring
    When thought of the snow long ago is forgot
    By sailor who bravely an odyssey wrought.

"Philosophy the helmsman of life" translates the Greek *Philosophia bioi kybernetes,* often abbreviated Phi Beta Kappa. The meaning could also be rendered "Love of wisdom [is] the steering-guide of life." The wisdom I'm trying to inculcate, in myself and anyone who con-verses with me, is the feeling-thought that rhythm in word song generates the speed-power to get the creative mind going. The "snow long ago" refers to the question raised by François Villon in his *"Ballade des dames du temps jadis"* ("Ballad of Ladies of Time Past"): *"Mais où sont les neiges d'antan?"* ("But where are the snows of yesteryear?"). I suggest that if you travel amphibrachically with me, you likely won't be troubled by such a question. Homer's Odysseus, my final line suggests, looked forward not backward; and we in our verse are even such mariners as he, or as Homer.

By the time we get to poem 20, I'll let my imagination wander as I create a fictional forebear-poet, a kabbalist conjurer with the Holy Names, who summons up a creature from the deep, fiery-bearded like himself, and flees from it in terror. Mental journeys are assuredly not without hazards, or I wouldn't need so write so many amphibrachic pep talks. The setbacks and obstacles can prove daunting, and in poem 9 I urge myself to keep steady the sense of a task both obligatory and worthy to perform:

The cold that's invading my home in the morning
Will generate motion, both warming and warning
    That ere we prepare for our narrowing home
    Far more must we pilgrims in caravan roam.

But the journeys of the versing wanderer can at times, like vacation trips, be refreshingly relaxing as well. So in the latter verses of section one, I offer sample verse letters I've actually sent as e-mails to friends over the years. It even struck me one day that the charm of most *limericks* resides in their amphibrachic rhythm!—so you get some of these, too. Even the lightest of light verse requires an artisanal, craftsmanlike mind.

II Anapest

That the anapest (la la LA) will rival the amphibrach in propulsive power may be suggested by the fact that just now, preparing myself with some coffee refreshment, while sitting in my rocker I heard the lines come to me:

In the aureorutilant dawn I arise
   To in-draw the fresh hue of the skies…

Right away, I'd been granted the gift I would need to write this next part of my preface. Three themes are presented in the fragment, all of them central to my offering of anapests. To explain them briefly will let me tell better my anapestic tale. The three themes are wit, color, and deep breathing.

Wit is a bridge-word connecting humor to power of invention. Poetry doesn't have to be profound—it's okay to be pro-funned, as I hope my limericks will have shown. Jocular poems 44, "Lim(b)ericks" and 45, "Joyce," are transitional pieces, leading into the section by demonstrating that a limerick may just as well have an anapestic as an amphibrachic structure. When I write "He a rational animal ain't" the humor, as we so often find, comes from incongruity—here, that of combining Aristotle's definition of the human creature with the goofy colloquial rhyme (for the biographic material in the poem, see *Joyce's* Ulysses: *The Most Dangerous Book* [2014] by Kevin Birmingham).

Word songs are music, and music itself is pro-funned (see poem 109), as I claim in the following lyric, which made a something of a hit on facebook with choristers and choir directors:

29. *Peccate Audaciter*

Peccate audaciter—that is the moral
The teacher wrote down. I've no reason to quarrel.
    "Sin boldly," I feared, mightn't quite be allowed
    But learned it meant "Sightreaders need to *sing
    loud!*"

How fitting: 'tis pointless to fear that an error
Will shame you, for music is joy and not terror.
    The ruler we name Evolution said, "Fun
    Will lengthen your life till your journey is done."

I truly believe it, dear reader: you see it
In all of my lines. Are they flawed? Well, so be it.
    They're fun to indite; let no censor indict
    My singing if something's not perfectly right.

I'm even so brave as to take the position
We're instruments, each, of a single Musician.
    Whoever's in charge of conducting the score
    Will power us now when our songs we outpour.

Music is pure pleasure: the "sin" of boldness in exuberant song is actually a deep faith in the goodness of the source it issued from.

    In my fragment above, the fun word "aureorutilant" might make the reader smile because the unexpected Latinate word for gold-red is incongruous with the simpler words around it—though here, as in the Joyce example, the odd word is carefully placed for craftsmanlike assonance, or vowel harmony. Artisanal shrewdness, though, can readily move from whimsical jest to a more pensive depth of inventive power. Metaphor itself, nearly as central to poetical effect as word song melody, results from exploratory resource. Poem 69, "Torch and Bucket," offers, in the story of the Sufi Islamic saint Rabi'a (who died in the year 801), a humorous invention to dramatize one of the most penetrating insights in the history of religion. She carries a bucket of water to quench hell and a torch to burn down heaven, so people will worship God for His sake alone, not for postmortal prizes:

When I prayed to be spared from the flaming of hell,
    Fires had seared me—I feel how they fell.
When I asked to gain heaven through sanctified grace
    I could see the door slam in my face.

The literalization of metaphor is the witty incongruity that makes you smile or laugh. And the propulsive strength of the anapestic meter may help the innovative opinion "memorize itself" in the reader's mind.
    "Aureorutilant" opens the way, also, to the theme of color, which gains prominence in this section to complement the foreground of tone. So in poem 46 you'll find

In the dawn or the twilight the colors will blend
    On the wavelets that shoreward extend,
And you'll love as you listen the pow'r of the tides
    Where the heartbeat, a-pounding, abides.

In another poem the theme of humor or laughter complements both color and tone:

51. Midnight Hymn

Though I haven't a theme, I am gladdened to start:
    Why did smiling arise in the heart?
There's a laughter inside me that wants to proclaim:
    Praise the Being that no one can name!

It has given my body an alchemy rare,
    That the element solar, most fair,
Which the morning awakes may transform what I write
    Into semblance of heaven's own light.

What is gold? The aurora, the aura, the or
    That with gules of the dawning our lore
Of the heroes of legend adorning is found:
    Red and yellow, on azurine ground.

In my spirit the primary colors are prime:
    O inspirers of rhythm and rhyme,
I will lift up my hands for the lauding of you—
    Sing at midnight, remanned, Hallelu!

Here's a fuller exposition of the color theme:

61. Life in Color

We can chant what we fancy. Our nature, in brief,
    Is to test hypothetic belief.
While we're singing a thing that we feel, it is true:
    Rain on leaves for a greening of blue.

You, in potency mainly, are All at the start,
    And when nourished, a flourishing heart
Will abound in the beauty of hymning the skies
    If you're treelike allowed to arise.

We the red in the warmth of the morning, crepusc-
    ular pink in the dawn or the dusk,
Raise from yellow and orange to white during noon:
    Gleaming blinds but the green is a boon.

Blue turns indigo, violet. Finally black
    The Unmanifest holds. Taken back,
With our odyssey done for the day we comply,
    Blessed breath to our Lover re-sigh.

I'm so reluctant to leave the spectrum motif that you'll find it still further elaborated in poem 265, "Half Asleep, and Later Answered."

    The third theme highlighted in the section on the anapest is deep breathing, which you find already in the poem just quoted. When we "re-sigh" our "blessed breath" to our "Lover," we are envisioned as replying, responding, to the breath that—in the mystical Sufi teaching of Ibn Arabi—created the world. God, according to this account, sighed out in lonely melancholy His longing for beings He might love; and the creative breath of that sigh, the imaginative yearning of the Divine Lover, imagined the beloved—the universe—into creation. My book often alludes to this theme, and in poem 76 I bring it into propinquity with the second section's opening motif of wit or humor, as the happiness of deep breathing leads me to laughter:

Deep the breath you inhale while you're waiting for
   thought:
    By no compass within is it caught.
It the palate will heighten—and brighten the eyes:
    Widened lungs will avail in their sighs.

Height will generate breadth, while the depth can beguile
    And the face may awaken to smile.
I'm beginning to laugh at the effort required
    To depict how I simply respired.

Wit, power of invention, humor, incongruity, laughter—all are related in mind, life, and writing. There's a childlike delight in the propulsive rhythms and often unpredictable rhymes awaked by the anapestic meter, which might have brought it into suspicion among poets of a more saturnine character. The fact is, music itself makes me laugh with happiness. At symphony concerts I always want to laugh when the music ends in triumph, though when I do so, I have at times feared to startle my neighbors in the audience. Singing Handel's *Messiah* last month, I controlled the temptation.

III Dactyl

The two things that appeal to me most about the dactyl (LA la la) are its vigor and conversational ease. Six beat (hexameter) dactylic lines were available for every purpose in the ancient world, and I would gladly make them so today. You can either write straight dactyls (the standard mode for epic in Greece and Rome), or you can write a modified lyrical variety organized in couplets—immensely popular in both these classical cultures—called elegiac or Ovidian distichs. Here's a standard dactyl: ONE and a, TWO and a, THREE and a, FOUR and a, FIVE and a, SIX and. The usual ancient dactylic line had a missing final syllable or catalexis, so we may call it a dactylic hexameter catalectic.

The modified dactylic form widely employed, i.e., the Ovidian distich, looks like this:

ONE and a, TWO and a, THREE and a, FOUR and a, FIVE and a, SIX and,
ONE and a, TWO and a, THREE   FOUR and a, FIVE, and a, SIX.

The two missing syllables in the middle of every second couplet-line give you a pleasant breathing space and pleasantly vary the music.

Dactylic lines of either the standard or modified type are perhaps the most vigorously animated of all the tri-syllabic metric forms. To me, the "ONE-and-a TWO-and-a" rhythm suggests, even more strongly than the amphibrach or anapest, the sound of a galloping or cantering horse. In poem 104 I use dactyls (without catalexes) to convey the dizzying rhythm of an Irish jig I love to play on fiddle, "Maggie Brown's Favorite": it is the fastest moving lyric I ever wrote. But even when more casual and relaxed, dactylic verse will promote lively-tempo'd narrative. Today's Americans will find it perfect for a Christmas or New Year's Newsletter, as I hope to have proved in my ambitiously newsy 12–stanza chronicle "101. A Month in Germany."

The conversational ease of the dactylic line and the Ovidian (dactylic) distich is truly remarkable. It makes the straight dactyl an ideal vehicle for pedagogical lyric writing, as in Vergil's *Bucolics* or *Eclogues,* telling how to lead a good life as a rustic shepherd; in his *Georgics,* where he explains how to run a farm; or in Lucretius' Roman speculative atomic theory textbook in the form of an epic poem (*De Rerum Natura,* or *On the Nature of Things*). In poem 80 I note other ancient writers who used the ever-popular dactylic meters.

If you want a feeling of youthful activity in your lyric writing, nothing is more uninhibited and chattier than the Ovidian distich. It will move you forward rapidly, so to speak, in your writing career. ("Chat" is an appealing verb, which the French have now borrowed: today I got an e-mail about some people allegedly waiting to "*tchatter"* with me.) Because it moves with agility and without fuss, the distich is perfect for long descriptions of the kind we often encounter in novels. In poem 91 I enthusiastically show in careful, colorful detail how a friend constructed a centerpiece for a Thanksgiving dinner party. Poem "94. Newsletter to Friends" tells how I was invited to teach

English for a month at a desert settlement in Egypt (one of the great adventures of my life). In poem "103. Summoned for Jury Duty" I offer a distichal memoir of a morning in city court.

Dialogue is the theme of my writing life, and nowhere is it easier to undertake with pleasure than in writing the Ovidian distich. In Poem "81. Being two people at once may lend energy perfect requital," I write:

Dialogue, then, for good planning's a help. But your psyche-division
 Also at times will occur quite independent of plan.
Being trans-ported, trace-lated in ecstasy means that a scission
 Comes: you are split, you are two. Truly "beside yourself."
 Man!
That's what the Greeks called ec-static! A *standing apart*! What precision!
 How to attain such a bliss? Here's how the rhapsodist can:

After completing a hymn that is bursting with lyrical feeling,
 Do something else for awhile. Later, returning, you'll see
Something occur that may stun you and leave you quite weak-kneed and reeling:
 How could this marvel have been written by someone like me?
Prostrate yourself to the gods, who their love for you, blest, are revealing:
 Rise! and with fire-word go forth, people by heart-warmth to free.

You'll notice here an additional kind of dialogue—the intimate response of the lines to each other, in rhyming. Ovidian distichs are rarely if ever rhymed, partly because the form stems from the ancient Greeks and Romans, none of whom ever rhymed anything. But why not be the first? I discuss the question in a couple of places, justifying rhyme in "53. Reading Helsinger on Hegel" and asking readers to comment on the value of rhymed dactyls in "80. Rhymes or blank verse for my couplet? No one will offer an answer." My own answer is, Do what you think best: do whatever you feel the moment and context demand.

One final note on chatty, conversational dialogue in dactylic writing. Not only do I blend the modern innovation of rhyme with the classic verse pattern, I end my demonstration of the alliance with yet another dialogic surprise. The italicized final line (see above) paraphrases closely the last couplet of "The Prophet" by Alexander Pushkin.

Triple and Duple Meters Combined

IV Third Asclepiadic

I don't know why the tri-syllable foot declined in the history of English verse; but equally sad, if not sadder, is the disappearance from our tradition of the highly appealing stanza forms where three-syllable units are combined in predictable patterns with those of two syllables. The ingenuity of these forms will delight and astonish the musical ear. They're as canorous as can be.

Before offering quick previews of the 6 kinds of composite forms I'll be focusing on in this collection, let me state the most important point to be made about them. The practical range of each—as of the three-syllable feet: amphibrach, anapest, dactyl—is vast, and it is capable of conveying all sorts of moods on every kind of topic. When I offer brief samples from the 6 categories, I'll be suggesting not only the variety of the rhythm patterns but the diverse applications of each. This book is a toolbox. It offers a total of 9 tool types, and with each of them you can do wonders.

Let's look at the first poem I offer where two- and three-syllable units are combined in a special way, repeated in every stanza. This kind of poem is called a "third asclepiadic" (the Greek Asklepias was a deity of healing):

106. Praise the gift of the hymn, found ere the seeker try

Here's the rhythm pattern. A slash is a STRONG syllable, an x is a weak one:

third asclepiadic
/x /x x/ - /x x/ x/
/x /x x/ - /x x/ x/
      x /x x/x
/x /x x/ x/.

Or you can say it out loud like this

ONE and, TWO and a, THREE—FOUR and a, FIVE and, SIX
ONE and, TWO and a, THREE—FOUR and a, FIVE and, SIX
        ONE and, TWO and a, THREE and,
        ONE and, TWO and a, THREE and, FOUR.

And, finally, you can print the opening stanza like this to help you hear the bracketed triplets, which I've marked with dashes connecting the words in each thee-syllable unit:

PRAISE the [GIFT-of-the] HYMN, [FOUND-ere-the] SEEKer
  TRY.
LAUD the [VIS-it-ant] VIM [GRANT-ed-to] LIFTed HANDS:
              MAKing [STRONG-er-the] WEAKer,
           RAISing [SONG-ful-the] SOUL from BANDS.

Now you're ready to read the whole poem aloud:

Praise the gift of the hymn, found ere the seeker try.
Laud the visitant vim, granted to lifted hands:
                  Making stronger the weaker,
            Raising songful the soul from bands.

Thank the chill for the brisk wind that we glad inhale.
Green let speak of the life dewy renewed in eye:
                  We're the oil-lamp Aladdin,
            Rug on runway to climb the sky.

Mars departed with March, comes Aphrodite near,
Rhododactyl the hand, henna'd the heaven rose:
                  Passion-grandeur, the mighty,
            Waked, unslaken, the chanter chose.

    Stanza one depicts the energy that fills the worshiper as a "visitant," something come from another, maybe preternatural, realm or level of being. In stanza two we're ready to step onto Aladdin's magic carpet for the next flight. In stanza three the ancient gods join our festivity. Mars the war god gave his name to the month of March: both god and month are departing. "April" comes from a variant of the name "Aphrodite," goddess of love and passion: these now enter the scene. Also hailing us while we rise will be the goddess of dawn, "rhododactyl" or "rosy-fingered," maybe with ornamental ruddy henna rubbed onto her palm as women in some Eastern cultures traditionally love to do.
    I've introduced into this opening poem an innovative feature: patterned rhyming. Notice how, in stanza one, "seeker" rhymes with "weaker"; in stanza two, "glad in-" rhymes with "Aladdin"; in stanza three, "Aphrodite" rhymes with "mighty." The ancients who invented and used the third asclepiadic didn't include this added adornment, which I hope you favor: I thought it might add to the charm of reciting. I rhyme in such a way a number of times in our section on this gracious and amenable word song form: poems 107–114 and 117–121 all contain the rhyme pattern.

In poem 117 I'm still enjoying the rhyme-breakthrough while contemplating with pleasure the vitality of the Hellenic achievement:

Not a mystery why ancient asclepiads,
Gliding tranquilly by, smoothly attain a pace
        Neither frantic nor sleepy—
    Smile-beguiling the human face:

First lines offer a way, metered, to show how thought
Sings a rhythm to fit pausing, or sudden run.
        Then, displaying the know-how
    Gained, relax: what we dared is done.

Fiery-wise were the Greeks, brave as a tribe could be.
Epic battle they'd chant, then lend a statue rest.
        What from them we imbibe would
    Ever better our very best.

What religion to choose? Hey, should I *be a Greek?*
Who such meter could make merits devotion true.
        What a splendid idea!
    Grecian tune I'll intone for you!

But I also want to emphasize how endlessly adaptable the ancient form is to whatever question—modern, or perennial—we wish to explore. In poem 111, as I'm lunching with a friend, we tackle the provocative topic of human immortality:

Lunch today with a friend. Topics would greatly range:
Life, and death, and the rest. Never a moment dull.
        Even livelier lately:
    More and better the themes to mull.

"I, at age eighty-three, hope there's an after-state,"
Charlie said. "I have just barely begun to learn."
        "Well," replying with laughter,
    I replied, "to the monkeys turn

Your attention: the ape, chimp, and gorilla must
Die—our simian tribe all to the dust are brought.
        Why suppose we fulfill a
    Stranger fate? A peculiar thought!

Gene-wise nearly a chimp, we're from the end exempt?
Why so lucky? I ask. You in a trap are caught!"
        "Country club! The agenda:
    Some are welcome, and others not."

Hah! This could be an anecdote from a TV or online comedy hour, don't you think? All we're adding are sundry pleasures for the mental and physical ear.

    Nor is whimsy lacking in poem 125, but I add to it the ambience of a fairy tale. Though a number of poems in this fourth part of the book (122–124) show a continuing interest in effects of painting and visual pleasure, this lyric returns to music, my greatest love:

Once had hymns to a boy told of a thing to be:
Every morning before dawn could illume the grass
        Magic tones unbeholden
    Would from heavenly creatures come.

They would sing him awake, phrasing in varied form
Chanting liquid and blue, fresher than cool of brook—
        Hid, unwearied musicians,
    Bearing news of a life to rise.

Dazzled then had he laughed, clapping the hands, oh
    loud!

"Sleeping Beauty" and "Snow White" never gave to him
 Anything to resemble
What would even the priest amaze.

V Fourth Asclepiadic

Let's ease our way into this lyric form with a poem featuring a relaxing, yet haunting refrain:

132. Be reborn in the random shell

Here's the rhythm pattern we'll be hearing throughout part five, again with a slash for a STRONG syllable and an x for a weak one:

fourth asclepiadic
 /x /x x/ x/
/x /x x/ - /x x/ x/
 /x /x x/ x/
/x /x x/ - /x x/ x/.

Said out loud, you'll hear this:

 ONE and, TWO and a, THREE and, FOUR
ONE and, TWO and a, THREE—FOUR and a, FIVE and, SIX
 ONE and, TWO and a, THREE and, FOUR
ONE and, TWO and a, THREE—FOUR and a, FIVE and, SIX.

Reciting now the words, you can see the tri-syllable groups in brackets:

 BE re- [BORN-in-the] RAN-dom SHELL,
WHERE the [TONE-that-you] HEAR—[ECH-oes-the] O-cean FLOOD—
 NOT re [CALLED-from-a] SOURCE-a FAR,
RATH-er HID-from-the EYE—[FLOW-from-the] BLOOD-in EAR.

Now we're set to recite the whole lyric:

> Be reborn in the random shell,
> Where the tone that you hear echoes the ocean flood
> > Not recalled from a source afar—
> Rather, hid from the eye, flow of the blood in ear.
>
> Be reborn in the random shell.
> Love the rush of the red, now till the end of days,
> > Favored tohu va-bohu tone
> Godly, momently gift, lent when the soul awoke.
>
> Be reborn in the random shell.
> Cosmic troubadour told, mission to follow vowed,
> > Servant pure of the streams within,
> Chant the tides of the moon, ruling the deep and high.
>
> Be reborn in the random shell.
> Be a tune to the folk, held to the ear of each,
> > Setting, merry, the heart astir,
> Filled with heavenly peace, lulled as the charméd wave.

The appeal of the refrain, the repeated opening stanza-line, is not only musical but intellectual and imaginative: How exactly can I be "reborn in the random shell"? Stanza one has startled most people I've shown this poem to. Your parents, or other grownups, probably told you early on that in a seashell you can hear the sound of the ocean. On a literal, factual level that is quite wrong. Researching the acoustics of the shell-experience I learned that what you hear is the *vastly amplified sound of the blood-flow in your own ear.* One of the epiphanic moments of my life, the feeling of that discovery will be treated again, with the ocean-flow of the hendecasyllabic (eleven-syllable line) in poem 164.

So now, in stanza two, I can offer a new meaning to the line "Be reborn in the random shell." You become mentally reborn, renewed, refreshed, when you shed the alleged literalism of the childhood myth and enjoy instead the scientific reality. But in losing a literal interpretation (you're not hearing the ocean that the shell had come from), you're gaining a metaphorical one that's far more exciting: the *ocean is with you, it's the flow of your blood.* In an encyclopedia I saw the structure of a shell acoustically diagrammed, showing the complex paths taken by the sound-bringing air waves when amplified: the confrontation of ear and shell is an elaborate happening from the engineering standpoint. And what a favor it confers—to hear the sound of your own circulating blood, the lovable "rush of the red," available till the "end of days"—of your own life, or of earth and its oceans. "Tohu va-bohu" is the Hebrew phrase in the Book of Genesis that means "null and void," referring to the chaos that was before the Creation. My point, though, is that chaos is *part of the living flow of a creation that is alive*; all cosmic creation is alive in being filled with risk and random chance in dialogue with temporarily perfected form. From that standpoint, chaos is part of the "godly" gift of creation as Genesis imagined it, a "momently" gift, meaning one given every moment (as "daily" means "every day"). And this gift was not only "lent when the soul awoke," when humans were first created in the scriptural account, but also "lent" (meaning "given" or "granted") when your own spirit awoke to life—the combined life of untamed force and perfected form.

In stanza three I suggested that if you want to be a world-aware and musical poet ("cosmic troubadour") who can foster for yourself and others a reverence (as "mission"-guided "servant pure") of the currents or "streams" of blood-flow "within," you might start by heralding, in hymn and psalm, the *mood, ruled by the tides* as we are by our tidal breathing. The lunar tides are my favored emblem of the lines of measured poetry, with a flow that's free but shaped, predictable in rhythm while liberated in meaning.

In the conclusion offered by stanza four I suggest that if your poetry becomes the song of the inner ocean that is the glory of your own blood-flow amplified in lyrics both written and sung, you'll be a seashell that both sets the blood astir and grants a deep and lasting peace, akin to the God-anchored serene tranquillity praised by John Milton when in "Hymn on the Morning of Christ's Nativity" he writes, "And birds of calm sat brooding on the charmèd wave."

Poem 133, immediately following, makes use of traditions from Christian apocrypha, Gnostic gospels, and Qur'anic narrative: the legend that Jesus molded a bird of clay and then breathed on it, making it live, belongs to both a Christian apocryphon and a sura (chapter, canto) of the Qur'an. But the saying, "Be reborn in the soul, people, and Beauty serve," the final line, is my own contribution. I like to think of poets as carrying on the tradition of ancient prophets, though always with the awareness that as servants of Beauty they can posit in imaginative lyrics a god or gods both imagined and imagining. That's what poem 134 proclaims. In poem 139 I suggest that you can write the extended parable of your own irreplaceable life by creating a bible, temple, symphony, or mural.

You'll recognize, in section five, adornments or supplementary features I've employed before: rhyming in poem 135 to embody birdsong, humor in the ending stanza of 136 to pay tribute to my late father's generous wit and caring nature. Poem 137 tells of my rediscoveries of ancient lyric forms: the free flow of the monologue shows how readily anything at all may be adapted to what might have seemed a resistant metric shape (granted, craft takes practice). After a series of fourth asclepiadics on wide-ranging topics, in rhyming poem 146 I suggest the form might become for you, borrowing the sobriquet attached to Arthur of the Round Table, a "once and future king," resurrected from ancient times to a new life. In more relaxed tone, I use 147 to reminisce about performing a taped violin-and-fiddle recital for the reunion of my high school graduating class; and then—once more in a loftier flight—poem 148 suggests that a poem in a meter like ours in section five resembles the drumming of a shaman or intermediary with the gods, a prophet-priest-poet whose ritual drum becomes a horse that, gallant chevalier, he rides while he "writes," composing in hoofbeat rhythm the epic narrative in verse of his own combat with evil spirits and of their eventual defeat, which he acts out for the hearers in an astonishing experience of group therapy.

A varied but unified group are shaped by poems 149–156, all concerned with aspects of the ten-day trip I took to Berlin in May–June 2017 to see Shahid Alam's exhibition of calligraphic paintings combining themes from all three of the Abrahamic religions: Judaism, Christianity, Islam. I lectured in German at the St. Thomas Lutheran Church on the topic of Jews and Christians in the Qur'an. In this lyric sequence you can hear my "diary entries" on the exhilarating journey. In poem 157 I'm feeling so refreshed that morning coffee becomes my mystical Sufi ardor-wine—before, in 158, I return earthward to contemplate the sadder phenomenon of unrestrained global warming. I partly recover in poem 160 to celebrate the remembered discovery of an extremely ancient monument to snake worship.

VI Stichic Strophes:
Fifth Asclepiadic and Hendecasyllabic

In section six, I offer something at once familiar and unheard of. This group of lyrics are all in "stichic strophes," meaning stanzas where all the lines have the same patterning of strong and weak syllables. The stanza (or "strophe") pattern is the same as the pattern of each individual verse line (Greek *stich*). Poems where all the lines have the same rhythm pattern are familiar to every reader of the sonnets of Shakespeare, in which every line-paradigm is iambic pentameter: x/ x/ x/ x/ x/. What's unheard of, in more modern writing, is to have a pattern that gives our ear the feeling of alternating two- and three-syllable rhythm units.

Part six will feature two of these types of stichic strophes: the fifth asclepiadic (16 syllables) and the hendecasyllabic (11 syllables). I'll demonstrate these in turn: because of their unchanging nature in each individual poem, each stichic strophe pattern is easy to get used to and enjoy. And to *write*—they are really fun to write.

165. Goddess entered the room, baby asleep, silent the night and calm

fifth asclepiadic
/x /x x/ /x x/ /x x/ x/
/x /x x/ /x x/ /x x/ x/
/x /x x/ /x x/ /x x/ x/
/x /x x/ /x x/ /x x/ x/

We start hearing the three-syllable units the line contains when we read aloud—four times over—the following:

ONE-and, TWO-and-a, THREE—FOUR-and-a FIVE—
   SIX-and-a SEV'N-and EIGHT

Now we can hear the bracketed three-syllable units when reciting the poem—same rhythm pattern in every line:

GOD-dess [EN-tered-the] ROOM, [BA-by-a-] SLEEP, [SI-
   lent-the] NIGHT-and CALM,
GIFT-se- [RENE-to-be-] STOW, [PRE-cious-to] HAVE,
   [YET-with-a] STRANGE-de- LAY.

FIN-ger [DIPPED-in-the] RARE [HON-ey-they] TASTE [ON-ly-who] NE-ver DIE,
SHE-the [LIPS-of-the] BABE [TOUCHED-and-a] CHARM [UT-tered-that] NONE-could HEAR.

Here's the whole poem 165 for reading aloud:

Goddess entered the room, baby asleep, silent the night and calm,
Gift serene to bestow, precious to have, yet with a strange delay.
Finger dipped in the rare honey they taste only who never die,
She the lips of the babe touched and a charm uttered that none could hear.

Sixty years would the deed sleep unrevealed, ev'n as the baby slept
Now who, rising refreshed, under the spell, naught of the gift would know.
This lay deep in the heart, even as if, hidden and strange to tell,
It in castle were kept, bolted and locked, guarded by thorn-trees 'round.

Shaken—earth and the sky, so that the man, white-haired and sixty-one,
Touched with lightning collapsed—days in a faint, finally raised alive,
Ears now filled with the tones Deity gave, hearing the Spirit-Name
Saved for coming of age, singing unsealed, free for the world to love.

Here I've begun with an ancient motif: in Antipatros' ode on Pindar a bee brings the great poet honey while he's yet in his cradle sleeping, a gift that will prophesy his later lyric sweetness. To this I've added the fairy tale motif from poem 128 above: the poet-gift remains hidden, as in the Sleeping Beauty tale I referenced in that earlier lyric. This time, the apocalyptically awoken bard is able to reveal the beauty of his lyric gift only after six decades of sleep. I borrow, in the final two lines, the Sufi tradition that when one or another of the 99 Names of God—possibly when personified in an angel or emissary—summons you, you're given to understand this Name as one that you can now embody in your own life-work if the Name attracts you. As it happens, my own life has much of the fairy tale quality of the newly made mythic legend: only after I got carpal tunnel syndrome and had to abstain from violin-playing till cured did I resolve to make music out of words as a substitute for melodic tones—and so discovered my own decades-long hidden god-gift.

In poem 169 I pay tribute to Horace for giving us the world-famous motto "Seize the day!" in a fifth asclepiadic he wrote. Then, in poem 170, another Horatian poem in this gorgeous meter stimulates me to write about Time in two quatrains with internal rhymes:

Some feel time in a stream, mind-soothing dream,
   bearing the soul to sea.
Others think it a storm, menace enorm, summoning
   heart to fight.
Some just call it a clock, fearing to balk, mild in the
   master-sight,
Others, dim with dismay, brush it away, turn to eternity.

Time's my lady of love—rhymes with above—under,
   surrounding, too:
Tidal rhapsody we, avid in spree, shape with a hallelu.
Meter speeding along, we with a song hymn when the
   birds are gone:

Teach the sun to believe, rhythmical heave, bodies the
  words of dawn.

These lines were my most blissful moment of fifth asclepiadic writing, and I owe Horace a huge debt for his entrancing example.

Now we'll look at the second kind of stichic strophe I mentioned, the hendecasyllabic. I've written 18 of these, contrasting with only 9 fifth asclepiadics, and that's probably because they're a bit easier. The syllables are fewer, and the meter is simpler—but I love this mode of writing none the less. Like our other stanza forms with tri-syllable rhythms throughout this book, it can do nearly anything. We'll sample four of the things it loves to convey: (1) compactly summed-up philosophic reflections; (2) a humorous comment on scripture; (3) a wry, urbane moment in ancient Roman conversation, and (4) a bit of lyrical meditative music.

Let's enter the hendecasyllabic scene with a few thoughts on why life is worthwhile:

178. Triple miracle rose for me awoken

hendecasyllabic
/x /x x/x /x /x

Easy to translate this into a language-line we can read aloud—four times over:

ONE-and, TWO-and, a-THREE-and, FOUR-and, FIVE-and.

We're ready to recite rhythmically, noting the three-syllable units in brackets:

TRIP-le [MIR-a-cle] ROSE-for ME-a- WO-ken:
AN-y [THING-in-ex-] IST-ence WHEN-there DID-n't

HAVE-to [BUR-geon-an] OB-ject, PLACE-or PER-son—
MERE-ly [BE-ing's-a] DAI-ly PRES-ent WON-der.

Now the whole poem:

Triple miracle rose for me awoken:
Any thing in existence when there didn't
Have to burgeon an object, place, or person—
Merely being's a daily present wonder.

People walking about a rounded planet,
Each one knowing a world, an earth horizon
Changing momently, sky direction upward—
Second wonder is creaturely awareness.

Members, we, of a boundless pluriversal:
Heaven getting in breath, each heart inhaling
This, and giving it back, in conversation,
Third of wonders will lend, no end, forever.

"Triple miracle" means three things to wonder at. Latin *miraculum* is a "thing of wonder," derived from *mirari,* meaning "to admire or wonder at." The first thing to wonder at is the existence of anything whatever, rather than nothing whatsoever. Why should there be anything at all, rather than absolute nothing? Nobody has figured this out. The second miracle is that we're all walking upright on a rounded planet, and somehow the sky is, practically speaking, "up" for everyone, even though since Isaac Newton the whole idea of "up" and "down" as real things (rather than ways of denoting apparent positional relationships) has been obsolete. Many people are still picturing a "heaven" which is "up," a "hell" which is "down," and an "earth" which is in between, a world-view left over from the fairy tales of childhood, a thought-pattern which is put into a separate brain-compartment locked for safekeeping when we enter physics or astronomy class at college. The third thing to be wondered at is breathing, our ability to take in sky and breathe it back out through our earth(l)y bodies, thus relating our micro-existence to the surrounding Boundless.

Next I'd like to sample the use of hendecasyllabic singing for a humorous thought on scripture:

181. If Mary Had Borne Twins

Matt. 5:29. "And if thy right eye offend thee, pluck it out, and cast it from thee: for it is profitable for thee that one of thy members should perish, and not that thy whole body should be cast into hell. 30. And if thy right hand offend thee, cut it off, and cast it from thee: for it is profitable to thee that one of thy members should perish, and not that thy whole body should be cast into hell."
18:8. "Wherefore, if thy hand or thy foot offend thee, cut them off and cast them from thee: it is better for thee to enter into life halt or maimed, rather than having two hands or two feet to be cast into everlasting fire. 9. And if thine eye offend thee, pluck it out, and cast it from thee: it is better for thee to enter life with one eye, rather than having two eyes to be cast into hell fire."
Mark 9:47. "And if thine eye offend thee, pluck it out: it is better for thee to enter into the kingdom of God with one eye, than having two eyes to be cast into hell fire...."

"Listen up! If your eye is getting greedy
Gouge it out! and you'll never have a problem.
Grabby hand? The solution's clear and waiting:
Hack it off! and you buy eternal freedom."

Jesus preached, and his darling sister listened.
He, so fond of Jazoola, hoped to help her.

"Moody? Brother, you tend to get depressive.
Comes the gloom, and you start to sound peculiar.
What you're claiming today is just plain wacko:
You'll be fine when the mental storm is over."

"Ah, Jazoola... You're right! It's true—no kidding:
I should talk to the womenfolk more often...."

Jesus comes off rather well, despite the narrator's wit, for in fact this revered teacher was ready to break well-established non-communication taboos precisely in order to speak with women—both the "respectable" and the scorned—as well as with children, Samaritans, tax collectors, and plenty of other members of excluded groups he thought he might helpfully counsel. For this reason Joseph Priestley, not only the co-discoverer of oxygen but a distinguished Unitarian historian and philosophic thinker, wrote, in an essay (admired by his contemporary Thomas Jefferson) which compared Jesus and Socrates as teachers, that Jesus deserved to be called the superior pedagogue since he would talk with anyone, whereas Socrates spoke almost entirely with young men of the Athenian elite.

The next use of hendecasyllabic writing I'd like to illustrate disclosed to me a series of treats not known before. It turns out that the poet Catullus, master of this kind of stichic strophe, conveys an exceptionally modern sense of complex, urbane, often ironic or satiric awareness; and he likes to cultivate reportorial fidelity in presenting subtle, convincing moments of ancient Roman conversation and personal interchange. I've dialogued with Catullus in poems 173, 175, 176, 177, 179, 185, and 186 and had a great time on each occasion, so it isn't easy to pick one sample. But you'll like this one. It isn't typical insofar as my Catullus dialogue poems usually involve more conversational input from me, while here I speak only two lines. But Catullus in this wry work is so clever you'll want to listen:

176. While Septimius held his lover Acme

Catullus 45

While Septimius held his lover Acme
Close to heart he declared: "If with abandon
I no longer can love, and prove unready
For a constant devotion though our lifetimes,
Then—as often as people perish lonesome
'Mid the Lybian heat, the searing swelter
Felt in India—then will I be going
Bold, undaunted, to meet the green-eyed lion."
Love, approval to show, was sneezing leftward
As it rightward had sneezed before, in answer.

Acme, bending her head in sign of welcome,
Eyes—infatuate—of her lover kissing—
Wine-red lips, a delight for him she favored—
Said, "Septimius, life of mine, so be it.
Servants may we remain of one great master,
Letting grander and keener passion kindle,
Burning soft in the marrow of your dear one."
Love, approval to show, was sneezing rightward
As it leftward had sneezed before, in answer.

Having so with a perfect omen started,
Thus they love and are loved in dulcet union,
Poor Septimius, lucky man, attached to
Acme—Syria, Britain both excelling.
As for Acme, she finds her every pleasure
In Septimius only, her beloved.
Who a happier couple could imagine?
Who a passion conceive, a love more blessèd?

Shall we seek for an answer? 'Tis a challenge...
Here's my double reply: "Good health! Gesundheit!"

Here the commentator has little to do: Catullus effectively holds the stage.

I don't think my final sample will need any clarifying either: just read it aloud and let yourself hear the lyrical music made possible by hendecasyllabic magic:

184. While the boughs of the arching willow tower

While the boughs of the arching willow tower,
Wands bow down to the farther ground of power.
Peace achieving, the tree is contemplating
Hunger, love, and the under-solace waiting.

Rousing fount with a waterfall combining,
Sky unbounded and ground-life unconfining,
Stately plant in palatial quiet captured,
Sculpture-brother of mine has mind enraptured.

Wind awaking to sway the branches riant
Leaves will breeze to demise with ease compliant,
Playful ways of the years of autumn showing:
Quick are we in our coming and our going.

Nature's art that can liberate from stricture
Sighing heart in a film will, tristful, picture.
Soul, inclining and rising, are you crying?
Flying children are dyed in hue undying.

VII Alcaic

From the beginning of my study of ancient lyric forms, the alcaic struck me as containing the most dramatic verve in every strophe: from the first two lines to the last two, the number of beats may diminish but line 3 is a powerful runway to the outburst that delights the ear in the always climactic line 4. The first of my alcaic samples, poem 189, will show this clearly, while adding the supplementary feature I love so much—a bit of anecdotal humor.

Let's begin, as always, with the scansion pattern, the rhythm chart:

alcaic
x/ x/ x/x x/ x/
x/ x/ x/x x/ x/
   x/x /x /x /x
     /x x/x x/x /x

Our speakable version will look like this, with tri-syllabic units bracketed:

and ONE-and, TWO-and, [THREE-and-a], FOUR-and, FIVE
and ONE-and, TWO-and, [THREE-and-a], FOUR-and, FIVE
       and-ONE-and, TWO-and, THREE-and, FOUR-and,
   [ONE-and-a,] [TWO-and-a], THREE-and, FOUR-and

Reciting our opening stanza, we get this:

al-JA-bir WROTE-in [FRONT-of-his] HOME-one DAY
that-IN-a LIT-tle [TOWN-by-the] DES-ert LAY
      when-PAST-him RAN-a HUN-dred CAM-els:
   [THUN-der-ing] [HOOVES-no-re-] STRIC-tion TRAM-mels.

And here, for reciting, is poem 189 (it helps to know that algebra is named for Al-Jábir):

Al-Jábir wrote in front of his home one day
That in a little town by the desert lay
      When past him ran a hundred camels:
   Thundering hooves no restriction trammels.

A rancher then arriving inquired, "Did you
By any chance a herd of my camels view?"
        "I noticed nothing," came the answer,
    "Loving your labor's a task enhancer."

The rancher, wild, replied, "Yet I see the dust
Has covered you! The animals ran, I trust!?"
        Al-Jábir looks: he can't deny it.
    Algebra dwells in a realm of quiet.

Despite the concluding words about calm, there is a visceral arousal in the last-line outburst with its double uprushing triplet. How could Anglo poets ever have forgotten such a vigorous invention? The Berlin exhibition at which I lectured on Jews and Christians in the Qur'an gave rise not only to poems 152–159 above but also to this algebra poem and to alcaics 192–198 and 201–206. It was Shahid Alam, the calligraphic painter and sculptor exhibiting his interfaith art works, who gave me the anecdote of the famed algebraist.

    The musical drama inherent in the meter of the alcaic strophe will doubtless help account for the stimulus that gave rise to so many alcaic poems about music in this collection. Either I simply respond to a given musical work in its context, or else I integrate thoughts about the work into a memoir- or diary-like account of what I was doing while listening. My sample to illustrate the first rubric may surprise you: poem 206 offers notes on the musical output of King Henry VIII.

203. Works two and thirty Henry the Eighth composed

Works thirty-two had Henry the Eighth composed,
Melodious-toned, that might by his life be glozed.
        In faith that merit love obtayneth
    Fate he bewayles when the maid desdayneth.

He'll many tunes devote to the claim of youth
To have its will in honor and cordial truth.
        If head and heart conflict, says Harry,
     Pray to the Lord when you're forced to tarry.

Strong lyric impulse here: when the solo sings,
An obbligato part will adorn the King's:
        She's ivy-like, in love entwining
     Flexible gesture, his own divining.

This *cortegiano,* master of courtly love,
Says Youth Will Rule, though bowing to pow'rs above.
        A church he founded. Morals foundered?
     Music had flowered if royals floundered.

Henry was genuinely talented as vocalist, lutanist, lyricist, and composer of enough works vocal and instrumental to fill a deeply rewarding CD.

    How did I develop as a violinist? Writing about this allowed me to attempt a mini-memoir while offering a few thoughts on a melody genre. The sample alcaic recollection of a musical youth-time can illustrate my second rubric, mixing autobiography with appreciation in poem 210:

I'm fourteen years of age and today I face
A wonder-prospect keeping the blood-beat high:
        Auditioning with Zathureczky,
     Russo-Hungarian music master.

I need to be accepted: with tensile heart
I'm practicing the piece he will want to hear—
        Achievement gauging, plus potential:
     Here is Corelli, with *La Folía.*

Fast-forward sixty years—came a compact disc;
Folías—more!—three centuries' worth of these!

Spain, Portugal, and France—the four-chord
Field is a "ground" for superb "divisions":

A march, lament, or brawl of a *branle*, or jig—
No limit for Marais or Martín y Coll
      With lute and bass or treble viol,
  Crisp castanets and a frenzied feeling.

Jordi Savall explained that *folía* means
Two near-related concepts in Portuguese:
      "Insanity" and "wild amusement"
  Equally suit me, today, recalling

The happiness brought on by the kindly smile
Of one who'd be my mentor and spirit-guide:
      I hear him yet, the Franck sonata
  Playing, his favorite madness-grandeur.

Blending music history with my own musical history allows the special satisfaction of feeling anchored in two kinds of meaningful past. I'll give you one final example of this unusual blending that seems to pay off particularly well when done in mellifluent alcaics. Here's poem 212:

A gray and drippy morning of early June
Would soon be lightened while, in a long massage,
      The muscle fiber tension devils
  Learned they'd be cudgeled away forever.

Returned, I found a treat: the computer screen
Revealed plump berries gathered from Sarah's yard.
      (The time is ripe—for Minnesota.)
  This I would mail to my friends—a present.

Next, brunch (delayed) for one who's forbidden jam:

Ezekiel toast and pesto with pine-nuts mild
        We top with fiery pickled mango,
    Sent to me here from a Hindu village.

My kitchen I with foods of a world away
Can fill: the *saag* or spinach and mustard greens,
        The *dal* of lentils, onion, eggplant—
    Save me the fare of the airplane travel.

The radio's beginning the final part
Of that Tchaikovsky symphony most admired
        By me, who loved it back in high school:
    Only the Fifth had a sudden breakthrough—

A theme in unrelentingly minor mode
Would—silenced—yield to marching in triple time
        That led the mood-swing transformation
    Turning our journey to manic gladness.

Who melancholy knew as a burden learned
That fate is molten down by the newly freed:
        A four-note bang on hammered anvil—
    Beethoven beat!—and the Fifth we answer.

The final four note *boom-boom-boom-BOOM!* which ends Tchaikovsky's Fifth Symphony I take to be an emblematic reply to the theme in that same rhythm which Beethoven made central to the first movement of his own Fifth. Beethoven interpreters have often equated it to Fate, and in the last lines of my poem I hear Tchaikovsky using it to climax a manically cheerful refutation of any pre-ordained, constraining destiny. The affirmation in the poem is sensual and physical as much as philosophic or spiritual since the whole poem interweaves body and mind, even as I find them interwoven in everything I do.

VIII Sapphic, Lesser and Greater

What we usually call simply the "sapphic" stanza form is one of two that are named to honor Sappho, the illustrious female poet by whom, tragically, only a few lyrics have survived. The sapphics popular in ancient Greece and Rome are in a sweetly attractive pattern I deeply love. The longer, "greater sapphic" strophe was evidently threatened with extinction in Rome already in the time of Horace (65 BCE—8 BCE), for only one poem of this kind can be found in his complete collected word songs. Yet that form, too, is attractive. We'll sample each, plus a poem combining the two. It could be said that my attempt to resurrect the "greater" sapphic is a plea to keep this endangered species of poetry alive today.

Our sample of the shorter sapphic form carries over the topic of melodious poems about musical works that was prominent in my alcaics. In poem 217 I study a sequence of brief cantatas by Dietrich Buxtehude, a work not well known but fascinating in the uncustomary use of love-song texts. First, the rhythm chart:

sapphic
/x /x /x x/x /x
/x /x /x x/x /x
/x /x /x x/x /x
 /x x/x

You'll find it pleasing and easy to chant this aloud:

ONE-and, TWO-and, [THREE-and-a], FOUR-and, FIVE-and
ONE-and, TWO-and, [THREE-and-a], FOUR-and, FIVE-and
ONE-and, TWO-and, [THREE-and-a], FOUR-and, FIVE-and
 [ONE-and-a] TWO-and

The flow of the melody in a sapphic will always be smooth because every line contains a triplet, a tri-syllable foot for a streaming, lulling effect:

BUX-te HU-dë's [*PASS-ion-*you] WELL-might CALL-it—
MEM-bra JE-su [*NOS-tri-*the] RIGHT-ful TI-tle:
FEET-knees, HANDS-side, [CHEST-and-the] HEART-and
     FACE-in
                              [SE-ven-can]- TA-tas.

Now we're ready to read aloud the descriptive lyric:

Buxtehudë's *Passion* you well might call it—
Membra Jesu Nostri the rightful title:
Feet, knees, hands, side, chest, and the heart and face in
                              Seven cantatas,

Holy madrigals of the sixteen eighties,
Each with prelude played by a viol consort,
Taught the grace of body-imagination,
                              Hearing, the human

Learns a Bible passage, the Introduction,
Then relates the thought to a deed of mercy,
Dwelling on the empathy of the Savior,
                              Martyr and mortal.

Ere the cloven side we in woe envision,
Solomonic word in a song will charm us:
Dove he calls to come from her hidden nest in
                              Rock-hollow, wall-crack.

Ere to heart we turn for a clement refuge,
"You my heart have wounded, O spouse, O sister,"
In his hymn King Solomon our companion
                              Begs for compassion.

Every kind of love we in Love are given
Let be shared—be sure they are brought together.
Every body part, when I pray, is praying;
                    Thanks, when I'm thankful.

Every song in the cycle is a tribute to one of the body parts (Latin *membra*) of Jesus and a hymn of gratitude for the benevolence involved in the sufferer's willingness to accept the role of that suffering body organ in his martyrdom. The intense visuality of the imaginative method draws Buxtehude quite near, in spirit and in visionary technique, to the instructions for detailed visualizing of the rosary-events that St. Ignatius Loyola recommends in *Spiritual Exercises.* Having just written, in my *A Lover's Art*, a tribute to the tradition of King Solomon's biblical Song of Songs in the history of love-hymns, I was charmed by the inclusion of motifs from Solomon in this touching homage to Jesus. Widening the range of reference even further, I allude in my final quatrain to Ibn Arabi's Sufi teaching that when you pray sincerely, every one of your body parts and organs prays with you, so that you become a mullah leading an entire corporeal congregation harmoniously chanting, enraptured.

Next we'll look at the rarer variety, the "greater" sapphic. Here the rhythm pattern governs the couplet, and we can make our own compositional choices regarding stanza length and number of couplets. Here's the pattern,

greater sapphic
            /x x/x /x
/x /x /x x/— /x x/x /x,

which we can easily chant as follows:

            [ONE-and-a], TWO-and, THREE-and,
ONE-and, TWO-and, [THREE-and-a] FOUR—[FIVE-and-a], SIX-&, SEV'N-and.

Looking at the opening stanza of my sample poem, we read aloud, noting the tri-syllables in brackets:

[EIGHTH-of-the] ODES-of HOR-ace—
THAT'S-the ON-ly [ONE-in-the] RARE—[FORM-of-the] GREAT-er SAPPH-ic.
[I-have-an] ENG-lish VER-sion
FOUND-where NOW-we [FIN-al-ly] LEARN: [WHAT-are-the] THEME-and TREAT-ment?

Boldly now we recite the poem as a whole:

226. Eighth of the odes of Horace

                Eighth of the odes of Horace—
That's the only one in the rare form of the greater sapphic.
                I have an English version
Found where now we finally learn: What are the theme and
    treatment?

                Lydia needs reproaching:
She allured young Sýbaris—quite torn from his love for action.
                Swimming and soldier-drilling,
Fighting, discus-throwing are *all* willfully shunned,
    abandoned.

                He, though a splendid athlete,
Far withdrawn is hidden away, totally sybaritic.
                Think of Achilles, hidden,
Fearing Trojan combat, disguised (shame!) in a maiden's
    garment.

                Thanks to a shrewd unmasking
Which the skilled Ulysses had planned, Greeks had a chance
    to triumph
                Since, in the Trojan conflict,

Gods made clear Achilles would bring—crucial—the secret
  weapon!

                                  Lydia, kindly listen!
Passion put aside, I entreat! Those whom the gods would ruin
                              First they afflict with madness.
Play no more the lyrical flute, sapping a manly valor!

The Horatian speaker is comically exasperated: Lydia, quit it! You're turning our best warriors into wanton luxury lovers with your alluring fluting! Three tri-syllables per couplet lend further rhythmic interest to that of the already exciting varied line lengths. I'd love to see the greater sapphic rapidly restored to favor.

    Shall we try, finally, to combine the two kinds of sapphic? Here's poem 232:

        What would happen, Chanter, if pen attempted
        Turning—skillful bird in a whimsied current,
        Loving windbreath-will in a deft surrender—
                      Every direction?

                         Credit your wings Icaric:
Here's a gust that telling of strength born in the chosen
   herald
                         Brings me, a cloud advancing
Gloried high in boreal pride, glassed in the ocean
   breakers.

        Now I'm dreamt by warmth in a blue suffusion,
        Drowsy-lulled, enwrapt in a gentle floating,
        Pinions kept aloft in the aided movement—
                      Breathe me, O heaven!

                     Weak and bereft of power,
Shifted off to northerly chill, victim of sudden wind-rush,

Mercy! I beg you—help me!
Heed my pure nephéliad pray'r—Grace to the faithful
   servant!

I reshaped myself into a nepheliad or cloud-spirit, feeling like the very breath of heaven, expecting to luxuriate in summer air of the upper sky, but the boreal northwind swept me away.

IX Experimental Rhythms with Duplets and Triplets

We can reward ourselves at last with a free-for-all, savoring the delights of two- and three-syllable feet in all sorts of invented structures. In poem 246, I offer a quick review of parts one, two, and three of this book, bringing together all the rhythms they taught:

246. Triplets Triply Considered

Line 1: x/x x/x x/x x/x
Line 5: xx/ xx/ xx/ xx/
Line 9 /xx /xx /xx /xx

The joy of the amphibrach: what's more engaging?
We rode at a canter, surveying the land—
Refreshed and receptive—the horse with free hand
Scarce guided, ungoaded, all tension assuaging.

But the anapest hastened the pace of the ride
As the winds became brisker and summoned with song:
When we hear them go by we accelerate—long
Is the road, and it's right!—the horizon is wide.

Dactyls, relaxing the speed of tetrameters,
Tell us to look. The inviting vicinity
Gladdens. The rhythm repeats the affinity
Galloping has with expanding parameters.

Roaming, and running, and roving, we say:
Here's catalexis, we'll call it a day.

    In poems 248–252 I invented a form which is such fun I stuck with it for five poems. In 254 I pick up a captivating meter from a rhythm suggested by verses of the Qur'an (tr. Pickthall) needing only slightly altered phrasing for rhythm's sake:

254. Building on Scriptural Rhythms

two and three-syllable rhythms
/x x/ x/x x/x

Qur'an 23:96. Repel evil with that which is better....
23:109. ...Thou art best of all who show mercy.

Evil repel with that which is better:
Thou art the best of all who show mercy.
Quickly supplanting lapse with improvement,
Proving good sense in action advancing,
Kind to your heart in smiling not weeping,
Shunning regret, lest ego-absorption
Make you neglect the path of the pilgrim,
Gladly admit: while living we're moving,
Leaving behind the past and its baggage.

Thou art the best of all who show mercy:
Evil repel with that which is better.
Straight is the path of steady intention—

Pardon what's done, make room for the future.
Wanderers we, who godlike in motion
That which we plan enact in our travel.
Emulate One Who world-life imagined,
Lauding in song the power 'tis granting
Dream to create, that earth may be heaven.

Everyday conversation is every bit as good as scripture when you're looking for a new shaping of double and triple units:

257. Getting a Haircut

2 amphibrachs, 2 iambs in each line
x/x x/x x/ x/
x/x x/x x/ x/
x/x x/x x/ x/
x/x x/x x/ x/

"My oldest is seven, Aurora." "Dawn?
How perfect—the sunrise, the waking day!
Is that what you had in your mind?" Can't say,
I once looked it up, but the time's long gone—

And Scarlett, my second, is three." "Oh my,
Another bright red in the morning sky!
From *Gone with the Wind*? Had you *that* in mind?"
"Well, no, but I hear it a lot, I find."

"A love for what shines—for the color red!—
What beautiful names: are they *like your own*?"
"I'm Jessica." "Nice, but the color-tone—
Not quite so predominant, I'd have said..."
"No, Jessica's *boring*. I thought: no more
Of that!—we'll have names that will *not, not bore*!"

I glanced in the mirror, my hair now done.
The colors, not dyed, would survive the test
Of boredom avoided. What sudden fun!
Hair black on the left, with the center white,
Then black—how symmetrical!—at the right.
I looked like a bird with a rising crest.

In poem 261 I even tried the first asclepiadic—a meter I wouldn't use often because of its brass band effect. But I'm talking about (the badness of) war, so the rhythm fits the topic. War is not only wicked but insidious, for the pleasures of comradeship can blind one to the fundamental evil of fighting:

261. Spoken by a Matriot

first asclepiadic, each line with 2 trochee-plus-iamb units for triplet effect
/, /, /x x/ /x x/ x/
/, /, /x x/ /x x/ x/
/, /, /x x/ /x x/ x/
/, /, /x x/ /x x/ x/

War! War! What is it for? Why do we send away
Joy filled boys to be killed! How can we stay so blind?
Weak, old, senile or sold, speak with a single mind:
"One—Grand—National Plan! Unity—come what may!"

Wait? No. Mate, you must go! Avarice, that's the ground:
Greed. Land. These will command, leading the bosses on,
Blithe, bright, smiling, and white. Followers cringe and
   fawn.
Doubt? Don't! Patriots won't! Pride is the fiend they've
   found.

Wild youth, childish, in truth—many of them—will hear:
"Fight! Serve! Smite, never swerve—hark to your
   country's call!
See? Stand! Heed the demand: tyrants will fail and fall!"
Bold, true, soldiers like *you*, comrades that hold you
   dear—

Fight—stride—right by your side: brother will run to
   shield
Blood warm brother from harm—friends, on the
   battlefield.

    Poems 266–274 employ autobiography—mostly in alternating three- and four-beat lines, with the usual mixture, for our concluding section, of two- and three-syllable rhythm units. Poem 268 may be the strangest of these; dreamlike is even the way I selected the title, for I was holding my grandmother's 1913 Ukrainian passport (written in Russian, with her four children's names transcribed as she pronounced them) before I began writing:

268. Passport

alternating trimeter and tetrameter lines, opening trochee option for triplet effect—
first quatrain:
    /x x/ x/
/x x/ x/ x/
   x/ x/ x/
/x x/ x/ x/

    Nineteen thirteen, the year.
Grandma and children, racked with fear
    (Eleven, nine, six, four),
Left the Ukraine. We may deplore

>Her fate, at thirty-five:
How could she keep the kids alive
>When, in Toronto, she
Saw her poor husband horribly

>Killed when he slid and fell
Off of his peddler-horse? They tell
>How she was left alone
With little she might call her own.

>She had to marry soon.
He was well off, a crucial boon.

>True, he was older—much.
But he could buy a house and such...
>Tenants would rent. She'd cook.
Her life took on another look.

>Though often she would shout—
A temper!—he would never pout—
>Patient (my cousins say),
And merely looked the other way.

>Passover Eve! How he
Had startled been when, suddenly,
>She weakened. Hospital.
Aged one-O-four, and sorrowful,

>He hanged himself. And she
Recovered fully, speedily.

I never forget for long about musical works. In poem 283 a piece on the radio gave me a chance to choreograph a melodic setting that would begin many lines with a triplet, as if it were a specially featured dance step, a recommended beginning to a measure of the orchestral interlude:

283. Minuet of the Will-o'-the-Wisps
from Hector Berlioz, The Damnation of Faust

iambic pentameter with optional trochee opener for triplet effect—
first quatrain:
/x x/ x/ x/ x/
/x x/ x/ x/ x/
x/ x/ x/ x/ x/
x/ x/ x/ x/ x/

Born of the rich corruption of the marsh,
Candle, the spirit of the dead, fool's fire,
They lead you slogging through the swampy mire
For treasure, quicksand, precipice. The harsh

Damned or indentured sparkles from a lyre
Learn an elaborately gallant dance—
Elegant, equable, the measured prance.
But watch: the flames that climb and flicker higher—

Dampened, confounded, baffled! Cloudy chords
Mean a complete obliteration by
Cold fog. Then quiet... Look again! Up—high
On thermal currents, leaping—see?—the hordes

Piccolo pitches reaching! blinding bright!—
Glittering, fluting sprite-swarms fill the night.

Finally, as in poem 254, I'd like to use material from scripture to present my closing example of duple rhythms varied for musical interest by optional line-opening triplets:

291. Scribal Error?

iambic lines with frequent opening trochees for triplet effect—
first quatrain:
/x x/ x/ x/ x/(x)
/x x/ x/ x/ x/
/x x/ x/ x/ x/
x/ x/ x/ x/ x/(x)

Or zaru'a la-tsaddik? Or zaraḥ la-tsaddik?

"Light is sown for the righteous": if we alter
Only a letter of the alphabet,
Changing the 'ayin simply to a ḥet,
Light "shines"! We've likely seen the scribe-pen falter.

How many kabbalistic plans were set
Happily, by that "error" in the psalter,
Finding a fall, and yet a heart-exalter,
In the resplendent metaphor they met!

Light that had shone up high is gone below,
Clipped in a shell, *klippáh*, a flaming seed.
Farther to seek the dark, the deep, we go:

Fallen, a force may be unfettered, freed.
Buried, it blazing upward now will burst:
Fountaining fire—how germinal a thirst!

  Looking over what we've surveyed, you'll find much to do if you'd like to apply any or the nine tools I've described and illustrated. Amphibrach, anapest, and dactyl are in themselves a feast of rhythms. The third, fourth, and fifth asclepiadic (plus the hendecasyllabic I've grouped together with the last of these) present three more categories of the best triplet-containing treasures ancient lyric ingenuity has to offer. The alcaic—most dramatic of the patterns—and the sapphic—most soothing and sweetly melodic—combine with the idea of placing duple and triple rhythms together in your own favorite ways to give you an additional threefold impetus to revive the vocal pleasures of the Greeks and Romans in crafting your own vibrant verses.

Enjoy! And please feel free to contact me at mbidney@binghamton.edu with your comments, which I'll read with vivid interest.

Acknowledgments: the respective references in poem 52 to Miles Tittle's essay "Illuminating Divergences: Morris, Burne-Jones, and the Two *Aeneids*" and in poem 53 to Elizabeth Helsinger's "Telling Time: Song's Rhythms in Morris' Late Work" are to the volume *To Build a Shadowy Isle of Bliss: William Morris' Radicalism and the Embodiment of Dreams*, edited by Michelle Weinroth and Paul Leduc Browne, Montreal/Kingston, Canada, McGill-Queens University Press, 2015, a book I reviewed in *Science & Society* 82.1 (January 2018): 154–156. All translations in this volume are mine unless otherwise indicated.

Explanatory note: all analyses of metric patterns in this book refer to the patterns as they are employed in modern (English, German, or Russian) verse, never to patterns with the same names which were used in ancient Greek or Latin verse. All the labels for metric feet (brief rhythmic structure units) or strophes (stanzas) that I use will always refer to structures that poets in the modern languages interpret according to their understanding of syllables regarded as either strong (heavy, emphatic, stressed) or weak (light, not emphasized, unstressed). Greek and Roman verse theory used entirely different (if analogous) criteria for classification, speaking rather of long versus short syllables. The word "triplet" as used in this book likewise refers to the musical effect produced and heard in the modern languages, not in the ancient ones.

PART ONE
Three Kinds of Triple Rhythms

I
Amphibrach

1. Weather Retort

amphibrachic tetrameter
x/x x/x x/x x/x
x/x x/x x/x x/x
    x/x x/x x/x x/
    x/x x/x x/x x/

Snowed in by the drift of the outer environs,
My spirit I lift with a vigor like Byron's
    Who, pacing the shoreline, the wrinkles marine
    Called free of all aging in glory pristine.

The river of time in your mind that is flowing,
Compliant, will feel that your spirit, bestowing
    The tempo, direction, and speed of the piece,
    Can grant from dull slowing a freedom-release.

I'll cover more space and more time in a minute
Should life to a triumph pay tribute within it
    And generate luck where no lack will be known
    If glory outpoured to the heaven be shown.

Philosophy, Helmsman, you aid in preparing
The ventures that Poetry soon will be daring
    When thought of the snow long ago is forgot
    By sailor who bravely an odyssey wrought.

2. Hail, Holy Light

amphibrachic tetrameter
x/x x/x x/x x/x
x/x x/x x/x x/x
    x/x x/x x/x x/
    x/x x/x x/x x/

Is time in control? Or am I? There's a question!
Let deity-picturing lend a suggestion:
    See Light of the Morning Apollo appear?
    He's mastered the craft of the charioteer.

You're also a reiner, a trainer, a rider,
Of sun-flaring steeds the director, provider:
    The bliss of the bridegroom you know, and the force
    You feel in the spirit is leading each horse.

How quick is a minute of living? Determine.
By verve are you spurred in the Word of your sermon.
    Your anthem is graphing your transit in time,
    Deep breathing in vigor with canorous rhyme.

Don't model your travel on Saturn, old Cronus,
Divest yourself well of dead memory onus,
    Hail future in aureate helial spree—
    And carry to Phoebus a greeting from me.

3. Within

amphibrachic tetrameter
x/x x/x x/x x/x
x/x x/x x/x x/x
   x/x x/x x/x x/
   x/x x/x x/x x/

The death in your mind is an enterprise failure.
Awake, be aware and stay heartstrong and hail your
    Bright origin-source in heliacal height,
    The sibling of billions in stellar-blest night.

The arch of your footstep in curving will mirror
The arc of the neck of your steed when you steer her
    In flight that the Pegasus hinted for you,
    Directed where no one before ever flew.

Let thud of your drum for your horse be the meter
That powers the speed which increasingly fleeter
    You feel when you spheres of the heaven
      transcend
    In peregrine pilgrimage never to end.

The struggle with time is unhelpful, so end it.
Yet struggle *within* it is fine, so befriend it.
    Who struggles with God an apprentice
      remains.
    Who struggles *within* Him a heaven attains.

4. The Jinns Are Winning

amphibrachic tetrameter
x/x x/x x/x x/x
x/x x/x x/x x/x
   x/x x/x x/x x/
   x/x x/x x/x x/

Time quiet, unmoved, might be uniform-seeming
Were billows not breaking the sea of our dreaming:
      I've dreamt of awaiting the flame of my work,
      But action-distractions are dangers that lurk.

Suppose that the strength of the day's obligation
Drained forces away from the morning's elation:
      I vividly think of the nightmare-like ill
      When worries long vanished keep plaguing me still.

I dreamt I was harried to bring to conclusion
A manuscript twenty years back, the confusion
      Arising from worries yet dragging along
      To doom through the fear of imputable wrong.

The jinns of our diffidence hunker and hanker
And moodily brood in timidity's rancor:
      How comical then that with slyness endued
      They waken, archaic, my craving of food!

5. March, April, May

amphibrachic tetrameter
x/x x/x x/x x/x
x/x x/x x/x x/x
    x/x x/x x/x x/
    x/x x/x x/x x/

Past ramparts of white I had walked to discover,
Had book-proof arrived of my *Art of a Lover?*—
    When sudden I heard, undismayed by defeat,
    A bird with a lilting, unspeakably sweet.

Another joined in, at a pace rather slower,
Yet pattern, repeated, the same, a bestower
    Of cheer, with a rapid ascensional slope
    As meant to prefigure a lesson of hope.

You birds won't surrender your mission so early!
Though Jove's a poor loser and pluvial-surly,
    He cannot turn back what is meant to occur,
    For April awaits, with her venery-whirr.

Though March is of Mars he must yield when defeated
To blithe Aphrodite whom April has greeted
    With promise, and Maytime awaits, unforsworn,
    Her deed to achieve, so more lovers are born.

6. *Ludus Tonalis*

amphibrachic tetrameter
x/x x/x x/x x/x
x/x x/x x/x x/x
    x/x x/x x/x x/
    x/x x/x x/x x/

The tone of your body you'll aid with a tonic.
You take it by making it. You are eu-phonic.
    Is tonic the note of a musical key?
    You bet—all the better the spirit to free.

Mirific the soul of our melody-forming
That light will extend with the heart-strings a-warming.
    Let seedling of st*art*le be sown by the art
    That, found at the center, will grounding impart.

The threes of the lines are the sweep of the swinging,
All burden aside to be flauntingly flinging,
    While fours are the vigor and thrust of the force
    That keeps you a pilgrim on privileged course.

You captain the vessel of health in your striding,
The font of your hymning inside you abiding:
    Aware of the mettle that's molten at core,
    Mellifluent, singing, you heavenward soar.

7. Twin Within

amphibrachic tetrameter
x/x x/x x/x x/x
x/x x/x x/x x/x
   x/x x/x x/x x/
   x/x x/x x/x x/

Rereading a lyric I'd recently written
I'm seeing the moment by which I'd been smitten
      Return when the voice that had given it word
      Made form of the hymn of my destiny heard.

The riverine singer, of Jordan the forder,
Was born as a giver and never a hoarder:
      He'll scatter as manna the sun and the dew,
      Aspersing a love and a mercy to you.

A form is a language and they who can speak it
Will find what to say without needing to seek it.
      Wait decades to hear it, should fate say you
         must:
      Your Name will be spoken, awoken from dust.

Trance-lation and transfer and transport convert you
To realms of ascension where hate cannot hurt you:
      Ecstatic, beside yourself, glad you impart
      A two that are one, to the saddened in heart.

8. Explanatory Amphibrachs

amphibrachic tetrameter
x/x x/x x/x x/x
x/x x/x x/x x/x
    x/x x/x x/x x/
    x/x x/x x/x x/

When God said, "I am what I am," He had meant it
To fire up the soul by the message He sent it.
    The flame of our Being is godly within:
    'Tis love for Creation. Why call it a sin?

The muchness to love is that Being is Making.
Creating to love shows the care you are taking
    With skill to ensure that the creature will yearn
    To praise what had made it: Creator Eterne.

What flames in the art of my arteried morning
Is one with the sunlight arising, aborning
    To cry with the beings that throneward will throng
    As once did the Sons of the Heaven in song.

To emulate One who's our Lover in splendor
We'll hasten to shape, for creations engender
    The love that is fruitful and multiplies well:
    Let's labor, then rest in a sabbatine spell.

"I am what I am!" cried the fire in his burning:
To him, to be vital, my strive-life is turning.
    I feel that, in reaching, my weakness recurs:
    Yet heaven-horizon the finer bestirs.

The flame when it flares will provide me the impulse
That powers the riverborne fish in a swim-pulse.
> The lack of regret when I errors have wrought
> Holds gravity quiet, lends pinion to thought.

The beast and the bird and the creature of ocean
Partake of the heard and the seen in their motion:
> Your blood is the flood that is roaring within.
> The shell that may tell it your wisdom can win.

Breathe deep and make room for the mood that is coming:
The beat of your art is the heart in his drumming.
> Chant love to the sky in the tongue of the sod—
> You're joining the choir of the voices of God.

9. March (An Imperative)

amphibrachic tetrameter
x/x x/x x/x x/x
x/x x/x x/x x/x
   x/x x/x x/x x/
   x/x x/x x/x x/

Snow covering earth in a frigorous blanket
Will stimulate vigorous thinking. So thank it!
      It pays to evade a mere "weather report."
      The makers are framing a better retort!

What's meteorology? *Meteor*'s "lofty."
You want to go high? Then be strong, not a softie.
      Nepheliads bend from their cloudy demesne
      And contemplate long the terrestrial scene.

The whiteness will compass all colors potential
That spring will unfold with a skill differential.
      And thus on the page that I contemplate here
      May colorful thoughts to the dreamer appear.

The cold that's invading my home in the morning
Will generate motion, both warming and warning
      That ere we prepare for our narrowing home
      Far more must we pilgrims in caravan roam.

10. Infinities

amphibrachic tetrameter
x/x x/x x/x x/x
x/x x/x x/x x/x
    x/x x/x x/x x/
    x/x x/x x/x x/

We center infinities—tinier, vaster,
We're moving toward them, and every day faster.
    More worldings we multiply, clustering stars,
    While speeded-up charges our tempo unbars.

Of billions one hundred the galaxies number,
But Hubble has barely awakened from slumber:
    The heaven the telescope hourly explores
    To space unimagined can open the doors.

The number of galaxies likely will double
When data come in from our conquering Hubble,
    And, too, the computer-realm Tiny expands
    And sparks per quadrillionth-of-second
        commands.

The poets who wrote of the chain of our being
Would barely believe what we're momently seeing:
    Each atom of Adam with glory might burst,
    Recalling each day is no worse than the first.

11. Nameless

amphibrachic tetrameter
x/x x/x x/x x/x
x/x x/x x/x x/x
   x/x x/x x/x x/
   x/x x/x x/x x/

If ocean be shoreless what dance would be dearer
Than simply to splash and immensities mirror
      To answer the thoughts of the twain in your play
      And hear, when the height meets the deep, what they say!

If both be in dark we reply to the glimmer
We yet can remember, still brilliant, not dimmer:
      Within are a depth and a height. That is why
      In you and in me are a sea and a sky.

The quiet and storm of the heaven and ocean
I share in my heart where the calm and commotion
      Contrasting and blending the day and the night
      Know death in the depth and the life in the light.

My blood is aroused while I bow in surrender
Acknowledging tidings tempestuous-tender
      Nor ever forget that the breath in my lungs
      To God-love directs what I'm telling in tongues.

12. Instruction

amphibrachic tetrameter
x/x x/x x/x x/x
x/x x/x x/x x/x
    x/x x/x x/x x/
    x/x x/x x/x x/

Events were contending to get my attention,
'Tween classic and folk-music held in suspension.
    Reception I love, but 'tis better to give:
    A voice from above said, "In singing you live.

You've played and you've listened to records forever—
That's part of you, heart-strength your age won't dissever.
    Within you it lived, but your musical youth
    Pray now resurrect in poetical truth.

Confronting the screen that the snowdrift will mirror
Begin and be favored with gifts for the hearer.
    His will you fulfill when the choirs in the heart
    Reply to desire in mellifluous art."

I thank you, Protector and Guide, for the moral
And avidly sing in a dithyramb choral:
    My organs of body and likewise of thought
    In organ recital their tribute have brought.

13. Solace Will Call Us

amphibrachic tetrameter
x/x x/x x/x x/x
x/x x/x x/x x/x
   x/x x/x x/x x/
   x/x x/x x/x x/

Who's bold the Unknown in a verse to encounter
From fatal may swerve as an Everest mounter
      And quickly be healed as a walker from wounds,
      For he will forsooth be a conjurer. Zounds!

The inner and outer exchanging their weather
Will make a duet of two players together,
      Developing moods they united enclose
      Concordant though fighting, and ordering those.

So long as a hearer be waiting in vision
No finding whatever is doomed to rescission
      But all are included in fugal array:
      "'Tis Bach, or the Devil," I heard a man say.

The wizard divined it with inner tuition—
Recurrent adversities yield to remission:
      Though folk may be trōthless, and hopeless you feel,
      Place hand on the bible you write. It can heal.

14. Zabur

amphibrachic tetrameter
x/x x/x x/x x/x
x/x x/x x/x x/x
    x/x x/x x/x x/
    x/x x/x x/x x/

The days of the psalmer aren't over, O Lover:
The rose may unfold to the soul-bird above her.
    So Persians have told in their poems of eld
    Where tone and aroma-strength heavenly meld.

The Hoopoe is known as it roams in the heather
To joy in the bringing of lovers together:
    It said to King Solomon, "Sheba the Queen
    Would welcome you gladly"—romantic the scene!

If God be a Lover, the world of creation
The being He loves, we'll discover elation
    From center diffuse when our petals unfold
    And ruddy-white bloom chant to azure and gold.

The stars who behold us will hymn in a chorus:
They know what we feel, seeing Eden before us.
    Their light that we view in the heaven today
    Was lent ere King David in cradle yet lay.

15. A Thank-you on Awaking

amphibrachic tetrameter
x/x x/x x/x x/x
x/x x/x x/x x/x
   x/x x/x x/x x/
   x/x x/x x/x x/

All night on my private Buraq had I ridden
Save when to a shrine I had resolute stridden...
    A scroll that I wrote I had sent to a friend:
    Advice would she kindly and helpful extend.

"Take time out to eat and to sleep," she suggested.
Yes, thank you! Good hours for them both I've invested:
    No risk is entailed by the things that I do—
    Well fed and well rested, low sugar count, too.

The only thing odd is my bodily rhythm:
When heart-love and mind-thought ascend, I go with 'em.
    'Tis best in the night-time, when folk are asleep,
    For then with the spirit I rendezvous keep.

I'm on the *qui vive* when my vigilant senses
Are lifted aloft—the suspension of tenses
    Will palpably hint, while the planets revolve,
    "By singing a hymn every problem you solve."

16. Sticktoitiveness and Stiffneckitude

amphibrachic tetrameter
x/x x/x x/x x/x
x/x x/x x/x x/x
    x/x x/x x/x x/
    x/x x/x x/x x/

Persistent remain in the face of the skeptic,
Your strength unrelenting in fit nympholeptic:
    The squares Mondrianic, Pollockian drips
    Win victory. That is the topmost of tips.

Matisse exhibitions, when thorough, are daunting,
For, year after year, he'll no triumph be vaunting:
    In room after room, what a gloom will dismay
    To view him a-wandering, finding his way.

Yet guided divinely and true to his yearning,
He'll treasures create after decades of learning,
    And he for Picasso will after a while
    Have proved both a source and a rival in style.

So write in a way that the height has directed—
And Hope, though it flutter, at length is protected:
    Let love persevere in a mode never known,
    That glory below be unfoldingly shown.

17. Freedom of Threedom

amphibrachic tetrameter
x/x x/x x/x x/x
x/x x/x x/x x/x
   x/x x/x x/x x/
   x/x x/x x/x x/

Your amphibrach mood may be tranquil, idyllic,
And likewise your lines anapestic, dactylic:
      Some poets arrive at their goal with dispatch,
      The slower ones up with the faster will catch.

Triplicity measures, felicity forming,
The spirit with rich authenticity warming,
      Will flourish one day when publicity comes
      To sum up the *summa* and calculate sums.

From Pushkin and Lérmontov learning of triples,
I'm higher than wine. When the taverner tipples
      A Russian contender may put on a show.
      Just let the flow bear you. (Flaubert? Yes I know...)

You'll find that the trinal designs are amusing,
Good humor with galloping amplitude fusing:
      The love of your tempo the self at its best
      Calls forth to perfection at heaven's behest.

18. Sermonette

amphibrachic tetrameter
x/x x/x x/x x/x
x/x x/x x/x x/x
   x/x x/x x/x x/
   x/x x/x x/x x/

A student, I ever worked best under pressure,
Of purging and splurging the ultimate mesher,
      The test if a soul be alert and alive
         Straight forward to stride and with fortune to strive.

Allegro con brio, con forza, con fuoco
Is made for the brave. *Ese tío—ah, loco!*
      The guy is plain crazy, they're likely to say—
      But go on your own, not behaving as they.

A sun in yourself, you're an energy center,
A temple that those are permitted to enter
      Whom true to your fate-as-creator you chose
      The holy of holies some day to disclose.

One's neighbor to love will evade the self-hater,
Respect for the self is a friendship creator:
      The self when essential's the body of love.
      Hate hides in a cave while the sunlight's above.

19. Gentleman-in-Waiting

amphibrachic tetrameter
x/x x/x x/x x/x
x/x x/x x/x x/x
   x/x x/x x/x x/
   x/x x/x x/x x/

The blended sensations of warming and cooling
Blest hands when they're clasped is intuitive schooling
    In quiet: attend to an entrance, prepare
    To make by accepting whatever is there.

I'll hymn to the spring, for today's the beginning:
Refusing to lose will be halfway to winning.
    Suspended and eager, the hand above keys:
    Ah, come to me, melody... (presently, please!)

I know it's arriving: the pressure that sent me
To grow in a striving the lesson had lent me
    That, diffidence banished, the spirit can't cease
    To bring to the seeking relief and release.

The heart, being happy, had sighed. And a smiling
Began, for the madrigal scan was beguiling,
    A victory chant I can never resist,
    A gift of the springtime—O hearken! O list!

20. Conjuror

amphibrachic tetrameter
x/x x/x x/x x/x
x/x x/x x/x x/x
    x/x x/x x/x x/
    x/x x/x x/x x/

The conjuror, though he was holy and pious,
Had shaven his face (as our fright may belie us):
    The beard that was red and the hair that was
        black
    Seemed rather ill-fitting, concinnity-lack.

He conjured with Names, for the rabbi who taught him
Had thought it a way to the One who begot him.
    He studied the numbers, he pondered the sum:
    Could—wonder of wonders—a visitant come?

It happened, of course, and the force of desiring
Will have, for an answer, what soul is requiring:
    The visitor shone with a brilliance combined
    Of radiant grace and a light that could blind.

But—trouble! The spirit in vision is gleaming
As red as that long-shaven beard unbeseeming!
    Asmodeus? Angel or devil? He fled
    With trembling of heart and with shaking of head.

21. Opening Adore

amphibrachic tetrameter
x/x x/x x/x x/x
x/x x/x x/x x/x
   x/x x/x x/x x/
   x/x x/x x/x x/

The birds are presenting a spring celebration,
Merkháh and *tupkháh* from the brave cantillation
    Of Torah, their laud to the heaven on high,
    The clouded gray-white of a buttermilk sky.

The cardinal, too, is a chorister ardent:
His bright upward glides, vernal fervor regardant,
    A teaching of hope in a melody tell,
    The shape of a shofar, the toll of a bell.

'Tis March into April. So Mars Aphrodite
Will summon, the lady in fever made flighty
    With frivolous whim that may Vulcan enrage,
    Yet lover-desires are inspiring the mage.

You birds that have come with a graceful arousal
Inclining the mind to a spirit-espousal
    Have made through me here an antiphonal song.
    Be blessèd your call!—it was never more strong.

22. Morning Paper

amphibrachic tetrameter
x/x x/x x/x x/x
x/x x/x x/x x/x
    x/x x/x x/x x/
    x/x x/x x/x x/

It seemed to be Shakespeare, but Marlowe is nearer:
The Faustian legend gets clearer and clearer.
    A pact was concluded indeed, and you'll see:
    Gehenna's ahead for the Party of T.

The henchmen of Trump with the Russians colluding
Are choking-aroma of sulfur exuding:
    He summoned the Russians to hack if they would,
    And Putin, usurper, the word understood.

The Trumpian lies are more bulkily clouding
The skies and the puppets for shelter are crowding,
    While helplessly pelted with sling-rocks of fact,
    To cover him up—unconvincing the act.

Impeachment may loom. And a character failure
At length will have taught him that once put in jail you're
    An opening given for light to stream in,
    And then may the time of redemption begin.

23. Anchorite? Not Quite Right

amphibrachic tetrameter
x/x x/x x/x x/x
x/x x/x x/x x/x
    x/x x/x x/x x/
    x/x x/x x/x x/

I'm reading a volume that deals with a hermit
Who decades had camped without seeking a permit
    And solitude sought, for with folk to collide
    Distracted, detracted from what must abide.

I'd posted a poem for facebook approval
But tempted had felt to resort to removal
    When time had gone by and no comment was seen;
    Uncertainty hurt. I'd prefer the serene...

I found a reply after patiently waiting—
'Twas great, but a question remained unabating:
    Just how independent from others are *you*?
    Poor half-hearted hermit, what weakness to rue!

Pure solitude, surely, would set me a-raving
When, childlike, attention I yet would be craving.
    I'd best not be trying my heart to deceive:
    In others' opinion I *partly* believe...

24. Bliss of Triplicity

amphibrachic tetrameter
x/x x/x x/x x/x
x/x x/x x/x x/x
    x/x x/x x/x x/
    x/x x/x x/x x/

The bliss of triplicity hits me with vigor!
To swiff away stiffness and frigorous rigor
    I wish, while I think of the strategy I'm
    Enraptured to catch as we trinally rhyme.

Astrology mustered the signs in an order:
Let each of four trios be element-warder.
    We thus will construct of zodiacal signs
    A brighter delight than heliacal wines.

A rapider tempo with circling and sweeping
And whirling and dashing more avid than leaping
    Will purge every remnant of errors and faults
    When stirring emerges the call of the waltz.

Come, partner! Be heartened, and let me embrace you:
In dream to elysian haven I'll race you!
    The slow and the cold and the old let aspire
    In fiery desire for the light of the higher!

25. Prolegomenon

amphibrachic tetrameter
x/x x/x x/x x/x
x/x x/x x/x x/x
   x/x x/x x/x x/
   x/x x/x x/x x/

O muse, Burgeoned Berry, sing hymns of the forest!
Good news, Virgin Mary, thou forth again pourest!
    A kingdom within will the human yet see
    When singing, by tune of the numen set free.

A wonder I'm learning from Goethe and Shakespeare:
The sun in its burning gave birth in the lakes, dear,
    To radiant blazes the heaven reversed
    Made gentle when blent and outspread and
        dispersed.

A love rose within me from Shakespeare and Goethe:
By nothing so quickly may heaven alert a
    Developing calyx more wealth to unfold
    As, whelming, a depth Danaëan of gold.

'Tis only a while the horizon may darken
Ere men resurrected to dawning ray hearken:
    The smile in the eye to the psalm will respond
    When deep calls to deep. Be our motto *Beyond*!

26. On a Phrase of Larry Lockridge

amphibrachic tetrameter
x/x x/x x/x x/x
x/x x/x x/x x/x
   x/x x/x x/x x/
   x/x x/x x/x x/

"Arcana remaindered"? The phrasing you've chosen
More treats may release than an orange well squozen:
      So gather your facts, re-create them with verve—
      And craftsmanly acts let elatedly serve.

Each trumpery tyrant, the bigots, belittlers
Are dead in the head as the dreadest of hitlers.
      Elated? Belated? Becoming will Be:
      I AM is the god that we cannot yet see.

We sing when we breathe; the Unending will answer
In ocean-wave seething and motion-brave dancer:
      For Adam the names of the angels availed—
      Abandon not ever the heaven inhaled.

Be carried along, to the daybreak replying:
When harried be strong, with the morningtide vying!
      Blest bridegroom, arise, and be rapid to race,
      High favor to savor, the granter of grace.

27. Spent years of my youth reading Pushkin and Goethe

amphibrachic tetrameter
x/x x/x x/x x/x
x/x x/x x/x x/x
    x/x x/x x/x x/
    x/x x/x x/x x/

Spent years of my youth reading Pushkin and Goethe,
Attention to melody ever alert, a
    Fine passion to catch when the рифмы текут
    Delighting the hearer, for счастие тут.

Entrancing the times when with ardor made fervent
I heard *glänzt die Sonne,* heart newly observant
    Cried out, in a frenzy enrapt, *lacht die Flur!*
    'Twas rhythm and rhyme made the pleasure so pure.

It seemed that in Eden, a deity speaking
Had found what he wanted, no need to go seeking:
    You're pained when by dart of the Cupid-boy smit?
    Sweet tunes will make Mozart-enjoyment of it.

I couldn't foresee that the day would befall me
When heav'n-dwelling angel by god-name would call me:
    Awake, yours the Poet-heart: profit by this!
    Once tearful, pure sower-art reap, finding bliss.

28. But why include wording in Russian and German?

amphibrachic tetrameter
x/x x/x x/x x/x
    x/x x/x x/x x/
x/x x/x x/x x/x
    x/x x/x x/x x/

"But why include wording in Russian and German?"
    A speaker inquires in my pondering brain.
"I'm wondering how we're supposed to determine
    Your meaning, unless we can speak them. Explain?"

I know it may seem like a prank, gentle reader,
    But cast your thought back to the poets of yore:
'Twas classical mastery made one a leader
    In vision and wisdom, they felt: though the door

To Latin or Greek might be closed to the hearer,
    They'd quote in those languages, gladly and proud:
Attracted admirers, they deemed, would come nearer—
    Assumption scarce doubted, and always allowed.

My quotes, not arcane, are but raising a question:
    Won't multiple languages writing enrich?
Excite curiosity!—there's my suggestion.
    Let's love local color—my salesmanlike pitch.

29. *Peccate Audaciter*

amphibrachic tetrameter
x/x x/x x/x x/x
x/x x/x x/x x/x
   x/x x/x x/x x/
   x/x x/x x/x x/

Peccate audaciter—that is the moral
The teacher wrote down. I've no reason to quarrel.
     "Sin boldly," I feared, mightn't quite be allowed
     But learned it meant "Sightreaders need to *sing loud!*"

How fitting: 'tis pointless to fear that an error
Will shame you, for music is joy and not terror.
     The ruler we name Evolution said, "Fun
     Will lengthen your life till your journey is done."

I truly believe it, dear reader: you see it
In all of my lines. Are they flawed? Well, so be it.
     They're fun to indite; let no censor indict
     My singing if something's not perfectly right.

I'm even so brave as to take the position
We're instruments, each, of a single Musician.
     Whoever's in charge of conducting the score
     Will power us now when our songs we outpour.

30. His Burden is Lite

amphibrachic trimeter
x/x x/x x/x
x/x x/x x/x
x/x x/x x/x
x/x x/x x/x

So what is the task of the poet?
You pick up a thought and you throw it.
It flies through the air and you sow it.
It falls in a furrow. You hoe it.

It germinates there and you grow it.
It rises like grass and you mow it.
It's ready for storing. You stow it.
It's nutritive, too—you can show it.

You're generous and you bestow it.
You compost a remnant, bestrow it.
You Coleridge it, or you Rousseau it.
You Whitman it, or you Thoreau it.

You Dickinson it, or you Poe it.
And that is the task of the poet.

31. Hymn of Thanksgiving

amphibrachic tetrameter
x/x x/x x/x x/x
x/x x/x x/x x/x
   x/x x/x x/x x/
   x/x x/x x/x x/

In thanks for the morning I gladly would number
My sugar: awaking reborn from my slumber
    Ere facing creation I take for a theme
    My own transformation by drumbeat of dream.

The total today is one hundred eleven:
With heaven it rhymes and, yet better, with sweven.
    The blood through my body more fleeting can flow
    When cheered by the count, the amount being low.

Thought Rilke, your god is a child you are raising.
If that be the case, find no danger in praising
    The power within that can blissfully grow,
    That tone may begin and a symphony show.

The lesser the number the more 'tis rewarding:
Be generous—gifts you receive don't be hoarding,
    For sweet moderation's the key to your health:
    More give than you take—'tis the ultimate wealth.

The truth of our youth will bestir us to duty:
We brighten, observing a person of beauty.
    May sun learn to smile from the shine in your eyes
    Well-blent with the merciful dew of the skies.

32. Insistent the world in besieging, besetting

amphibrachic tetrameter
x/x x/x x/x x/x
x/x x/x x/x x/x
   x/x x/x x/x x/
   x/x x/x x/x x/

Insistent the world in besieging, besetting!
When solitude calls, a relief we'll be getting.
      When sounds grew around him with media rife
      The Prodigal Son had to flee for his life.

Though Promised the Land is our wandering dearer:
In quiet the pilgrim to soul can draw nearer.
      A border to thwart and the Jordan to ford
      We're destined ere welcoming Temple Reward.

The strength to instill in our melody making
Derives from the orientation we're taking.
      Let weather be riant or tristful—who cares?
      Our Nature—how changeful the raiment she wears!

The heart in its ardor, the carmine auroral—
We blissful combine them in dithyramb choral:
      Be jubilant, people! Be joyful, O crowd!
      Psalm Hundred and Fifty—intone it aloud!

I speak to a group, but I'm solitude praising.
A paradox, true? Yet no problem I'm raising.
    Priest, rabbi, or mullah, we congregants find:
    Who's praying? Each part of your body and mind.

You're never alone as you wander exploring.
While windows you're winning and doors are adoring,
    The organs within you unsilent will laud
    The One Whom your solitude hearkens to, awed.

33. When Shakespeare and I wrote our sonnets for pleasure

amphibrachic tetrameter
x/x x/x x/x x/x
x/x x/x x/x x/x
   x/x x/x x/x x/
   x/x x/x x/x x/

When Shakespeare and I wrote our sonnets for pleasure
We knew we were doing what humans would treasure:
     We no one would bother—with care and with tact
     We singing made vigorous, craft made exact.

While slower boys labored, their Latin construing,
Friend William and I different aims were pursuing:
     To let the god sing what was in him to tell,
     We dowsed in the desert and found us a well.

The god settles in and your body is lighter:
The hymn you exhale is of his a requiter,
     For none can deny what the spirit instilled:
     They others enthrall who themselves have been thrilled.

Assemblies of tone the beloved will muster
Who know that encased in the clay is a luster
     That fell from the sky in a time that is gone
     Yet ample can rise, rhododactyl the dawn.

34. Inconclusion

amphibrachic tetrameter
x/x x/x x/x x/x
x/x x/x x/x x/x
   x/x x/x x/x x/
   x/x x/x x/x x/

Though faster I dance, I'm alone in my castle:
So many deft minds are half buried in hassle!
    What's keeping the poets I'm reading today
    From sweeping and soaring and floating away?

Swift triplets are rare, and they're getting extincter:
How stiffened the sphinx! How constricting the sphincter!
    With joy of the golden-age world in its prime
    Be bolder, O sage! Be enlivened in rhyme!

The space will make way when we're flying together:
Hibernal and vernal, eternal the weather
    Available here as we sail in our room!
    Elijah with Mary the sky will assume.

Though one in the body, in spirit I'm double:
The houri-and-muse in the aster-glad Hubble
    I use when perusing the universe-bloom
    The white of our galaxy-milk may illume.

35. So Plato was right when he claimed that the poet could not

amphibrachic pentameter
x/x x/x x/x x/x x/(x)
x/x x/x x/x x/x x/(x)
x/x x/x x/x x/x x/(x)
x/x x/x x/x x/x x/(x)

So Plato was right when he claimed that the poet could not
Control the high soul-gift when led by the god to the brink.
Green tea's all I've taken. And what would a nympholept think?
The soma, nepenthe, the sweet panacea he sought,

The lotos ambrosial, the heavenly nectar, the potion
That leading me dreamward in lavalike Lethe would lave
Which Neptune had swept from the nereid zone of the ocean
Would rival the reed of the Syrinx when Jupiter'd rave.

Green tea laced with juice of the orange an organ made vocal
Recalls when the angel descended on thinking he'd heard
In famed St. Cecilia's toccata the fatherly word
Of God in the heaven, but lo! 'twas a prelude more local.

You hear how the power aroused by the hum of the sea
In Homer is echoed at home in a cup of green tea.

36. Amphibrachic Reply to Annie Finch
lamenting my inability to translate a long poem in rhymed amphibrachs

amphibrachic tetrameter
x/x x/x x/x x/(x)
x/x x/x x/x x/(x)
x/x x/x x/x x/(x)
x/x x/x x/x x/(x)

Thanks, Annie. Kapóvich I know I've neglected.
I'm sorry I failed to write sooner. The rhymes!
They're beautiful, yet—at the finest of times—
Beyond me. It's something I never expected.

She's given me one of the sweetest of meters—
A skill I appreciate, gratefully savor.
She's done, for the reader, an excellent favor.
But even espresso-aid, several liters,

Would leave me, inevitably, at a loss.
The cantering, bantering, chanting—delightful.
I cannot, however, deliver the rightful,
The lithe acrobatics. Far simpler to toss

Blithe casual rhymes in the air without thinking
Of liters of coffee I'd have to be drinking.

37. Song for Paul Jordan

amphibrachic tetrameter catalectic
x/x x/x x/x x/
x/x x/x x/x x/
x/x x/x x/x x/
x/x x/x x/x x/

Exciting! If only I'm able to sleep…
We're playing again in the morning. I'll need
A pilot's flight-readiness: fiendish indeed,
For sightreaders, tricky transitions; the leap

You make beyond logic when ledger lines rise
So high and so many—no counting them! New
Connections of neurons are forming for you.
No flagging, reflecting, or lagging! The wise

Unwearied musician by listening learns
That rhythm and harmony hints in the air
In patterns are floating, enough and to spare,
In cello, piano, viola. He earns

A rapt satisfaction who, catching the clues,
Can trust to the neurons: they'll know what to use.

38. Song for Johanna Masters

amphibrachic tetrameter catalectic
x/x x/x x/x x/
x/x x/x x/x x/
x/x x/x x/x x/
x/x x/x x/x x/

johanna dot masters at yahoo dot com—
An amphibrach-ramble arising revives!
The limpid élan of the rhythm contrives
More intricate imprint than Omar Khayyam.

With wing irresistible flying we show
We fling aside habit. An amplitude, calm,
A galloping ambling, relaxing, a psalm
Of ringing triplicity hymn-singing drives.

Enlivened, not racing but praising, I play
With pause and rapidity, altering by
A breathing-like stress-then-a-resting, a sigh,

And then inhalation, more motion. We go
Along where the current may carry and sway
Soft-rocked by the wind as it wanders away.

39. Birthday Limericks for Larissa Shmailo

amphibrachic lines regular and catalectic
x/x x/x x/
x/x x/x x/
    x/x x/x
    x/x x/x
x/x x/x x/

So now you are sixty—hooray!
With feeling unmixed we can say,
    A middle-aged sixty,
    Betweeny-betwixty,
Means "Wisely I'm seizing the day!"

And while I am at it, I'll add:
Five dozen—that isn't half bad.
    Another five dozen
    I'm wishing you, cousin,
For that's what the Moses-man had.

40. Lecture on the Limerick
for Katharina Mommsen

amphibrachic lines regular and catalectic
x/x x/x x/(x)
x/x x/x x/(x)
    x/x x/(x)
    x/x x/(x)
x/x x/x x/(x)

Der Knüppel liegt immer beim Hund?
Why worry? *Es giebt keinen Grund.*
    Relax for a minute,
    There's happiness in it.
The work is abyssal—*ein Schlund!*

I'd like to do versing in German,
But errors would earn me a sermon.
    My best—macaronic.
    The test is a tonic:
Its worth, connoisseurs will determine.

The limerick tune's amphibrachic
And anacreontic and bacchic.
    The meter assures
    The cheerfulness cures
Your bilious ills or stomachic.

The form of the lines in the middle
Is something I'll quickly unriddle:
    A shape catalectic

>   Will make them less hectic,
> More gentle—an air on the fiddle.
>
> The galloping, rollicking measure
> Will grant you a frolicking pleasure,
> >   And metrical pause
> >   You'll welcome because
> The resting's a genuine treasure.
>
> Perfection in metrical craft,
> A practical topic, not daft,
> >   I've treated awhile
> >   In elegant style
> And frequently happily laughed.
>
> My letter the lesson will send;
> Farewell, my poetical friend!
> >   May every impression
> >   Your energy freshen—
> And strength to your pen let it lend.

41. Limericks for Richard

amphibrachic lines catalectic
x/x x/x x/
x/x x/x x/
    x/x x/
    x/x x/
x/x x/x x/

A limerick needs to be slim.
Yet thinness won't mean that it's flim-
    sy. Better to say:
    Where's a will there's a way.
Let rigor be tempered with whim.

        Panegymeric
for a genealogist of his own paternal lineage

Of Boswellological lore
Than Richard none ever knew more.
    If that's what you seek,
    Be glad, for unique,
You'll see, is the treasure in store.

42. Lives of the Poets

amphibrachic lines regular and catalectic
x/x x/x x/x
x/x x/x x/x
    x/x x/
    x/x x/
x/x x/x x/x

He wanted a rhyme for Nantucket,
This poet, but such was his luck it
    Took over a year.
    He uttered a cheer
Exultant but—whoops!—kicked the bucket.

43. An Upbeat, Three Triplets, and Ringingly

amphibrachic lines with syllable added or subtracted
x/x x/x x/xx
x/x x/x x/
x/x x/x x/xx
x/x x/x x/

An upbeat, three triplets, and ringingly,
First bird of the vernal I heard.
He versed it with verve, and so springingly
It perfectly turns into word.

Fatigued, I the "Seven Beatitudes"
Had only just finished this morn.
His heavenly anthem of gratitudes
Then thrillingly willed me reborn.

An interval sequence repeatedly
Awoke—sing and hear it with me:
c / D-e-c / D-e-c / D-e-c.
Behold: we're a glee club of three!

*II
Anapest*

44. Lim(b)ericks

anapestic lines regular and catalectic
xx/ xx/ xx/(x)
xx/ xx/ xx/(x)
    xx/ xx/(x)
    xx/ xx/(x)
xx/ xx/ xx/(x)

When the time came to leave Queen Calypso,
Sad Ulysses would not leave her lips, so
    He at length made it clear
    It was only the fear
Of Penelope's wrath moved the ships so.

Things were never much better with Circe.
Turning men into animals—mercy!
    It was misery for
    The new bull, bear, and boar.
But I've made it a well-metered verse, see?

Now the way that Ulysses went after
The Cyclopean eye would bring laughter
    To the arrogant few,
    But with little ado
He'd have hanged the young punk from the rafter.

Then Ulysses came home. It is hard.
"What I need is a narrative bard.
    And he's got to bring with him
    A good sense of rhythm

Or likely be feathered and tarred."

Dear Ulysses, I'll be at your service,
Not a thing on the planet can swerve us.
   I am handy and gallant
   And, banding our talent,
We'll know that no foe can unnerve us.

What you want is a Musical Master.
You have found one. I'll work all the faster.
     But while feeling the need
     For a suitable speed
I'll write featly. No fear of disaster.

I'm a Minstrel, a merry métier,
And I really rev up when I play
     On my limerick lyre,
     Plink the lyrical wire,
And with daring desire have my way.

Epilogue
*for Peter and Terry, in the hope that
you'll like the limerick lecture*

Light verse for you, and may it lighten
The hours with newly-spawning sun,
For if we will our mind-time righten
'Twill help make eve and dawning one.

Calendrical manipulation
Is like the planning of a tune:

We choose a metric application
Of solar measure, or of moon.

If we our tempo by a star
Should gauge, it may appear absorbed,
While atom-orbit rhythm far
More quick would be than planet orbed.

Perhaps the beating of the heart
A finer timepiece were than all:
The body's horologic art
Has lent me clock and watchman-call.

45. James Joyce

anapest
xx/ xx/ xx/
xx/ xx/ xx/
    xx/ xx/
    xx/ xx/
xx/ xx/ xx/

Superstitious? A rat makes him faint.
(He a "rational animal" ain't.)
    He was flummoxed by thunder
    And sure 'tis no wonder,
He wasn't exactly a saint.

46. Invitation to the Dance

alternating anapestic tetrameter and trimeter
xx/ xx/ xx/ xx/
    xx/ xx/ xx/
xx/ xx/ xx/ xx/
    xx/ xx/ xx/

As from Pushkin's "The Cloud" I'd of amphibrachs
   learned
      And to quick emulation had turned,
Poet Lérmontov's "Angel" and "Raven" had set
      An example I'd never forget

Of another triplicity, anapest named,
      That in many a ballad acclaimed
(Think of "Mermaid"—O blest!—which I deeply
   admire)
      Soon would school me a lilt to acquire.

Since the triples have died in American verse
      I'll a favorite urging rehearse:
Come and dance with me, Friend, on the poetry
   shore
      And awaken a melody-lore.

In the dawn or the twilight the colors will blend
      On the wavelets that shoreward extend,
And you'll love as you listen the pow'r of the tides
      Where the heartbeat, a-pounding, abides.

47. Three Lermontovian Seekers
in "Angel," "Desire," "Mermaid"

alternating anapestic tetrameter and trimeter
xx/ xx/ xx/ xx/
   xx/ xx/ xx/
xx/ xx/ xx/ xx/
   xx/ xx/ xx/

For the "Angel" contentment no better is known
    Than to circle the heavenly throne
And to chant to the Lord in seraphical way—
    But the Soul it has borne cannot stay.

It descends to the earth and may wistfully yearn,
    When the misery ends, to return.
Much more lucky, the Raven may fly, if it please,
    To the westernmost isle in the seas.

Yet the poet, not raven-like, sadly is left
    Back in Russia, of mentor bereft.
For his forebear, a Scot, came to settle in snow
    Whence the fettered descendant can't go.

Like the angel-borne Soul he'll be stuck where he's found.
    So the Mermaid her dolor will sound:
She'll the Sailor bewail, for her love he'll forsake:
    He is dead and may never awake.

48. Pharaoh Accepts Allah
written after hearing a talk by Bart D. Ehrman

alternating anapestic tetrameter and trimeter
xx/ xx/ xx/ xx/
    xx/ xx/ xx/
xx/ xx/ xx/ xx/
    xx/ xx/ xx/

There's a gospel, in Coptic, where Pilate repents—
    And the meaning, for him, is immense:
Seeming pure as a lamb and untouched by a taint
    He's promoted at once to a saint.

In the gospels of Mark, Matthew, Luke, and of John
    More attractive he got further on
Than he'd earlier been. So the tactic they'd use
    Would cast more and more blame on the Jews.

In the legend of Jesus if Pilate's a saint
    In the Moses account may we paint
Evil Pharaoh as likewise converting to be
    What we'd wish, in our Eden, to see?

The Qur'an, in verse ten, ninety-one will disclose
    That, confronting his drowning, he chose
To "surrender" to faith in the God Moses taught
    Though in Him indignation he wrought.

49. Asiyah Accepts Allah

alternating anapestic tetrameter and trimeter
xx/ xx/ xx/ xx/
    xx/ xx/ xx/
xx/ xx/ xx/ xx/
    xx/ xx/ xx/

Well so much for the Pharaoh, but what of his wife?
    She'd convert—for a radiant life!
To the teaching Mosaic she turned, the Qur'an
    Will affirm. (She to heaven has gone,

And with Mary, Khadijah, and Fátima she,
    Says tradition, forever will be.)
Sixty-six, that's the chapter; eleven the verse:
    To the Better she turns from the worse.

Though when Pharaoh converts, God's a little upset
    Since the trouble He cannot forget
That the former had caused: the conversion, if true,
    Is a strange alteration of view.

But Asiyah, the Queen, isn't hard to believe:
    How sincere her entreaty! We grieve
When she prays to be saved from the king and his folk
    Who'd been nothing but burden and yoke.

50. Asiya Welcomes Moses

alternating anapestic tetrameter and trimeter
xx/ xx/ xx/ xx/
    xx/ xx/ xx/
xx/ xx/ xx/ xx/
    xx/ xx/ xx/

Now a flashback: the boy from the river was brought—
    Baby Moses—and straightaway caught
The attention of kindly Asiya, the Queen—
    In her motherly loving serene.

In the twenty-eighth sura, verse nine, she declares
    He'll provide "consolation" from cares:
"For a son" "we may choose him," she adds—it is clear
    From the start, how she held him so dear!

I would like, just a little, to speculate now
    If the liberty you may allow:
I would guess that the seed of the faith in the Lord
    That she'd later maintain was reward

For her tender compassion: heart godly I see.
    As "Beneficent," "Merciful" He
Who created the worlds in Qur'an is acclaimed,
    Blest in Being, the Ninety-Nine-Named.

51. Midnight Hymn

alternating anapestic tetrameter and trimeter
xx/ xx/ xx/ xx/
    xx/ xx/ xx/
xx/ xx/ xx/ xx/
    xx/ xx/ xx/

Though I haven't a theme, I am gladdened to start:
    Why did smiling arise in the heart?
There's a laughter inside me that wants to proclaim:
    Praise the Being that no one can name!

It has given my body an alchemy rare,
    That the element solar, most fair,
Which the morning awakes may transform what I write
    Into semblance of heaven's own light.

What is gold? The aurora, the aura, the or
    That with gules of the dawning our lore
Of the heroes of legend adorning is found:
    Red and yellow, on azurine ground.

In my spirit the primary colors are prime:
    O inspirers of rhythm and rhyme,
I will lift up my hands for the lauding of you—
    Sing at midnight, remanned, Hallelu!

52. Reading Miles Tittle on William Morris

alternating anapestic tetrameter and trimeter
xx/ xx/ xx/ xx/
    xx/ xx/ xx/
xx/ xx/ xx/ xx/
    xx/ xx/ xx/

I am reading this evening a tome to review
    Where an essay was writ to renew
An awareness of something long vanished, unknown,
    That was sold, "private property" grown:

An unfinished *Aeneid* where Morris had scribed
    Latin verse that Burne-Jones had imbibed
In the spirit and lyrical paintings had made,
    Helping Vergil his legend unlade.

It remained incomplete, for the styles had diverged
    When a change in their thought had emerged:
Figures languid and bent and pre-Raphaelite
    Were for Norse-loving Morris not right.

He went on, a translation to make on his own
    Where the sources he hoped to have shown
That preceded the polished Vergilian art
    And would speak to a northerly heart.

53. Reading Helsinger on Hegel

alternating anapestic tetrameter and trimeter
xx/ xx/ xx/ xx/
    xx/ xx/ xx/
xx/ xx/ xx/ xx/
    xx/ xx/ xx/

The abstracting awareness of metrical scheme
    Will a thinking perceiver beseem,
But the metrical feeling it generates, too,
    Brings our bodily strength into view.

Borne along by the beat we are conscious of *time*
    While it forward is flowing. Through rhyme,
Which repeatedly pauses, reflection to aid,
    Of our *thought* we more conscious are made.

So from body to spirit we focus advance,
    Yet in both they'll each other enhance:
Half-abstractive is body-strong meter, we saw—
    Half-concrete is the rhyming tones' law.

Who would unify body and spirit in one
    And with wisdom would live 'neath the sun
Will have energies wedded and vigor unloosed—
    Holy Being rejoiced and rejuiced.

54. A Thought from Lao-Tse

alternating anapestic tetrameter and trimeter
xx/ xx/ xx/ xx/
    xx/ xx/ xx/
xx/ xx/ xx/ xx/
    xx/ xx/ xx/

As you never can lose what you hadn't possessed
    Let the spirit be moved but at rest.
Worried fear had infected the angel that fell
    And he hasn't been doing too well.

"What will so-and-so, high and exalted, of me
    Be supposing? Rebuke may I see
When I look in his eye, who the judgment will call?
    Will I favor acquire? Will I fall?"

Be alerted: stern eyes are but mirroring you
    When you're judged by whatever they do.
And they each in a carnival fun-house appear
    Where the forms are distorted by fear.

And your growth is aborted whenever you think
    That your fortunes are made, or will sink,
In proportion as forms at the carnival change
    While the portraits your heart-life estrange.

55. A Stray Bird from Tagore

alternating anapestic tetrameter and trimeter
xx/ xx/ xx/ xx/
    xx/ xx/ xx/
xx/ xx/ xx/ xx/
    xx/ xx/ xx/

World a vastier mask having doffed for awhile
    Would the mind in the quiet beguile.
Subatomical dervishes, too, become still
    When the tiny's divined what you will.

As a cat on the chair of her person-friend purrs
    That to revel in presence prefers,
Tell a lesson, dear Mentor, when rain in the trees
    Will to spirit be speaking of ease.

Primal love which exploded, exploring the dawn,
    In the Binghamton Bang lingers on:
As the heart of the hearer expands in the dark,
    Holds the eye, from the solar, a spark.

They are never bereft, as I yesterday said,
    Who behold, not possess, and are led
To the scripture of breathing. We're scribing aright:
    Blood and bone become flood-tone in light.

56. Wave

alternating anapestic tetrameter and trimeter
xx/ xx/ xx/ xx/
    xx/ xx/ xx/
xx/ xx/ xx/ xx/
    xx/ xx/ xx/

I'm a wave and of up and of down am I made,
    High and low, by the light and the shade,
In my passion to rise, then collapse on the shore,
    Sliding back to the source evermore.

How I swell in the noontide, subside in the night!
    Blent by melding of dark and of bright
To the sun I must climb, drawn aside by the moon,
    Whirled in multidirectional swoon!

When from cloud-rumble spawning the droplets come down
    They're upraised in me, wave, ere they drown.
From my crest will the spume and the spindrift illume
    Plenilunary gaze in the gloom.

One-and-multiple wills of the meetings in me
    Rush assurgent as wind in the tree.
I will mirror your face over sand that I lave:
    We are siblings, a wind and a wave.

57. Hippo

alternating anapestic tetrameter and trimeter
xx/ xx/ xx/ xx/
    xx/ xx/ xx/
xx/ xx/ xx/ xx/
    xx/ xx/ xx/

An Egyptian clay hippo I lovingly view
    With her multiple lotus tattoo.
Every stage in the growth of the plant may be seen
    For a hippo-like symbol serene.

It is glazed in the vivid and sumptuous hue
    Of a sky rich in brightness of blue.
Who the riddle of hippo and lotus can know
    May enriched by fertility grow.

Stems awave in the wind and new-budded in spring
    Hymn the blessing that pregnancies bring.
And it happened that on the computer today
    Blissful hippos were floating my way.

To the emblems attend: let fecundity come
    By the Nile—hear a thunderbolt drum!
Be the eye of Osiris amenable to
    Productivity-season for you!

58. Beard

alternating anapestic tetrameter and trimeter
xx/ xx/ xx/ xx/
    xx/ xx/ xx/
xx/ xx/ xx/ xx/
    xx/ xx/ xx/

I'm resculpting my face, vernal spirit to soothe,
    'Tis the place and the time to feel smooth.
With the cut "number one" a few decades you shed:
    Let to spring-mood be memory led.

Though the photos remain that I'd never erase,
    With a forest-growth framing the face,
Yet the wintry-big thicket (Walt Whitman, Karl Marx)
    I would trade for "Wot larx, Pip, wot larx!"

To recapture the past, present doldrum to fix,
    I'm remaking my age: twenty-six.
I would then wear a beard in a style that was trim
    (Though my mother said "No!" and looked
        grim).

I am eager to act at the weather's behest
    And adapt Mother Nature's bequest:
Find in season a reason: may each be a spice,
    Finer taste for our life to entice.

59. *Cor Ma(t)ris*

alternating anapestic tetrameter and trimeter
xx/ xx/ xx/ xx/
    xx/ xx/ xx/
xx/ xx/ xx/ xx/
    xx/ xx/ xx/

How peculiar that meaning should music these lines
    If the words be conceptual signs.
When I play violin there's no verb and no noun:
    Even adjective, adverb might frown.

It is meter that urges me, present, intense,
    While awaiting conceptual sense.
And the sweeter it surges me, more grows the faith
    Which a body may lend to the wraith.

Steady beat of the tides of the sea, there abides
    In your heart, dear my Mother, what hides
Till the wind-swell be clad in a body made glad
    Chanting praise of awaking, half mad.

Words emotion enwreathed when the spirit-wind breathed:
    Light awoken from earth have they sheathed.
They arise from the ocean, the world's beating heart,
    Whence the life and the soul of my art.

60. Haydn's *De Angustiis* and Fauré's *Requiem*

for Bruce Borton, our Binghamton University Chorus conductor, with 13 years' worth of gratitude

alternating anapestic tetrameter and trimeter
xx/ xx/ xx/ xx/
    xx/ xx/ xx/
xx/ xx/ xx/ xx/
    xx/ xx/ xx/

Every psalm that I sing in the hundred-voiced choir
    Joys in calm- or in thunder-desire.
Troubled times in the Haydn, grave care in Fauré,
    Horrid burdens that world-night affray,

Are re-moaned and redeemed: you re-travel the waves
    When a mage with a tone-gift embraves.
All the moods that awake I remake in my heart—
    For Cecilia would sainthood impart

When the poet-composer a testament sung,
    Whom the tides of the ocean kept young.
They are lifeblood within, as you'll readily hear
    When you lift up a shell to the ear.

If a parent should say you are hearing the sea,
    Reply smiling, "The ocean's *in me*.
Through much-amplified echo this object I hold
    Can my ear's tonal blood-flow make bold."

61. Life in Color

alternating anapestic tetrameter and trimeter
xx/ xx/ xx/ xx/
*   xx/ xx/ xx/*
xx/ xx/ xx/ xx/
*   xx/ xx/ xx/*

We can chant what we fancy. Our nature, in brief,
    Is to test hypothetic belief.
While we're singing a thing that we feel, it is true:
    Rain on leaves for a greening of blue.

You, in potency mainly, are All at the start,
    And when nourished, a flourishing heart
Will abound in the beauty of hymning the skies
    If you're treelike allowed to arise.

We the red in the warmth of the morning, crepusc-
    ular pink in the dawn or the dusk,
Raise from yellow and orange to white during noon:
    Gleaming blinds but the green is a boon.

Blue turns indigo, violet. Finally black
    The Unmanifest holds. Taken back,
With our odyssey done for the day we comply,
    Blessed breath to our Lover re-sigh.

62. Indef(l)ectible

alternating anapestic tetrameter and trimeter
xx/ xx/ xx/ xx/
    xx/ xx/ xx/
xx/ xx/ xx/ xx/
    xx/ xx/ xx/

Till the last of my days I'll be waiting for you
    And be swayed in a vast hallelu:
When the first of the robins of spring I could view
    In the morning burst forth, I sang too.

It is tricky to picture a species of bird
    Called "the critic," whose tone would be heard
'Midst the choir in their hymnody: freedom and fate
    Swell the throats of the folk we elate.

As in stretching to heaven the sprouts will become
    What their total potential may sum,
So the robin aquiver with love that can't rest
    Had by destiny sighed for a quest.

That each person might happy in homestead abide,
    Has the world been created so wide
(Waldo Emerson wrote). Follow boldly your star
    And be true to the Being you are.

63. Staying Power

alternating anapestic tetrameter and trimeter
xx/ xx/ xx/ xx/
  xx/ xx/ xx/
xx/ xx/ xx/ xx/
  xx/ xx/ xx/

In arranging your flowers take maximal care:
   Time will pass and your work yet be there.
Unregarding of age, never petal will fall:
   Fate no color may earthward re-call.

It is claimed that our flowers and friendship will fade
   As the leaves in their graveyard are laid.
For both science and poetry—doleful mistake:
   Stubborn error's a bane—let's awake.

With serene immobility stands the bouquet
   I have greeted—four years—every day:
We symmetrical balance in curvature learn
   And for grace, the unburdener, yearn.

Who from mission won't flinch nor at shadow will
  g(r)asp—
   Happy time-world these folk will enclasp.
They're more calm than a psalm in the summery
  sun
   With, in winter, their force not fordone.

64. Thanksgiving Wreath

alternating anapestic tetrameter and trimeter
xx/ xx/ xx/ xx/
    xx/ xx/ xx/
xx/ xx/ xx/ xx/
    xx/ xx/ xx/

Branches rounding my wreath have a willow-wand look
    Whence the craftsman a color-plan took—
Fruit and wheat-seed and ribbon configured in plaid
    Well enwound in the bow-cloth are clad

In a goldening bronze to envelop the whole:
    "Be a Solomon-seal for the soul,
Be a welcomer! At your receptive behest
    Let my homestead be greeting the guest!"

It is true that, although you three years had survived
    While the elements vainly had strived
To outdo all the features of fall in their strength
    Till they savagely felled you at length,

You undamaged collapsed (with the fastener torn)
    And once more by the door might be worn...
Yet your presence adorning my room is so dear
    I'm reluctant to move you. Stay here.

65. I Sing, Therefore I Am

alternating anapestic tetrameter and trimeter
xx/ xx/ xx/ xx/
    xx/ xx/ xx/
xx/ xx/ xx/ xx/
    xx/ xx/ xx/

Trade my poetry posy for Prozacky prose?
    Thank you, no. It is not what I chose
When my lips by the goddess with honey were smoothed
    And my soul by the moly well soothed.

Panacea Pangea provided for me
    By the myrtle and laurel, each tree
Being sacred—to Venus or Phoebus—and why?
    Love and verse are aspersed from on high.

Of a lisper who whispered in numbers I've heard
    But myself had to wait for the word
So appealing in sweetness by deity's gift
    To awake and my spirit to lift.

Sleeping beauty was Poesy, dormant within
    Till the bard should be hailed and begin
With a daily prostration to speak to the gods:
    Grace and patience have beaten the odds.

66. Song on a Saying

*"So tut jeder an seinem Platz, was ihm von Oben her
aufgetragen ist."*
—Katharina Mommsen

alternating anapestic tetrameter and trimeter
xx/ xx/ xx/ xx/
    xx/ xx/ xx/
xx/ xx/ xx/ xx/
    xx/ xx/ xx/

If while true to oneself, both in labor and love,
    We do freely things cherished above,
Ever easy the burden, and light is the yoke—
    So the acorn ascends to be oak.

Who have focused their goal on producing their fruit
    Feel a strength welling up from the root
That to scrutinize mindfully glad they postpone
    Till to makers and shapers they've grown.

What's immortal in each allegorical tree?
    'Tis a story of learning to be.
Focused upward and outward it hears from within:
    Be- is half of a daily Begin.

Undismayed by a plague of rebuke and regret,
    They're intent on their mission: Beget.
So Begin to Beget and in Wisdom you'll *Be*.
    This I feel when I think of a Tree.

67. Chant

alternating anapestic tetrameter and trimeter
xx/ xx/ xx/ xx/
    xx/ xx/ xx/
xx/ xx/ xx/ xx/
    xx/ xx/ xx/

All my thoughts have I chanted, in hope to enchant.
    Can a dogma be had? No, it can't.
Gnome and oracle, proverb and adage I craft:
    When they're wise have I cried as I laughed.

Should apostle-epistle, apocalypse be
    Ever credited, later, to me,
Never name me the way or the truth or the light:
    No indeed. That is pride. 'Tisn't right.

Should a feud of interpreters ever arise—
    Is it A, then, or B?—pray advise
The contenders the fertile reply will be Yes.
    'Tis the deep-dreaming self that I bless.

Don't promote me to god or to saint—a bit much,
    I would think: should your feeling be such
That you'd favor creating a song on your own,
    Rest assured you are never alone.

68. Style

alternating anapestic tetrameter and trimeter
xx/ xx/ xx/ xx/
    xx/ xx/ xx/
xx/ xx/ xx/ xx/
    xx/ xx/ xx/

Lengthy notes? I will never compose them—ah, no…
    Likewise *widthy* and *depthy* must go.
Close proximity—phrase that one ought to eschew
    Till the distant kind's brought into view.

And proximity's meaning? Pure nextness, I fear:
    "In propinquity" merely means near.
And *the media is*? Well, a medium is,
    But keep media plural. Gee whiz!

I am told I should "tweet like a girl tweets"—oh, yike!
    "As she tweets" would be better than "like."
And my point is, is never to lie to the press.
    Why repeat the main verb? Who can guess?

I am always relieved, splendid essay to read
    Where for *arguably* there's no need.
Never increase, or growth, in our prose anymore:
    Unrelenting, the *uptick*s outpour.

69. Torch and Bucket

alternating anapestic tetrameter and trimeter
xx/ xx/ xx/ xx/
    xx/ xx/ xx/
xx/ xx/ xx/ xx/
    xx/ xx/ xx/

When with water-filled pail and a torch burning bright
    Lady Rábi'a walked, she'd incite
Many questioners: "Pray, would you kindly explain—
    What's the goal that you hope to attain?"

"When I prayed to be spared from the flaming of hell,
    Fires had seared me—I feel how they fell.
When I asked to gain heaven through sanctified grace
    I could see the door slam in my face.

As I love my Lord God for His nature alone
    I no other reward want to own.
Since I love my Lord God for His nature held dear
    There's no hell that I ever can fear.

With my bucket I plan all the hell fire to drench
    And its very idea to quench.
And I want with my torch to set heaven ablaze
    In the hope not a trace of it stays."

70. The Cats of Istanbul
after the movie "Jedi"

alternating anapestic tetrameter and trimeter
xx/ xx/ xx/ xx/
    xx/ xx/ xx/
xx/ xx/ xx/ xx/
    xx/ xx/ xx/

"Cats are conscious of God—so my parents would
  tell.
       Dogs think people are deities. Well—
We're just middlemen—cats are aware of it, so
       They are grateful, but know what they know."

"And the females have elegance—really, I'd say
       It is gone from most women today.
When you look at a cat, though, at last you begin
       To awake the wild creature within."

"They're like people—controlling, or bashful, or slow,
       Or—aristocrats—won't say hello.
Now the one I just love is a psychopath cat,
       She's the boss, and you've got to like *that*!

And her husband she guards! Him she'll fiercely
  protect
       So he'll treat her with fear and respect.
He compliantly waits till her dinner is done:
       Only then will his own have begun."

"All my cats I adore. Says my therapist, I'm
    Healing wounds of my own every time
I take care of them, feed them. The wounds must be bad—
    Not yet healed—but a cat makes me glad."

"If some water you might in the Afterlife need,
    These containers keep filled, and pay heed.
Than my grandma my cat was more precious to me—
    Yes, the feline more 'heaven' would be."

"All your surplus of energy cats will receive—
    And the field-soil does, too, some believe.
In my praying-beads daily a strength I can find
    Just to leave all my troubles behind."

"Folks who cannot love cats don't love people. It's true!
    When a cat's looking upward at you,
Life itself you feel smiling. I've watched them for hours,
    And they've got supernatural pow'rs."

71. Preoccupied Mind

alternating anapestic tetrameter and trimeter
xx/ xx/ xx/ xx/
    xx/ xx/ xx/x
xx/ xx/ xx/ xx/
    xx/ xx/ xx/x

The preoccupied mind, a solution to find
    To a problem that's dourly remembered
May forget to breathe deep, all attention will keep
    On a realm where the Mays are Novembered.

A conception is not what we've captured and caught
    But more often controls the conceiver.
And of glory the thief is a hoary belief,
    Hidden, tortuous reef, a bereaver.

Let your breath remain free, that a meaning may be
    By the steady refreshment protected,
For the motion you feel may an ocean reveal:
    By the tide is our life resurrected.

Every minute the taste of our living in haste
    We neglect for its wasting reflection
In a sentence begot by the remnants of thought.
    Lend the sweven a friendly affection!

72. An Apostle Epistle
to Larry Lockridge

anapestic tetrameter
xx/ xx/ xx/ xx/
xx/ xx/ xx/ xx/
xx/ xx/ xx/ xx/
xx/ xx/ xx/ xx/

How delightful the praise! but how sad the lament!
As my spirit you lift by the wit you have sent
Be assured that your conquest of muteness will be
Perfect treasure forever extended to me.

What's an author? I'm paying a nominal fee
For each amazon printing: so far, readers three
(You included) to August have happiness lent
As my value they've triply confirmed. Thus it went

With my earlier writings that amazon placed
In the world: they've with profit quite modestly
   graced
Humble striver whose mind has in rhapsody raced.

Thus I chant, and my bread on the waters I cast,
And when days upon days have on calendar passed
I shall see it again (claims the Preacher) at last.

73. I'm beginning to write, and again as before

Each playful bear—
A nature pray'r.

anapestic tetrameter
xx/ xx/ xx/ xx/
xx/ xx/ xx/ xx/
xx/ xx/ xx/ xx/
xx/ xx/ xx/ xx/

I'm beginning to write and again as before
Waken energies dormant, a morning-tide sign:
I'm so filled with the will to sing forth, I a door
Have to open: let melody exit, divine!

O be praised that the gift of the maker is mine!
To the Nameless One blessing unending I pour—
Every summoner muster! Eyes, ears I incline,
For the calling will come: speak the "and," say the
    "or"!

Never harvest I hoard, for the heart will restore—
In the time that can, subtle and supple, combine
By the whirl of the spiral the circle and line—

What I viewed in the friendship of bears on the shore
Of the river in film on computer screen: more
They exuberance proved than the nightingale's wine.

74. Should the time and the clime and sky be exciting

anapestic tetrameter
xx/ xx/ xx/ xx/x
xx/ xx/ xx/ xx/
xx/ xx/ xx/ xx/x
xx/ xx/ xx/ xx/

Should the time and the clime and the sky be exciting
And the ground be resounding with motion unknown,
It is then you will ken that a power's inviting
What in summer had slept till the summons were shown.

There are lives to arrive, so be open, awaken
What you'd dared not to think, so oblivious grown:
From your lethargied Lethe by storm-thrust be shaken
When the maple-top watches the high, the Alone.

Be the darkness no Nil but a Nile overflowing;
Of the silence of Night hear the deep-hidden tone:
To the dark of your soul be a hearkener, going
Where the ways of the Maker shape air and form stone.

More receptive than wax, more than marble retaining,
Let the gift you were granted be manifest boon:
In the brain may the *lares, penates* remaining
Give their aid to the shaman in Mercury-shoon.

75. I've with pleasure described the contentment of cats

alternating anapestic tetrameter and trimeter
xx/ xx/ xx/ xx/
    xx/ xx/ xx/
xx/ xx/ xx/ xx/
    xx/ xx/ xx/

I've with pleasure described the contentment of cats
    When they calmly consider their lives.
They apply (as I've learned) a capacity that's
    Meant to strengthen what's liked and survives.

By a scent quite distinctive the feline ensures
    It will recognize where it has lain.
Where the fragrance identifies, comfort endures
    And return's a recognizant gain.

After delicate pheromones reverie wake
    Revelation ensues: think of Proust.
The olfactory organs an artifice make
    Of the memories richly unloosed.

With the finding of lines that I'd written before
    A volupty voluminous comes.
Vivid sense can re-thrill from a long-hidden store
    While the muse on her dulcimer thrums.

We are told that the cat is a creature of place:
    That is true when aromas are lent.
In poetical mood with enveloping grace
    Words at length may reveal what they meant.

76. Deep the breath you inhale while you're waiting for thought

alternating anapestic tetrameter and trimeter
xx/ xx/ xx/ xx/
   xx/ xx/ xx/
xx/ xx/ xx/ xx/
   xx/ xx/ xx/

Deep the breath you inhale while you're waiting for thought:
    By no compass within is it caught.
It the palate will heighten—and brighten the eyes:
    Widened lungs will avail in the sighs.

Height will generate breadth, while the depth can beguile
    And the face may awaken to smile.
I'm beginning to laugh at the effort required
    To depict how I simply respired.

When the psalmist wrote, "Lift up your heads, O ye gates,"
    He had shown what occurs: one awaits
What will come to the mind, but the journey to thought
    Is the best of the pleasure that's brought.

'Tis the Jordan we swim, while the shoreline our sight
    'Mid the chill may more finely delight:

We more treasure the meadows that effort will reach
    When we've swum and have come to the
        beach.

O the tone of the breakers, the surf on the sand,
    When we're gently approaching the land!
I am borne on the swell of the wave while the Lord
    Is Himself the impórtuned reward.

77. Excerpt from "To Saul Levin, a Letter in Sonnets"

anapestic trimeter
xx/ xx/ xx/(x)
xx/ xx/ xx/(x)
xx/ xx/ xx/(x)
xx/ xx/ xx/(x)

"To Saul Levin, a letter in sonnets"—
Anapestic, it swirled into song!
Tripping trimeters move me along.
If Stokowsky, André Kostelanetz,

Leonard Bernstein (an athlete!), or, say,
If Nuréyev had known, to their leaping
They'd have added ('tis really in keeping
With performative antics) a way

To keep viewer and hearer delighted,
Namely myriad sonnets by me,
Each a dance, like a wave of the sea:
Minuet, ländler, polska—I've cited

Three more triplets in order to show
Primigenial rhythms mean "Go!"

78. Glossolaliology

anapestic tetrameter
xx/ xx/ xx/ xx/(x)(x)
xx/ xx/ xx/ xx/(x)(x)
xx/ xx/ xx/ xx/(x)(x)
xx/ xx/ xx/ xx/(x)(x)

With a gadget for gauging cephalic geography
A neurologist wonders what triggers the lungs
To a seeming-disorderly speaking-in-tongues:
Single photon emission computed tomography

Is a powerful tool to create three-dimensional
(Volumetric) portrayals of X-rays of brains.
With a radioactive injection in veins
Comes a CAT scan suggesting the words aren't intentional.

For the frontal lobes, usual speech-control center,
Into grand glossolalias never will enter.
But no scientist knows what had made them arise.

Glossolaliological findings are scant.
We would like to know more, but right now we just can't—
Patient waiting, the only right role of the wise.

III
Dactyl

79. Why should we write in the form of dactylic Ovidian distich?

Ovidian distich
/xx /xx /xx /xx /xx /x
/xx /xx / - /xx /xx /

Why should we write in the form of dactylic Ovidian distich?
    Ambling, relaxing the tone—rambling and casual chat.
Practical-minded the mode of the rapidly metered logistic,
    Feeling so natural-grown—major, the pleasure in *that*!
Perfectly suited for each personality, cynic to mystic.
    Planning and scanning well known, purr and be calm as a cat.

Ancient the rhythm, but Grecians and Romans weren't given to rhyming.
    Would you prefer that we rhyme—or that the versing be blank?
Music won't suffer, whatever your choice, for the lines will be crafted,
    Harmony ever kept sweet—vowel or consonant placed
Fitly to grant what we savor, alliterative, assonantal
    Patterns to comfort the ear, ev'n while delighting the mind.

Since in our fourteen-lined sonnet-like form the conclusion's arriving
    Soon, would you write me what you, personally, would prefer?

80. Rhymes or blank verse for my couplet? Well, no one will offer an answer

Ovidian distich
/xx /xx /xx /xx /xx /x
/xx /xx / - /xx /xx /

Rhymes or blank verse for my couplet? Well, no one will offer an answer.
    Why not assume that they're *both* viable? That's what I'll do.
Problem resolved. I'm aware that in Hegel's *Aesthetics* he argued
    Rhyming is highly unwise when it's a question of forms
Which for millennia hadn't been rhymed, as their founding idea
    Can't be combined with a thought suited to times later on
Smoothly and fittingly. Novelty's bad when it's mere contradiction.
    Hegel, I hear you—and yet, cannot accept what you claim.
While you were speaking, Euterpë came in and said *Look to the future:*
    Present and past may be blent—serving the purpose of each.
Hegel the owl of Minerva consulted, who only at evening
    Spread out her wings for a flight. Seek you the robin of dawn.

Isn't it fun to be reading when meter is gliding and flowing?
    I'd be prepared to contend writing it doubles the joy.
Solon, Theognis, Tyrtaeus, Callimachus—even wise Plato
    Tried it, and later we find Romans who loved it no less:
Ovid, Propertius, Tibullus... In Germany, Goethe a memoir—
    Telling how love had in Rome freed him from duty and care—
Wrote in the classical form; and the "Metamorphosë der Pflanzen,"
    Where the evolving of plants he would attempt to explain—
That has Ovidian melody, too. Now the question arises:
    Why don't the Anglo's take part? Why I am chanting alone?
Baffled, one needn't be sad: we'll move on and do something productive,
    Being alive to what lives. Forward, with Orpheus' aid!

81. Being two people at once may lend energy perfect requital

Ovidian distich
/xx /xx /xx /xx /xx /x
/xx /xx / - /xx /xx /

Being two people at once may lend energy perfect requital.
      Selfhood is boring? And yet—self when divided in two
Offers a colloquy. Shared, the perspectives of both are more vital.
      Love you will give and will win. Double advantage for you!
Reading the scripture within him, Muhammad in triumph-recital,
      Teacher and learner combined, showed us, each one, what
      to do.

Two are the ways that the doubling is done. In a mind-conversation,
      A had suggested to *B* (both of them dwell in my brain),
"How about proofreading twenty-five lyrics and blogs? A summation
      Then you may, confident, write: this will the Preface contain.
Work through the night and they're finished. Okay?" *B* replied with
      elation,
      "Sure, let's get busy! No prob! Pleasure with maximal gain!"

Dialogue, then, for good planning's a help. But your psyche-division
      Also at times will occur quite independent of plan.
Being trans-ported, trace-lated in ecstasy means that a scission
      Comes: you are split, you are two. Truly "beside yourself."
      Man!
That's what the Greeks called ec-static! A *standing apart*! What
      precision!
      How to attain such a bliss? Here's how the rhapsodist can:

After completing a hymn that is bursting with lyrical feeling,
> Do something else for awhile. Later, returning, you'll see
Something occur that may stun you and leave you quite weak-kneed and reeling:
> How could this marvel have been written by someone like me?
Prostrate yourself to the gods, who their love for you, blest, are revealing:
> *Rise! and with fire-word go forth, people by heart-warmth to free.*

82. Long have I wanted to see in the mind as a painting the prophet

Ovidian distich
/xx /xx /xx /xx /xx /x
/xx /xx / - /xx /xx /

Long have I wanted to see in the mind as a painting the prophet
    Whom, writing first-person lines, Pushkin had made us behold.
After the angel his tongue had removed, and inserted the snake-tongue,
    Watch him upraise it, two prongs, wet in the venomous mouth.
Double tines needed for stereo-smell make it hard to imagine
    How he could utter a word, even at angel-command.
Deadly potential maintained by the flickering forked apparatus,
    Shall we perceive it emerge—splurt!—from the lips of a man?
Try as you will, though, to google the picture that I am describing,
    Nothing at all will you find. Maybe the theme lacks appeal?
Surely, in future portrayal, we'll view it in brave animation,
    Darting and two-tined and dark, fit not to speak but to kill.

Next I'll consider the fire-flaming coal that the angel inserted
    After the sufferer's heart he, hand ensanguined, removed.
Avid, the cavity, even though filled, is remaining wide open—
    Otherwise wouldn't the flame, covered with flesh-weight, expire?
How can the organ that's formed of a coal start to beat and empower
    Blood to flow smoothly throughout all of the body, revived?
Serpent-tongues never can speak, and a coal won't allow circulation:
    Now that reality's dead, super-reality wakes,

Coal in the chest and a snake-tongue in mouth—a surrealist
  painting:
    That's what we're offered. And so, reasonably I conclude:
Pushkin indeed is portraying a "prophet," whose wording can burn us
    Only when issuing forth, crazed, from the brush of Dalí.

"God" for the poet was father and czar, ugly double-tongued censor:
    What would rebellion then be? Stunned, we behold it right
      here.
Calling a cyborg with snake-flame components a "prophet" is
  prankish—
    Born from the dream-world, a joke—bellowed resentful in hell.
What's the command from the Lord? Just to word-burn the hearts of
  the people.
    Nothing of love or delight mentioned. *The burn, just the burn.*

83. Parable of the Squirrel

Ovidian distich
/xx /xx /xx /xx /xx /x
/xx /xx / - /xx /xx /

"Let us unearth what we buried last fall—now's the time," thought
  the squirrel.
    "Brain power focused on goal may the observer amaze.
Gratification delayed means we doubly enjoy the deferral
    That with imagining wise brightened the frigorous days.
Many folk 'grab it all now'—to their style I'd convey a demurral.
    Prudent, preserve in the depth what you much later can
      raise.

'Prudence,' I hear it objected, 'is timid, retarding your action.
    Trust to the future? Good luck! No one the future can know.
Winter may freeze you before you have eaten. For quick satisfaction,
    Banquet today, and be sure. Winds of the killer let blow—
Maybe they'll hit you and maybe they won't. You'll have lived! No
  retraction,
    Once you are fed, can be asked. Never procrastinate. No!'

Hunger in spring will be greater, however, when once I have rested—
    Just when the acorns I love cannot new-fallen appear.
Life is a journey, conceive it as such. For the pilgrims who've quested
    Foresight will lend a reward—pictured, kept well, and held
      dear.
Putting aside the attainments of youth for awhile, we'll have bested
    Rivals and challenges all—prudent, the bold needn't fear."

What have I learned from the squirrel? My poems through decades
  abounding

> I could accumulate, calm, while in hibernal repose
> They would be patient to wait till I'd further matured and a grounding
> > Gained for a way to re-win that which the spring would disclose.
> Racers may fail, while the pilgrimage-taker's not foundering, founding
> > Rather a method to show: where are things hidden?—he knows!

84. Why do religions live on? In the brain we've an organ for oneness

Ovidian distich
/xx /xx /xx /xx /xx /x
/xx /xx / - /xx /xx /

Why do religions live on? In the brain we've an organ for oneness.
    Jill Bolte Taylor described living with *that* in command—
She, having all of the functions of willing and goal-planning damaged,
    Given a Buddha-like peace, feeling of unity blest.
Now we can well comprehend why the brain-wave effects when they're measured
    Prove meditation techniques lend a tranquillity deep.
Ego, when blended with all that's around us, can make one reluctant
    Ever to wish to restore problems "normality" brings.
Taylor the "healing" achieved, and I'm happy she did, for her journey
    Opened a door that may now lead to poetical thought.

Things being blended, the I being Youniverse, all appears *living*.
    Einstein may tell me the same—matter seems energy calmed;
Energy, matter revivified. Interconvertible seemings,
    Then, are the motion and peace, contrast apparent not real.
Hills join the goat and the lamb in their leaping, the psalmer had told us...
    That's their *potential*, indeed: endless the energy stored.
Dogs that would shepherd the waves though the "sheep" in their whiteness may vanish
    Offer a psalm of their own, blending a feeling with deed.
Matter and force or Becoming and Being are one, they're unsundered.
    Metaphors merely remorph. Make of yourself what you will.

85. Seeking a melody fittingly handsome I need to be hearsome

Ovidian distich
/xx /xx /xx /xx /xx /x
/xx /xx / - /xx /xx /

Seeking a melody fittingly handsome I need to be hearsome,
    Hearkening, ready to shape all that is granted to me.
No, the strange word in the opening line isn't new, it may cheer some
    Readers to learn—and yet why not a neologist be?

People alerted to see may pursue an event to the sequel,
    Persons encouraged to touch might a toccata compose.
Folk more attracted to smell should beware: other things being equal,
    Odor of sanctity won't come from the saint that you chose.

Taste is amazing: it often is linked to the arts. Being tasteful
    May advantageous be deemed, too, in an elegant dress.
I would grateful, as well, if my hearer were careful, not hasteful
    (Aye, that's a coinage of mine), showing a kindly largesse.

Most of the lyric you've heard was a little excursion etymic.
Even if partly original, still I need wordwork to mimic.

86. Cold makes the birds a bit quieter: why should my words follow after?

Ovidian distich
/xx /xx /xx /xx /xx /x
/xx /xx / - /xx /xx /

Cold makes the birds a bit quieter: why should my words follow after?
    Pink and the gray of the brain picturing gold in the blue,
Chanting a hymn of the morning in warmth, may reply with a laughter
    Lighting the clouds that abide—seemingly piercing them through!
Thoughts travel faster than pinion might sail. May the resolute crafter,
    Shaping a day made to like, offer an alternate view.

Chilly it is, I admit, but the sky became orange and yellow
    While I was writing, and now: birds in their chamber group chat,
Maybe conversing in bafflement—how should a spring-minded fellow
    Deal with the cold and the damp? *I'd* be discouraged by that...
Let's check again—I can't see them but, yes, affirmations are mellow,
    Plans underway, we may guess—mind-bright though color be matt.

Branches are fallen and scattered—not hopes. If the grasses are growing
    Slowly, that's better than fast: lawns that are perfect to view
Likely were treated with chemicals. Noxious potential they're sowing
    Who, for the brightest of green, prudence unkindly eschew.
Louder, emphatic the singers!—how fine! With a fervor they're showing
    Melody makers are blest... Thanks for that vast hallelu!

87. Here's how the hours of the therapy went. Though the dream would be altered

Ovidian distich
/xx /xx /xx /xx /xx /x
/xx /xx / - /xx /xx /

Here's how the hours of the therapy went. Though the dream would
 be altered,
    Theme wouldn't vary at all: fully a night's worth of shame.
Always I'd failed in a strange obligation: I'd fatedly faltered...
    Remedy? Efforts to help...compensate? Burden of blame
Wouldn't and couldn't be lifted. With labor constricted and haltered
    On would I plod till the time ripe for awakening came.

Changes of episode rose when a movement too restless had made me
    Turn from the right to the left, say—and the brain took a
 break.
Yet, when the mood proved relentless, I knew that the ones who'd
 waylaid me
    Nothing could sway from their course—justice infernal at
 stake!
Court is in session! Dead parents had brandished their right to
 invade me:
    Nobodad, Phantomom—*rise*! Ready revenge they might take.

Gogol's novella "The Nose" made a comedy out of his dreaming.
    There, when our hero got up, horrid a flatness appeared
Right in the spot where the nose ought to be. And the fears that were
 teeming
    Wouldn't abate, for the man, quite understandably, feared
He would not only be mocked at the workplace, the ladies would,
 screaming,
    Call the police, and, oh Lord! Horrible! Here something weird

Happened: the chapter just *ended!*—the dream and the theme, though, progressing.

    Look, it's—the Nose! But behold: driving a carriage through town!

Oh!, and his uniform showing a really high rank—no addressing

    Someone promoted so high—might have been wearing a crown!

Now he dismounts. The cathedral he's entered, requesting a blessing...

    [Frowning? I wanted to *smile*! Nightmares are getting me down.]

88. Nature Preserve
for Julian Shepherd

Ovidian distich
/xx /xx /xx /xx /xx /x
/xx /xx / - /xx /xx /

Heavy and brownish and slothful and monkey-like, sparkling with
    quill-frost,
        High on a hemlock's bare branch piercing midwinter's pure
        blue,
Napping, the porcupine wakes—you can watch how he's groping and
    stretching.
        Want to predict what he'll think? Glance at the damage below:

Look at the sugar-pine punched full of holes, half demolished, a
    ravage;
        That's because, year after year, pileate woodpeckers banged,
Jolted, concussed the hard husk, having hoped for a beetle-grub
    feast-day.
        Standing in snow-covered marsh, only one willow remains:

All the less lucky were felled by the beavers that, hapless at walking,
        Like to have dinner at home, bringing the wood to the wet.
Now, though, a dam they created when all the doomed others went
    under,
        Weakening, coming apart, letting new water pour through,

Makes a fresh forest arise: came the aspens, impatient invaders,
        Then the intrepid white pines, branches low-spreading out wide.
Seeing familiar destroyers revisit—the beaver included
        (Banished a century back, harried by fashion-mad hats),

Caught in the maundering muddle of wondering where we are going,
        Grateful, we come to a stop, stirred by the rule of return.

89. Helpful Counsel: Versifying a Letter from Anni Johnson

Ovidian distich
/xx /xx /xx /xx /xx /x
/xx /xx / - /xx /xx /

"While you are doing your kitchen remodel with dishwasher maybe
    Off of the dining room French doors you could also put in.
Then you could have a raised deck in the back to sit out on below the
    Willow-tree boughs. You could grow wonderful flowering vines,
Fragrant, and climbing on trellises, offering privacy from the
    Neighbors (for all I can tell, no one will ever show up).
Oh... then a grill you could get, on the deck—grilling shrimp, maybe scallops..."

Yes, and remember last night? That's when you showed "we could change
    Things in the kitchen, the stove be made central, completely replacing
Island and counter—they're gone!—multiple cupboards removed;
    That would make room and admit flowing light and cool air from the windows..."

Wholly absorbed in the plan, quiet yet eager you were,
    Gently let fantasy wander, a child that a picture of Christmas
Drew in the air of a dream, painting a haven, and free.

90. Colors of the Day: Versifying a Letter from Anni Johnson
sitting on Bill's front porch and reading Edward Hirsch's Transforming Vision

Ovidian distich
/xx /xx /xx /xx /xx /x
/xx /xx / - /xx /xx /

No, it is not to be likened to *Order of Angels* by Kiefer,
    Though I have tried it. The day's greener, with yellow and red.
Can't call it blue. Yet the crow's cawing louder than all of the pretty
    Birds that were missing on Grande Jatte when Seurat painted dots.
Autumn-red leaves—can I spy them in this "devout off'ring to summer's
    God"? Where'd the little ones go? Top of the tree's become bare.
Meanwhile the eyes were so easily drawn to the swimming of yellow
    Making me think: Jasper Johns—he would have made it abstract.
Cool is the wind that is blowing the oak where the curling and drying
    Leaves turning up will converse. What are they saying to me?
Wake, smell the earth, hear the rustle! How soon we will all turn to compost.
    Think of the garden snakes warm, under the rotting remains—
Late-summer harvest—mouse drowned—and the bunny quite happily eating
    All the tomatoes that hugged, close, unavailing, the ground.
Safe!—remain safe on your southerly journey, my angel-wing'd hummers:
    Nectar in ample supply now I'll lay by for the days,
Longer, in spring—for the signal, the whiff of the sweet honeysuckle.
    Meanwhile I waiting will make angels of snow with Monet

(Think of Sandvika) and look at *Before the Aquarium* with the
    Goldfish and woman Matisse painted. I'm rocking, at rest,
Near to the room that I love, with no more than a thin pane of glass
  and,
    Too, my religion to keep night and the northwind away.

91. Watching Anni Make a Table Centerpiece
for Anni, Hannah, Julian, Kyle, Lee, Tim, and Ute

Ovidian distich
/xx /xx /xx /xx /xx /x
/xx /xx / - /xx /xx /

Poetry used to be practical—Vergil in country "bucolics"
    Told of the shepherding life. "Georgics" would offer you help
("George" means a farmer) in plowing the earth or in guarding your beehives.
    How to make handbooks a treat? How to make manuals fun?
Once you have chosen a topic, try light conversational rhythm—
    Casual, calming, relaxed... Amble, or saunter, at ease.

Yesterday Anni had made, for Thanksgiving, a centerpiece lovely.
    First she a pumpkin scooped out (we will be saving the seeds,
Baking them till they are crunchy and snackable). Yet when it came to
    Cutting the top of the sphere, she had determined the lid
Partly would still be attached, for the shape was attractive, and also
    Part of the stem would be kept, sculptural driftwood in form.

Then she a holder of water would set in the hollowed-out pumpkin:
    This on the bottom would rest—floral-green moss put on top.
Flowers with wiry and durable stems would be planted in moss-block—
    Dampened and bright are they all, aptly with water supplied,
Daisy-like, themed in magenta and burgundy—downy green centers...
    Rose and carnation would vie, red, with the lily-white pure.

Verdure was added by greenery softer than kale in its color,
        Tenderer texture as well—maybe surprising to find,
Also, an apple, returning the note of the carmine, diverting...
        Loosestrife, white dots on a bent, lengthened, and flexible cone,
Leaves that are sizable, perky, assertive. Tan raffia, trailing
        Streamer and strand, will complete, raffish, the picture I paint.

Singers in English, I'm eager to ask you: what folksier meter,
        Swinging and loping along—glad to be wild—could you find?
Write—find delight—in Ovidian couplet, hexameter dactyl!
        Gladly I'd read them at morn, walking, or resting at eve.
Thanks be to Anni, who started me off on my painterly journey:
        Thanks to the classical bards, too, for their metrical map.

92. Sonnet of Classical Distichs for Louise Fairfax

Ovidian distich
/xx /xx /xx /xx /xx /x
/xx /xx / - /xx /xx /

Be not amazed, dear Louise, that I use the Ovidian distich:
    Schiller and Goethe have shown how I might melody gain.
Prose never suited me—no, not at all: in a previous lifetime
    I in Eleusis a vow made, that I'll never betray.
First let me empathy offer; the stormy, subtropical moisture
    Havoc has wrought, and I see: weakened as well is your health.
All the Hercúlean labors together, the twelve of them, taxing,
    Gather, demanding, to plague someone deserving no grief.

(Light my profession has been, though Augéan the stables for cleaning
    Viewed when my students would write—those whom the gods turned away.)
Nature and culture at once, it appears, are exacting their tribute:
    Mulcher, computer, and sound system declining, in spite.
Added to allergies, fungi (to lungs, what a peril!), exhaustion,
    Much have you had to endure; all must the hearer lament.
Glad you'll be getting to *Figaro* (not *Rigoletto*, yet worthy)...
    Birthday of Kirsten, and then: boys with a carol of cheer!

Bruce' coming birthday as well, and Yelena arriving by airplane—
    Great is the reason for cheer: some of the deities—kind.
I, as you may have suspected, am keeping quite busy with writing:
    Elegies Roman-composed, Goethe's, I render each day.
Hundreds of lines elegiac I'll soon have completed with pleasure!
    Christmas and New Year enjoy! Many the happy returns!

Starting the middle of Jan., I am planning a visit to Egypt:
    There I a month will remain, writing a lyric per day.
Sauntering under the palms I'll remember the wassail in Vestal:
    Often the good with the good comes, and the bad with the bad.
Both have I happened to know in a life that is varied and checkered.
    Time to conclude, it appears: couplets I've finished fourteen.

93. Making Jeff's Party the Epic It Is

Ovidian distich
/xx /xx /xx /xx /xx /x
/xx /xx / - /xx /xx /

Sing in me, muse Mandolina, nor ever the project abandon,
    Those to extol whom the mood zephyral-wingéd will aid
Feelings of heart to outpour, of our generous Maytime adorant.
    Whiskey, farewell, for a tune sprightlier tonic may bring!

Now is the time: fly away!—never wait for the last hallelujah!
    Who is the player, the played? Surely the fiddle is each.
Ask of the wind if the mover and moved can be ever distinguished!
    Hark to the clearing, whose green hymn to the springtime one hears!

Flourish and prosper, live long! Let the many guitars be exalted,
    Clothesline and broomstick and pail—old-timey bass made of these—
Cello, accordion, dulcimer—all who in tribute responded—

    Help me, O goddess, to laud: epic by tunesmith is made.
Who is Ulysses today but a melody-making of Homer?
    Hero-and-minstrel I name shaper of epic in Tone!

94. Newsletter to Friends

Ovidian distich
/xx /xx /xx /xx /xx /x
/xx /xx / - /xx /xx /

How did it happen, my travel to Egypt? It's quite a narration,
    Pleasanter offered in verse, classical-rhythmed and quick.
Friend Katharina, you see—Dr. Mommsen, Emerita, Stanford—
    Kindly suggested a task, once, in a letter to me:
Might I be willing to render famed Goethe's *West-östlicher Divan*?
    Earlier version, it seemed, hadn't been up to the mark.
Plus: "Notes and Essays," the hundred-and-eighty-page helpful appendix,
    Never was rendered before—ever—in English. Indeed!
Yes, I replied. And I did it (with aid Peter Anton von Arnim
    Offered in "Essays and Notes"), adding some poems (my own).

Now we'll fast-forward: Katrina is having her generous birthday.
    Party in Weimar! What fine fortune—I'm meeting her friends.
Here's Dr. Íbrahim Ábouleish, founder of Sekem near Cairo:
    Kíbbutz, I'd call it: superb, eco-sustainable farms—
Settlement, though in the desert yet flourishing, making a profit.
    He had to Austria gone, seeking his higher degrees;
Falling in love with a Catholic woman, he'd asked for instruction:
    "Give me a scriptural text, make Christianity plain."
She had suggested "Our Father," which reading, the man had concluded:
    "Everything here can be called perfectly Muslim. We're set!"

So they were married. To me Dr. Abouleish now posed a question:
    "Christians 'Our Father' have prized. Muslims 'The Opening' love.

Is there in Jewish tradition a text that is parallel, central?"
    Yes, I replied and declaimed, glad, the "Shemá Yisraél."
Next I repeated the same, but in English—and then he suggested:
    "What would you say to a month's visit at Sekem with us?"
That was to prove such a blessing I'd call it the gift of a lifetime:
    Ninety the lyrics I penned during my residence there.
I was a teacher of English at Sekem to teachers of English.
    They were my pedagogues, too: happy our colloquies brave.

95. Homage to Bach

Ovidian distich
/xx /xx /xx /xx /xx /x
/xx /xx / - /xx /xx /

Now that I'm into my sixties, a life-writing whim-drive arises—
    Think of a moment that sowed light in awakening days:
Magianly musical. One in particular brightly comprises
    What from a fire-seed may grow, branching in ramified praise.

Wholly engrossed in a library music-tape archive recording,
    I, yet in high school, intent fully on hearing each part,
Voices, alone and together, polyphony-rapture affording,
    Avidly trying to find what was alluring my heart—

Bach, *Musikalisches Opfer*, the trio sonata, I wanted
    Truly, completely, to hear, *feel* every note in the score.
Movement? The second, *Allegro*, arrestingly jaunty, had haunted
    Me and my friends who had played, often, the work, but the more,

Now, that I willed that my brain might contain what the Master had written,
    Lord! all the fainter I felt—loved!—overpowered—and smitten!

96. Andrei Guruianu's "Text Page Three" Versified with Reply

Ovidian distich
/xx /xx /xx /xx /xx /x
/xx /xx / - /xx /xx /

Drinking the wine of the gypsies I work with my head full of grieving.
    Books on the shelf: some to Christ, some to the devil
      would kneel;
All look aesthetically pleasing, no order at all. Some on tea and
    Marmalade dine; some the knife sharpen on stone for the
      meal
When there were promises made and the promises broken. They're
  bored, the
    Virtuous, bored with the night. Moon they will prosecute.
    She's
Innocent, let her hang anyway. Feels like you're cheating at times
  when—
    Sip and a wafer, no wait: all are forgiven—a breeze.

Reply

Grief and intensity both can be draining, and therefore I halted:
    Text number three, it appeared, begged for a tribute of tune.
Beckett (recall *How It Is*?) will in parallel manner a meter
    Often suggest for awhile, slogging through comical swamp.
"Comical? How can you say it?" Well, that's how it is: the musician
    Wrote what had entered the mind, cheering and charming
      the ear.
I am already redeemed. So the knight in the lyric by Pushkin,
    Bored with the father and son, yet to the lady was true.

97. Video-Sonnet
for Tom Head

Ovidian distich
/xx /xx /xx /xx /xx /x
/xx /xx / - /xx /xx /

Riding the memory seahorse, the vehicle named hippocampus,
    Later the squirrel, we learned, ninety percent of the pine
Nuts he had buried can blithely recover, although thirty thousand
    Well he had scattered and hid. Grand is the Canyon indeed
Where at his leisure a scientist watching the natural marvel
    Learns of a kinship with bird cousins he long had disowned.

Studying comparably the amígdala mighty in feeling,
    Now the researcher a boy told of a task to be done—
Quickly and easily (so he explained) as the others had done it.
    Ah!, but in setting the clock, he was enacting a lie,
Making the deadline arrive at an earlier time than he'd stated.
    Next an orangutan, too, he would on purpose betray.

This would enable their "shame" to be studied: head fallen, slumped shoulder...
    Knowledge—and sorrow. Pray stop! *I* am already ashamed.

98. Letter to Johanna Masters

Ovidian distich
/xx /xx /xx /xx /xx /x
/xx /xx / - /xx /xx /

Sorry this morning my lyric is late, dear Johanna, I badly
        Needed recuperative rest from an action-packed week,
Writing, recording, and singing in chorus, with energy, tension,
        Leaving me "plumb tuckered out" (rural expression to use).
Ever uplifting as well, composition in classical meters:
        Why, you have asked, did I switch, answering verse from a friend
(Asclepiadic), with strange, unawaited Ovidian distichs?
        Philipp requested the change: that is a rhythm he loves.

Pleasing, the latest of meters that Philipp and I were exploring:
        First came asclepiad third, followed quite soon by the fourth;
Then we had sapphic, and now (as you notice) the distichal measure,
        Keeping the melody rich—thought (so I'm hoping) as well—
Adding a bit of hybridity, also, in lines elegiac,
        Mixing my "sonnetry" in: grouping of eight, then of six.

99. Letter to Johann Wolfgang von Goethe

after my translation of his East-West Divan, *to which I'd appended a commentary-verse divan of my own*

Ovidian distich
/xx /xx /xx /xx /xx /x
/xx /xx / - /xx /xx /

Back from the afternoon music—accordion, mandolin, fiddle—
    Viewing Venetian delights, typing away in my chair,
Gladly reminding my reader, in casual epigram comment,
    Themes will recur (we have met dreamy Armida once more),
Taking a break as I think about starting the next, ninety-seven,
    Wolf, what a pleasure it is—chatting with *you*, treasured twin!

No one can ever deprive me of this, walking on with my comrade,
    Certainly never the strange theory some entertain,
Stating the dead should be kept by themselves, unaddressed by the living,
    "Pure" and enshrined in a fane, idolized high and sublime...
No one may stop us from partnership-writing, no scholar, no critic.
    "Poets today," some have said, "valued may be, and the past
Writers we deem to be classic are always approvable, truly;
    Yet they may never consort: clear segregation's required.

How can the master, who's dead, and the living aspirer be drinking
    Water derived from the same fountain, although they are friends?
Races of people unequal: the sacred, the student-usurper!
    Dialogue? Perish the thought! Holy the *genius*—alone."
Wolf, while I live I'll remember: we walk in Elysium daily.
    Sometimes your lines will excel, other times mine are the best.
I will be writing our dialogues down, not withdraw as a coward.
    Better to die than retreat, cowed into silence, and quit.

Nor will I sit at the back of the bus in poetical heaven:
> I, till the day of my death, yet shall be speaking with *you*.

Brother, this lyric I give for a seal of perpetual friendship:
> Twin of my spirit and wise, Mentor, accept my embrace!

100. A Sunflower

dactylic pentameter catalectic
/xx /xx /xx /xx /
/xx /xx /xx /xx /
/xx /xx /xx /xx /
/xx /xx /xx /xx /

Half of the sunflowers, hiding her face while she bent
Getting the proper container, gold petal-wealth lent,
Crowded, surrounding each blossoming pupil of eye,
Made me respond with—unplanned and exultant—a cry.

"Oh! They're so beautiful, aren't they?" Face lifted, she turned
Slightly toward me, and smiled in a manner that earned
Thanks from the flowers, and me, and the world, with her eyes
Smiling so bright as without her I'd never surmise.

Born to be lovers, we're known, I'm beginning to think,
Deep in the hearts that are fountains where beauty will drink.
These are the maidens who light up the soul with their glow.
God they create by their presence wherever they go.

101. A Month in Germany
with gratitude to the Alam family and to all my new friends: a newsletter-poem

"It is an absolute perfection and as it were divine
for a man to know how to enjoy his being loyally."
Michel de Montaigne, tr. John Florio

"Laß uns, o höchster Gott, das Jahr vollbringen,
Damit das Ende so, wie dessen Anfang sei."
from a cantata by J. S. Bach

Ovidian distich
/xx /xx /xx /xx /xx /x
/xx /xx / - /xx /xx /

Kindly assistance providing, the home of the Álams of Stolberg
    Proved the most fruitful domain, writerly aim to pursue.
During the time I was there I wrote dialogues, seventy-seven:
    Couplets made tranquil, relaxed, daily a diligent mind.
Rapt conversations I had with the towering spirit of Rückert,
    Poet and friend of the East, man of a stature immense.

Thanks be to Sháhid, my mentor and friend in the Sufi tradition,
    Also to Barbara—wise, hóspitable, and serene.
Charming how Ámena—lively and sprightly, their twelve-year-old daughter,
    Read me a story aloud, making the characters live,
Who, in their travels from Bristol by plane to the distant New Zealand,
    Shone in the beauty of fine English recited with ease.

Christmas—the reels and the jigs that I played with the skillful Jan-Philipp—

Fiddle-piano duets—tunes of O'Carolan blind—
Sweet even now to my ear the remembrance of "Planxty John
     Drury"—
          Also your singing so deft, telling "the levee was dry."
Amena, Barbara danced to the rapid and triple-timed music.
          Oh, and the carols I heard! Joys never sampled before:

Ánwar, twin brother to Philipp, had earlier come, with his mother
          Silke, and Róshan, her son. Anwar, on fiddle, to me
Offered delight that the holiday season made ever more pleasant,
          Things with a humorous twist, or with canonical grace.
Anwar and I tried "Take Five,"—what a splendid parodical Brubeck...
          Don't forget Telemann, too, perfect in festive baroque.

What of Sylvester? For that is the name that the Germans give New
     Year's
          Eve—when the fireworks upbúrst, frenzied, all over the town.
Shahid and Barbara hosted a party, and most of the neighbors
          Hummed "Auld Lang Syne" in a choir, even when words were
          unclear.
Toasted were friends and companions, and friend Katharina had
     sent us
          Fitting champagne for the rite—relished by one and by all.

Ansche, who'd come for the fest from her splendid Tyrolean homeland,
          Wanted to watch (and I'm glad!) how Zubin Mehta conducts
Famed philharmonic musicians to honor the year in a manner
          So Viennese that I'm still drunken with polka and waltz.
Often a dance would have sounds that were clownish with nutty
     percussion,
          Bird-calls and such, till the end came with "Radeczky"
          applause.

Barbara Brötz, with a gentleness linked to her practice of healing,
          Liked to hear songs that were played, wholly absorbed in
          the mood.

She and Sebastian, the surgeon, liked hymns from the States and
from England.
Thanks be to music that brings feeling alive in the heart—
Also I'm happy to say that whenever I'm singing in Yiddish,
No explanation's required: all's comprehended at once.

Wholly unclouded, the sky, as with Shahid I rode in a carriage
Touring the city of Bruges, gleaming benign in its blue,
Greeted us, joining the people we viewed—by the smooth-trotting
horses
Gladly alerted. How strange!—here is a place of the past—
No modern structures allowed, an eight-century building-museum!
(Brussels? It rained, but we still strolled in the shopping
arcade.)

Flörsheim—an evening salon at the home of the family Petters:
Poetry, music, and art here were discussed and enjoyed.
Vocals with fiddle I offered, and Shahid's Arabian writing
Shone as from names of the guests artful calligraphies came.
I from the Scotsman John Clark got a cup with some dancers
depicted.
He is a "painter on glass." That was the "name" he preferred.

Two more adventures remain to be told. At the Rückert Museum
Christel explained what we saw, giving the context desired.
Later her husband, Klaus Rückert, the poet and scholar's great-
grandson,
Told of the lands he had known, languages learned. And the
desk
Made for the poet was really a lectern—he liked to write standing.
Two meters tall, he had been. Desktop few people could use!

Overnight stay in the home of this writer I daily converse with—
Here is a high point of life. Rooms had been left as they were.
Lofty the ceiling, floor wooden—hurrah for the resonant echo!
Both of our hosts have a love, fervent, for music and verse.

Present and past interwoven in culture and wide understanding—
> You, Klaus and Christel, will be friends ever treasured and dear.

Nürnberg—and here I am charmed by historical lore of Franconia,
> Lives of the saints, and the tales blazoned in fabular frames,

Vivid stained glass of the Church of St. Lawrence, with Biblical symbols,
> Clarified, rich in detail—thank you, good Manfred, so much!

Raised in traditions of which Lautenschlagers had long been partaking,
> You in one day quite reshaped how I envision the past.

Envoi

Twelve were my strophes (though here's the 13th) like the 12 days of Christmas:
> Festal the time that I spent—blest be the people I met.

All of my chanting I offer you now as an anthem of tribute:
> Here then my melody ends, grateful to friends and to joy.

Dearly I hope that the year which in happiness now is beginning
> All may complete with the same cheer that in friendship I feel.

102. A Thought for Singers of Handel

Ps. 24:7. Lift up your heads, O ye gates; and be ye lift up, ye everlasting doors; and the King of glory shall come in.
8. Who is this King of glory? The Lord strong and mighty, the Lord mighty in battle.
9. Lift up your heads, O ye gates; even lift them up, ye everlasting doors; and the King of glory shall come in.
10. Who is this King of glory? The Lord of hosts, he is the King of glory. Selah.

dactylic trimeter catalectic
/xx /xx /
/xx /xx /
/xx /xx /
/xx /xx /

Lift up your heads, O ye gates!
How can a gate have a head?
Riddle solution awaits.
Think of a human instead.

You are the gate—it is you!
Let the Almighty come in!
Give Him a way to get through.
Then may the entry begin.

Folk bending over confine
Entryway into the chest.
Stand up erect! The Divine
Likes you, when highest, the best.

Lift up your eyes to a hill.
Quiet, breathe deeply. Then sing,
Ready His goal to fulfill.
Welcome the glorious King!

103. Summoned for Jury Duty

Ovidian distich
/xx /xx /xx /xx /xx /x
/xx /xx / - /xx /xx /

Groggy with marathon sleeping enforced by a viral infection,
    Yet I showed up as required. Lottery-wheel being turned,
Eight were the names of the chosen who, taking their seats near the court bench,
    Briefly were interviewed. One woman I'll never forget:
Mother of four, she'd another one coming, she smilingly told us;
    Never a person could seem granted more wealth of the heart.
Some of the jurors were sad while they told of their family stories.
    Only one man was turned down: too many lawyers he'd known.

Dickens reported the doings at trials—good training for writers.
    How I'd have liked to hear more, say, of the woman whose life
Even from earliest age was devoted to caring for children—
    Four generations of these! Here's what intrigued me the most:
"Where's Caprice Venerable? Is there anyone here who has seen her?
    Someone know where she might be?" *Her* I would like to have heard.

104. "Maggie Brown's Favorite": Irish Folk Jig Sonnet

dactylic tetrameter
lxx lxx lxx lxx
lxx lxx lxx lxx
lxx lxx lxx lxx
lxx lxx lxx lxx

Steadily venturing—simple, habitual—
Bland, undemanding, though handily danceable—
Melody mellow and mildly enhanceable—
Planned, unelaborate rhythmical ritual—

Feeling of galloping, prancing, and cantering—
Triple-time fiddling to cheer you relaxingly:
Festive, equestrian, gently—untaxingly—
Rapidly chanting and happily bantering.

Presently, then, what was pleasantly pillowing
Confident calm, a predictable, merrily
Singable thing became crazily, scarily
Swaying and raving, a breaker-wave billowing—

Rearing and rising!—then sinking, subsiding.
Fine!—I survived it, inspired by the riding!

105. Mem'ry engendering music machine!

dactylic tetrameter catalectic
/xx /xx /xx /
/xx /xx /xx /
/xx /xx /xx /
/xx /xx /xx /

Mem'ry engendering music machine!
Waltzing, my sonnet refashions the ball
Given by emigré Russians, the hall
Filled with the silken, the fur, the sateen.

Rushing and swishing, enchanted, entranced,
All were aware of the range of the space.
Chandelier-scattered, the light on your face
Liveliness, handsomeness, happy enhanced.

Grandeur—in sweep of the arms when they swung
Feminine figures that moved to the high
Fever the orchestra fanned—we'd descry
Fanciful gowns black tuxedos among!

Wondrous and lovely the lesson I'd had:
Breathing so fast, I was never so glad!

PART TWO
Triple and Duple Meters Combined

IV
Third Asclepiadic

106. Praise the gift of the hymn, found ere the seeker try

third asclepiadic
/ x / x x/ / x x/ x/
/ x / x x/ / x x/ x/
     / x / x x/ x
/ x / x x/ x/

Praise the gift of the hymn, found ere the seeker try.
Laud the visitant vim, granted to lifted hands:
    Making stronger the weaker,
    Raising songful the soul from bands.

Thank the chill for the brisk wind that we glad
   inhale.
Green let speak of the life dewy renewed in eye:
    We're the oil-lamp Aladdin,
    Rug on runway to climb the sky.

Mars departed with March, comes Aphrodite near,
Rhododactyl the hand, henna'd the heaven rose:
    Passion-grandeur, the mighty,
    Waked, unslaken, the chanter chose.

107. Kept the sugar count low— favor bestowed a sigh

third asclepiadic
/x /x x/ /x x/ x/
/x /x x/ /x x/ x/
      /x /x x/x
/x /x x/ x/

Kept the sugar count low—favor bestowed a sigh.
Said kombucha to me, You I reward with cheer:
    Keep your word, you unload a
  Burden—*tabula rasa,* clear.

Spring has meant that today clouds would awaken
  brave.
Swept with shadow the grass, briefly—to light re-
  turned:
    Vigor living unshaken,
  Chill of winter the will unlearned.

Why then look at the news? Who such a gloomer
  needs?
Truths are known from of old. That's where my love
  belongs.
    Turn from gossip and rumor.
  Read with ease in the Song of Songs.

108. "Here's a lyric event, Thursday, it's four to five"

third asclepiadic
/ x / x x/ / x x/ x/
/ x / x x/ / x x/ x/
      / x / x x/ x
/ x / x x/ x/

"Here's a lyric event, Thursday, it's four to five,"
Science Library wrote: "Come and recite your lines!"
    I have plenty of lore to
Share: one theme, with entwined designs.

"Google, how many brain célls do I own?" Reply:
"Hundred billion." "And, pray, how many galaxies
    In the universe?" "Lonely?
Hundred billion!" With speed and ease,

Rhymes I started to write—then, I could hardly cease.
What I sang? You can hear—true scientific bliss!—
    All my thinking. A bardly
Gift to me!—many thanks for this!

109. What? My lines aren't profound? Well, they're at least pro-funned

third asclepiadic
/x /x x/ /x x/ x/
/x /x x/ /x x/ x/
        /x /x x/x
/x /x x/ x/

What? my lines aren't profound? Well, they're at least
   pro-*funned*.
Made for play are they all! I'm but a white-haired
   clown!
            Leaven, making the yeast grow,
      Turns to levity growl and frown.

Daily sodden, the ground. Sod are we too, indeed.
Yet we've air in our lungs, grand when we sing a
   tune!
            Must lugubrity ruin
      Bliss of Harlequin, Pantaloon?

Swing we bravely between doom and the deepest
   height:
Laughing, crying at once. Quick, the distinction
   dies...
            Thou, comedian, weepest?
      I'm a lover that smiling sighs.

110. Take a look at the sky. Light that we view in stars

third asclepiadic
/ x / x x/ / x x/ x/
/ x / x x/ / x x/ x/
    / x / x x/x
/ x / x x/ x/

Take a look at the sky. Light that we view in stars
Meant one never could say we in "the present" dwell.
    What those light rays were doin'
Can a heavenly lesson tell.

Past is what they depict. Light years of travel time
Each one took to arrive, here, to delight your eyes.
    All their journeys unravel
Things we're learning in wild surprise.

Thirteen hundreds of years flew the Orion light,
Knowing *you*'d be alive, seeking to favor you
    With a message undyin':
"I, if old, may your sight renew."

111. Lunch today with a friend. Topics would greatly range

third asclepiadic
/x /x x/ /x x/ x/
/x /x x/ /x x/ x/
    /x /x x/ x
/x /x x/ x/

Lunch today with a friend. Topics would greatly
  range:
Life, and death, and the rest. Never a moment dull.
      Even livelier lately:
  More and better the themes to mull.

"I, at age eighty-three, hope there's an after-state,"
Charlie said. "I have just barely begun to learn."
      "Well," replying with laughter,
  I replied, "to the monkeys turn

Your attention: the ape, chimp, and gorilla must
Die—our simian tribe all to the dust are brought.
      Why suppose we fulfill a
  Stranger fate? A peculiar thought!

Gene-wise nearly a chimp, we're from the end
  exempt?
Why so lucky? I ask. You in a trap are caught!"
      "Country club! The agenda:
  Some are welcome, and others not."

112. Blest, I'm seventy-four. Cup runneth over, Lord

third asclepiadic
/ x / x x/ / x x/ x/
/ x / x x/ / x x/ x/
    / x / x x/ x
/ x / x x/ x/

Blest, I'm seventy-four. Cup runneth over, Lord:
Surely mercy and good follow me all my days.
    Pilgrim-soul is a rover,
  Meant to wander the hidden ways.

Hymns' continual chant lending a splendor yet,
Honey-touch on the lips granted me newly-born
    Means I ever will render
  Rhapsode tunes to the rorid morn.

Triumph riant will know one whom the Spirit chose
Daily singing to greet Him who will soon arise.
    He's approaching—I hear it.
  Dew has filled my awoken eyes.

113. Venevítinov wrote, He whom the deities

third asclepiadic
/x /x x/ /x x/ x/
/x /x x/ /x x/ x/
　　　/x /x x/x
/x /x x/ x/

Venevítinov wrote, He whom the deities
Early love effloresced granted to one that sings
　　　Well may quietly be a
　　Servant, meek, of eternal things.

Kept apart at a height, solemn, of hidden thought,
If, excited, he burst out in a stream of speech,
　　　He'd the impulse unbidden
　　Soon regret. 'Twould a lesson teach.

Anger kills me, indeed. *That* would I gladly shun.
Quiet isolates, though. Where might I welcomed be?
　　　Bellow out—even madly—
　　Sounding tones in a melody.

Somber-sober, as well, never could I remain.
Witty joke will the mind quickly with might re-
　　charge.
　　　　Sporting—spritely and fiery—
　　Aids me waiting at heaven-marge.

114. Raise the shell to your ear. Why's there an ocean tone?

third asclepiadic
/ x / x x/ / x x/ x/
/ x / x x/ / x x/ x/
  / x / x x/ x
/ x / x x/ x/

Raise the shell to your ear. Why's there an ocean tone?
Is it really the sea? No, we reply—and yes.
      What you hear is the motion,
   Amplified, of our blood-largesse.

Were we learning a lie? Tale of the "sea"—untrue?
No, there's ocean, and yet—not as we thought we "knew"!
      Cosmic change Galilean:
   You're the center—the sea *in you.*

Blood in the ear will sing, making the lulling sound—
Tone you needed to hear, helped by the friendly shell:
      Can't cease pondering, mulling:
   What deep news could our comrade tell!

115. Twofold elegy sent, lately, a friend to me

for Grace Cavalieri

third asclepiadic
/ x / x x/ / x x/ x/
/ x / x x/ / x x/ x/
*　　　　/ x / x x/ x*
／x / x x/ x/

Twofold elegy sent, lately, a friend to me.
Death of one did it mark, whom in her heart she saw
　　　　Purple mist-cloud-surrounded,
　　Rising up from the greenyard bloom.

Elegiac, the tone proved to be yet alive
What was made in the old Bion-and-Moschan time:
　　　　Elegy for Adonis,
　　Tribute paid to the fine and young.

Shelley wished to behold, watching the earth-soul
　grow
Up from soil in the spring, Keats come alive again.
　　　　Yet real gone-ness aggrieved him:
　　So, in hope, to eternal height

Shelley lifted him. Feel, sweet, the maternal smile!
Too, the latter of those poems I glad received
　　　　Showed the youth in ambrosial
　　Cloud ascend to a hymn of bliss.

116. Loud the bird in the height, crying! A strength intense

third asclepiadic
/x /x x/ /x x/ x/
/x /x x/ /x x/ x/
    /x /x x/x
/x /x x/ x/

Loud the bird in the height, crying! A strength
  intense,
Never-ending the drive, rending the body small:
    Feel the sequences lengthen—
    Herald bright in the Father Hall!

Love is come to the world—hear and awaken! Pray!
Spurred and spermed and bestirred, "Opening" time
  recite!—
    Thirst of bird-life unslaken
    Till the loved one arise in light!

Barefoot walk in the dew. Jungle-ambition grows,
Tropic-wet underfoot, climbing the spiry grass:
    April-fest ebullition
    Fed with damp as we gently pass.

Moist and luscious and cool! Joyful a thunder
  pounds,
Filled with want, yet aware nothing can love excel—
    Up, around us, and under:
    That's what—madly—the bird cries tell!

117. Not a mystery why ancient asclepiads

third asclepiadic
/x /x x/ /x x/ x/
/x /x x/ /x x/ x/
      /x /x x/x
/x /x x/ x/

Not a mystery why ancient asclepiads,
Gliding tranquilly by, smoothly attain a pace
      Neither frantic nor sleepy—
Smile-beguiling the human face:

First lines offer a way, metered, to show how thought
Sings a rhythm to fit pausing, or sudden run.
      Then, displaying the know-how
Gained, relax: what we dared is done.

Fiery-wise were the Greeks, brave as a tribe could be.
Epic battle they'd chant, then lend a statue rest.
      What from them we imbibe would
Ever better our very best.

What religion to choose? Hey, should I *be a Greek?*
Who such meter could make merits devotion true.
      What a splendid idea!
Grecian tune I'll intone for you!

118. Lo! arose in the land one whom the surf-rush trees

third asclepiadic
/x /x x/ /x x/ x/
/x /x x/ /x x/ x/
      /x /x x/ x
/x /x x/ x/

Lo! arose in the land one whom the surf-rush trees
Taught to sing as had wished, inward, the violin.
      Meads a-greening and turf-lush
Anthemed, "Be is but half. Begin!"

Feet are hands that can walk. Hands than the feet
  more far
Need to travel upon keyboard, the lamb-leap hill,
      Mental creatures to greet more
Strange and grand than the angel-will.

Ear's an eye that can turn color a timbre-tone.
"Speak to me with a gold-azurely dawning voice,
      Gleaming even as amber,"
Asked the man, "and the rhyme make choice."

Who shall answer him, then? One who'll reply in
  kind?
Where's the Shulamite whom Solomon hopes to view?
      Lonesome he as a lion,
  Striped with fire as a tiger, too.

119. Move me, lunary height, orrery for a bard

third asclepiadic
/x /x x/ /x x/ x/
/x /x x/ /x x/ x/
      /x /x x/x
/x /x x/ x/

Move me, lunary height, orrery for a bard
Raise to mind when you sway words in a roomy
   swoon:
      Under flood may the flora
   Smile beguiled by the *clair de lune.*

Stately, measured the sweep silken of royal robe
Call to ear when you shape wave in majestic laud:
      Soul, to rhythm be loyal,
   While your voice you are lifting, awed.

Beauty, ever of you let me the servant stay,
Day and night to attend, faithful as thane of yore:
      Heart, in ardor be fervent,
   When in love you her praise outpour.

Currrents come and they go—we, in the spirit, too,
Sally forth and return, song of a wave-pale swan:
      Blest command, let me hear it!
   Glad the travel we carry on.

120. What is meant by a crown? Simple, enwreathing leaves

third asclepiadic
/x /x x/ /x x/ x/
/x /x x/ /x x/ x/
    /x /x x/x
/x /x x/ x/

What is meant by a crown? Simple, enwreathing leaves
May have been, at the start, mark of respect well
  earned:
        Wreaths are healthfully breathing—
  Gift of life they have thus returned.

Much-loved Laura would fade, struck by a fatal
  plague
(Ringing, rounding the rose: ashes, we all fall down).
        Yet she's daily re-natal—
  Love Petrarchan, with laurel crown.

Lord-called man who'd compete, seeking the winner-
  prize,
Hymn-performer who'd strive, loving Olympic fun—
        Triumph, outer and inner,
  They attain when the day is done.

Pindar, praising in ode athlete of major skill,
Those who read him in Greek say is the man
  supreme.
        Let me, pray, be the wager,
  Here, of peace for the chanter's dream.

121. Three-year classical ode colloquy I review

third asclepiadic
/x /x x/ /x x/ x/
/x /x x/ /x x/ x/
　　　/x /x x/x
/x /x x/ x/

Three-year classical ode colloquy I review:
Sweet the taste of the words, paling an Eden fruit—
　　　Airy, watery, fiery,
　　Earth-gift bliss from the wisdom-root.

Orchard, paradise-name, well may you claim to be
Heaven-metaphor made, daily the food to taste
　　　That in phrasing we aim to
　　Give, in psalm by the dawning graced.

Relay runners are we, handing the glowing torch
Back and forth as we write, helped by the mentor-
　　friend
　　　Looking on while we're showing
　　Each in turn what the worlds commend.

122. Morning portrait: a cat, placed for the painter-brush

third asclepiadic
/x /x x/ /x x/ x/
/x /x x/ /x x/ x/
    /x /x x/x
/x /x x/ x/

Morning portrait: a cat, placed for the painter-
  brush—
Flattened railing of wood making a spot for rest,
        White the paws, and the orange
    Body matched with the tanned light tint

Which as background will serve, framing the central
  brick
Backdrop, muted the red melded with gentle brown.
        Perfect studio picture,
    Model, he, of the calm of spring.

Bit of grooming to do, tiniest movement we
Like observing—the touch offers the eye a charm
        Lending casual pleasure
    'Mid the umber, the green of trees.

123. Color patches and then delicate brush you need

third asclepiadic
/x /x x/ /x x/ x/
/x /x x/ /x x/ x/
　　　/x /x x/x
/x /x x/ x/

Color patches and then delicate brush you need,
Black or white to portray form that will move in air:
　　　　Jewel hues of the youthful
　　Day excite—for a lither dance!—

Limber way to create art as Raoul Dufy
Learned in ways that relate—quick!—to the tonal
　mood.
　　　　Watercolor musician!
　　Violins on the canvas play.

Touch a key and believe word is a pitch and two
Words are half of a tune, played by the painter hand,
　　　　Sculpted servant of beauty,
　　Ninety-nine on the palms engraved.

124. Gone the wrongful rebuke, damning Narcissal doom
reading Simon Schama, The Face of Britain

third asclepiadic
/x /x x/ /x x/ x/
/x /x x/ /x x/ x/
  /x /x x/x
 /x /x x/ x/

Gone the wrongful rebuke, damning Narcissal doom.
One who'd fallen in love, thus, with the lake
   transformed
      Dream-bright into an image
   Rather deem the rewarded youth.

Worship surface—remain wholly immersed in gift
Brought to you by the light, water, and shape of joy:
      Gold, white, petaled, and centered,
   You and painting are heaven grown.

When a field of the high daffodils came uncalled,
Depth would enter the eyes, tired, of the seeker old,
      Light-filled body awoken
   Then at last of the child restored.

125. Once had hymns to a boy told of a thing to be

third asclepiadic
/x /x x/ /x x/ x/
/x /x x/ /x x/ x/
      /x /x x/x
/x /x x/ x/

Once had hymns to a boy told of a thing to be:
Every morning before dawn could illume the grass
      Magic tones unbeholden
   Would from heavenly creatures come.

They would sing him awake, phrasing in varied form
Chanting liquid and blue, fresher than cool of
   brook—
      Hid, unwearied musicians,
   Bearing news of a life to rise.

Dazzled then had he laughed, clapping the hands, oh
   loud!
"Sleeping Beauty" and "Snow White" never gave to
   him
      Anything to resemble
   What would even the priest amaze.

126. Keep the rhythm in mind. That is the key to life

third asclepiadic
/x /x x/ /x x/ x/
/x /x x/ /x x/ x/
    /x /x x/x
/x /x x/ x/

Keep the rhythm in mind. That is the key to life.
Think of Salahuddín Zárkub, the master-friend
    Who had hammered a gold piece
At the fair in a meter sweet,

Which when Rumi the great, mystic of leaping fire,
Happened, gladly, to hear, seized he the gifted hand,
    Whirled him 'round in a circle
Viewed today in the dervish rite—

Patrons, both, for me here, writing a dance that
  died—
So 'twas deemed—with the Greeks, now given life
  once more.
    Ears, awake from your slumber!
Free of mortal encasement, Flame!

127. "Make the phrase like a fish, gliding, with central swell"
for William E. Culverhouse

third asclepiadic
/x /x x/ /x x/ x/
/x /x x/ /x x/ x/
    /x /x x/x
/x /x x/ x/

"Make the phrase like a fish, gliding, with central
    swell."
How'd we fare? "It was too rapidly big and round—
    Try a trout, not a sunfish."
    Quick with image, a guide who'd smile,

He the contest for new Choral Director won
After showing the choir how many shapes could take
    Half a line of the music.
    We were learning to mold the clay,

Frame a changeable mind, sculpting a form as might
One who wanted to show alternate ways to feel:
    School the pliable phraser,
    Do a favor to heart and brain.

128. Breathe what meter you will, body's attentive grown

third asclepiadic
/x /x x/ /x x/ x/
/x /x x/ /x x/ x/
    /x /x x/x
/x /x x/ x/

Breathe what meter you will, body's attentive grown,
Fingers arched over keys, blood in the feet more
  swift,
        Lungs beginning the thinking
    Shaping air when the mouth inhales.

Whisperlike, the unpitched hum-tone that came to
  shield
Mind from silence entire, firm with a building
  strength,
        Aid to focus and motion,
    Kind may cushion the carpet-flight.

Thrilling, how it has helped, making aware the soul:
Rhythmic pattern of eld, waiting the birth of me,
        Wanting only a sacred
    Heart made wide in surrender-time.

129. Drinking coffee today, pondering themes, I heard

third asclepiadic
/x /x x/ /x x/ x/
/x /x x/ /x x/ x/
    /x /x x/x
/x /x x/ x/

Drinking coffee today, pondering themes, I heard
You, Asclepiad Three, singing a lissome tune!—
    Then, phantasmal, the fiddle
Took it up, and the bow hand moved.

YouTube—that was the next thought that arrived to cheer.
Sing them, play them, and oh!—ask for a dancer, too.
    Maybe several people?
Improvising, perhaps? Inquire!

Coffee, blest, hallelu! Better than Sufi wine,
You in rocking-chair grant plans that will bloom— and soon!
    Firm in resolute fervor,
Let me treasure the lesson lent.

130. Mind won't stop, and the view, bright, on the saver screen

third asclepiadic
/x /x x/ /x x/ x/
/x /x x/ /x x/ x/
      /x /x x/x
/x /x x/ x/

Mind won't stop, and the view, bright, on the saver screen
Threefold movement conveys, keeping the brain a-dance:
      Runner, glad, on the seashore,
  Scudding cloud, and the surf-drawn wave.

Pilgrim elements all, filling the cosmic dream,
Be you ever a hymn, too, for the One where we,
      Vision heirs of the Making,
  Dreamt have learnt what we hear to sing.

Skull-formed globe where the cells tapestry-flames appear,
Heart that joins them below, chanting the ocean proud,
      Blend with me in surrender,
  Prelude-fugue of the vast chorale!

131. Gabrieli's *"Jubilate Deo"*: Metric Modulation

third asclepiadic
/x /x x/ /x x/ x/
/x /x x/ /x x/ x/
     /x /x x/x
/x /x x/ x/

Four-part chorus? It can't quiet the heaven drive.
Two such choirs will compete: *then* may the concords
  fill
      So entirely the brain-case
  Heart-perfection will be achieved.

Will it? No, I forgot something I need to add:
Double shift of his thought: first in a three-beat
  scheme,
      Then to rhythm in two-count,
  Calm to threes coming back at last.

Swift chameleons, we—loving a world of change.
Rhythm, harmony both—food for the hungry soul
      Growing are the providers:
  Altars alter! The tune make new!

V
Fourth Asclepiadic

132. Be reborn in the random shell

fourth asclepiadic
```
      /x /x x/ x/
/x /x x/   /x x/ x/
      /x /x x/ x/
/x /x x/   /x x/ x/
```

      Be reborn in the random shell,
Where the tone that you hear echoes the ocean flood
      Not recalled from a source afar—
Rather, hid from the eye, flow of the blood in ear.

      Be reborn in the random shell.
Love the rush of the red, now till the end of days,
      Favored tohu va-bohu tone
Godly, momently gift, lent when the soul awoke.

      Be reborn in the random shell.
Cosmic troubadour told, mission to follow vowed,
      Servant pure of the streams within,
Chant the tides of the moon, ruling the deep and high.

      Be reborn in the random shell.
Be a tune to the folk, held to the ear of each,
      Setting, merry, the heart astir,
Filled with heavenly peace, lulled as the charmèd wave.

133. There's a gospel, a marvel, called

fourth asclepiadic
```
      /x /x x/ x/
/x /x x/  /x x/ x/
      /x /x x/ x/
/x /x x/  /x x/ x/
```

    There's a gospel, a marvel, called
Trinal Mystery-love Hidden in Beauty's Realm.
    Here we're taught of the early truth
Jesus youthful attained, waiting his hour to teach.

    Thomas-Didymus-Jude, the twin
Ever deeply admired, tells of the blessed goal
    Which his brother enamored of
Song of Solomon, warm, dowered with zeal achieved.

    He who later to Luke would show
Perfect masterly art, many a year had spent
    Painting views of the Garden life
Spice-aroma'd and rich—cardamom, nard, and
  myrrh.

    Font of joy in his Eden-heart,
Ninety-nine were the scenes he of the lovers drew.
    Apple, flagon, and oaken bed,
Silken pillow in high Heaven-approved abode.

    I in vision prophetic heard
Tidings true that I sing, Shula, to you alone:

In the desert, beneath a cave,
Slept a scriptural book, telling of things to be.

You've been told of the bird of clay
Jesus made that awoke, living, and flew afar:
Here we learn of the wingéd art
He'd perfected in long trial unknown to men.

Word will, too, from a slumber wake
(This I heard in the dream, sung by the honey-
  tongued)
Found, unearthed by a shepherd soon:
"Be reborn in the soul, people, and Beauty serve."

134. Harbor harvest the Lord had lent

fourth asclepiadic
    /x /x x/ x/
/x /x x/ /x x/ x/
    /x /x x/ x/
/x /x x/ /x x/ x/

    Harbor harvest the Lord had lent:
Where's completeness in lack? 'Twill from production come.
    Mind needs parable rays to shine,
Blindfold so to remove, letting the past come back.

    Should you daily a lyric shape,
Hundreds then you create. Such parabolic song
    Tells of what for the undismayed
Yet may serve as the one fable that never fails.

    Let the folk, when you're dead (not gone)
Say, He never would plunge, pleasing the lemmings loud.
    Skyward gaze. From the sphere must all
Lines lead up, on a path not to be trod again.

    Let the blessing, a shock, intrude,
Set asunder the blocks built of a structure planned.
    Widen heart for the light forgot,
Let the eyes of the mind welcome the heaven dew.

    Take command of the reins of time,

Breast the Jordan and ride, roaring to farther shore—
    Resting, raising the grateful arms,
Rainbow-arch, to the blue, crying, The heav'n be praised!

135. Comes the cardinal: threes and fours

fourth asclepiadic
>/x /x x/ x/
/x /x x/ /x x/ x/
>/x /x x/ x/
/x /x x/ /x x/ x/

>Comes the cardinal: threes and fours
Gliding upward or down, speaking as if to cheer
>Night-wed poet who dawn adores—
Lovely gift, keep it up, bird whom I hold most dear!

>While I wrote and could only hear
What I made for the page, rhyming and metered
> right,
>You continued your singing clear,
Prophesying the end, soon to arise, of night.

>Chant your tune to the dark, don't fear
Your envisioning, bold, won't to the light appear!
>I will enter your holy sphere,
Nor depart, but in heart lend a rememb'ring ear.

136. Weather Theater comes to us

fourth asclepiadic
    / x / x x/ x/
/ x / x x/   / x x/ x/
    / x / x x/ x/
/ x / x x/   / x x/ x/

    Weather Theater comes to us
Every day as a treat, natural moods to share.
    If the kitchen's electric lamp
Oddly wavers a bit, so does the lightning mild.

    Burke and Kant the sublime described:
Pre-assumed is a place carefully guarded. Then
    Master-minded we deem ourselves
Who at tranquil remove calmly the storm observe.

    We a *hortus conclusus* need.
Folk who dwell on the bank, facing a river flood,
    Note their theater quite destroyed:
Picturesque though the view long had remained, 'tis gone.

    I a house on a hill had bought:
Cozy, warm the retreat, best for a weather show.
    Twoscore years when I reached, my dad
Paid the rest of the cash, ending the mortgage due.

    Much relieved by the thoughtful act,
Not a moment I lost, rendering heartfelt thanks.
    Answered he, "In the graveyard I
Don't desire to be called 'wealthiest man that's here.'"

137. Who's my teacher of olden tunes?

fourth asclepiadic
/x /x x/ x/
/x /x x/ /x x/ x/
/x /x x/ x/
/x /x x/ /x x/ x/

    Who's my teacher of olden tunes?
No one coming with hid treasure from centuries
        Gone, from Chaucer to Auden, showed
Fitting tools to apply, shaping an ode for you.

    Generations of chosen youth
Deemed the best of their day, Cambridge- and
  Oxford-bound,
        Set to work and with fervor read
Fond in rhythm the hymns Horace had writ in Rome.

    Why not give us in English, too,
Songs urbane and relaxed, wisdom in tranquil mode,
        Set in rhythmic Horatian form?
Where's the update of what pupils were daily shown?

    Hopeless! No one would answer me.
Yet—who cares? I could find models from which to get
        Clear tutorial scansion maps.
"Write whatever the charts tell you of metric stress."

    Rose-wreath'd Houri and classic Muse,
Holy Spirit as well—perfect my teachers three,
        Counseled, "Use the computer! Go!"
That is where I acquired training in ancient craft.

138. You of life can a bible write

fourth asclepiadic
/x /x x/ x/
/x /x x/ /x x/ x/
    /x /x x/ x/
/x /x x/ /x x/ x/

     You of life can a bible write,
Gospel tale with a plot, letters on what you've learned,
     Book of acts for your travel notes,
Then apocalypse dream, telling of what's to come.

     You of life can a temple build,
Big cathedral enspired, dwarfing the hordes that crowd,
     Rosy pane where a smiling lass,
Now remembered for aye, gave you a courage word.

     You of life an orchestral world
Too can form where the four symphony sections blend,
     Themes recalling of which a hint
Given first will expand, filling the hall with light.

     You of life may a mural paint,
Showing how the divine flame could in upburst rise,
     Learn in circle to whirl 'round One
Who the lesson had told: Those that behold will shine.

139. Here is one of the finer things

fourth asclepiadic
    /x /x x/ x/
/x /x x/   /x x/ x/
    /x /x x/ x/
/x /x x/   /x x/ x/

    Here is one of the finer things
Human beings may try, tired of the *déjà vu*.
    You'll discover a theme that's new:
Be determined to use, knowing the wealth it brings,

    Some wild metaphor yet unsought.
"Meta": "over," "beyond," going beyond the pale,
    Shouting "Freedom!" and breaking jail.
Next, the "phor" will imply "carrying" out your
  thought.

    What's the metaphor I employ?
Grafted plants, or a mixed-marvelous living beast.
    Try it, risk it: the very least
You'll attain is a rush: boundary-bursting joy.

    Greek-plus-Shakespeare is what? Behold:
Hybrid sonnet. The beat? Ásclepiadic, bold!

140. Biggest underground tomb in Greece

fourth asclepiadic
/x /x x/ x/
/x /x x/   /x x/ x/
   /x /x x/ x/
/x /x x/   /x x/ x/

      Biggest underground tomb in Greece,
Found in Pella, the place Alex the Great was born,
      Here the nobles reposed in peace.
Light blue, golden, and red—hues of the early morn...

      Just before the surprise report
Accidentally one *more* unexpected tomb
      Meant for men of the royal court:
Sixty-third in the Kings' Valley was viewed—a room.

      I in Greece, and in Egypt, too,
Toured the temples and graves, weighted with powers
   past,
      Thought how vanishing lives may last:
      Art, religion, *and verse.* Renew

Forms long thought to be dead. Bring them alive.
   Enwreathe,
Clasp, embrace them again. See, they begin to
   breathe!

141. Holy mage of the healing arts

fourth asclepiadic
    /x /x x/ x/
/x /x x/ /x x/ x/
    /x /x x/ x/
/x /x x/ /x x/ x/

    Holy mage of the healing arts,
Scalpel-skilled are you called, clearly a man of parts:
    Milkweed good for a fever pain
Patients even today praise when relief they gain.

    Root for pleurisy cooled the lung—
Cure *Asclepias* all name in Linnaeus' tongue.
    You're a famed constellation made—
Stars have granted a shape, stature that cannot fade:

    "Serpent-bearer," with snake-rod meant
Pleasantly to recall snakes in the temple pent,
    Calming, healthily sliding on
Over suppurant skin, lovely as gliding swan.

Snake-touch, tranquil massage, milkweed, and poetry—
These are means that combine well in the mind, for me.

142. Bony snout, and with hollow rings

fourth asclepiadic
>/ x / x x/ x/
/ x / x x/   / x x/ x/
>/ x / x x/ x/
/ x / x x/   / x x/ x/

>Bony snout, and with hollow rings,
New Guanlóng have they found—lizard, about ten feet,
>Clearly one of the Chinese "kings,"
Three-toed, much like a bird, predator fierce and fleet.

>"Guan" means "crown," and the giant mold
Some compare to the elk's antler, the peacock's tail.
>Flashy, sexual, potent, cold!
Feathers may have adorned further the rock-hard mail.

>Ninety millions of years T. Rex
Took, to get from guanlóng. Fourfold his length increased.
>Killer heat, or another hex?
Fifteen million or more years—and he quickly ceased.

These we mourn, but the King Dragons abound today.
Paintings keep them alive, papery kites for play.

143. Keep it simple, the bird outside

fourth asclepiadic
```
        /x /x x/ x/
/x /x x/   /x x/ x/
        /x /x x/ x/
/x /x x/   /x x/ x/
```

    Keep it simple, the bird outside
Chanted—three-noted call, savored and never
   changed.
    Just the thing for a man who spent
Every hour of the night living in former selves.

    Villanelles had I proofread first,
Then to Rilke had turned, dialogue partner loved,
    Whom inhabiting I'd been shaped
Into someone he helped make, with the Houri's aid.

    Moving back to asclepiads,
I'm refreshed and perplexed: how will they sound to
   you?
    Glad they come in an easy flow:
I'm not quite who I was twenty-four hours ago.

144. Waked at last from the longest dream

fourth asclepiadic
    /x /x x/ x/
/x /x x/ /x x/ x/
    /x /x x/ x/
/x /x x/ /x x/ x/

    Waked at last from the longest dream!
Sounds incredible—yet, really, I could have sworn
    I'd prepared, in a feeling-state
Gone, and not to be brought back to the waking mind,

    Waiting, watching the time go by
Till the thing should occur which was appointed me:
    Death by lethal injection. *What?*
Death by lethal—explain, *someone*! Indeed, I'd seen

    News reports in the last few days,
Each with drawn-out account telling of problems caused
    When officials in Arkansas
Found their stock running low, so that the fatal drug

    Might no more be available.
I remember the ire flooding my heart and brain:
    Execution is murder, too!
These American men slay in the name of law!?

    Now in mind I again revive:
In my twenties, the news came of a Buddhist monk
    Who his body had set aflame.
I—it happened, I swear!—dreamt I had copied *him*.

145. Rilke, heading for Venice where

fourth asclepiadic
    /x /x x/ x/
/x /x x/ /x x/ x/
    /x /x x/ x/
/x /x x/ /x x/ x/

    Rilke, heading for Venice where
I had also repaired several years before,
    Let a phase of my travel there
Timely rise to the mind, memories bold outpour.

    Some equipped with a camera go
Here and there and record things they on cell phone
    saw:
    He and I can a poem show—
"Lasting longer than bronze"? Gently correct each
    flaw...

    Have to laugh: a Horatian boast—
Who would make it today? Friends can at least enjoy
    What we write. So I'll raise a toast:
Praise the notebook! And pray epic survive each Troy.

146. You've survived from the ancient time

fourth asclepiadic
    /x /x x/ x/
/x /x x/ /x x/ x/
    /x /x x/ x/
/x /x x/ /x x/ x/

    You, revived from the ancient time,
Quondam rex may I call, *rexque futurus* name.
    Ash-arisen, transcending, climb
Now again to the height whither in spring you came!

    Quam ridiculi termini—
Borders risible which folk from their kin divide!
    Past from present as well, I see,
Folly great would it be, blinded from life to hide.

    Fourth asclepiad, you I praise:
Let your lovable tone offer a honey taste
    Made for pleasure in gloomy days!
Go, my lyric, and cheer friends with your aid, in haste!

147. Meter, mood, even pitch compete

fourth asclepiadic
>/ x / x x/ x/
/ x / x x/   / x x/ x/
>>/ x / x x/ x/
/ x / x x/   / x x/ x/

    Meter, mood, even pitch compete:
Time to utter some praise, loud, to the engineer,
    Videographer, schoolmates, all
Who on YouTube a gift rendered: accept my thanks!

    When I first had begun my song,
Tunes were running around, still, in the wakened
    brain:
    Handel, Telemann, Cárolán—
Strange "Lord Moira" strathspéy, then, in a bluegrass
    mode

    (Scottish forebear of this, at least),
"Miss Jane Cooper," the reel aided by Wanda's
    dance!—
    "Baptist Johnston," a tune well named
After someone who gave food to a minstrel blind.

    Now they've gone for awhile, and I
Write to you in a form, old, with a brand-new beat.
    Read the ditty aloud—you'll note
How the singable words dance in your mind at once!

Prosper, flourish, and happy years
Many more may you spend, Univee friends of mine!
　　　Let the spirit of cheer abound,
Sounding loud to the height, Bloomington, much-
　loved home!

148. Shaman-named is a showman known

fourth asclepiadic
> /x /x x/ x/
/x /x x/ /x x/ x/
> /x /x x/ x/
/x /x x/ /x x/ x/

    Shaman-named is a showman known.
Turn your drum to a horse, ride through the upper sky,
    Force the foe through your better strength
Loud to moan when his hope fades from the battle lost.

    Actor, author, producer you
Trinal roles will combine, voicing in low and high
    Timbre-register every turn
Action, roused in the joust, takes, that your might be proved.

    Superego and id by plain
English quickly reveal: It and the Over-I,
    New Mardúk versus Tiamat,
Light must fight the Abyss—trophy of soul to win.

    Beat that drum! Let the conflict rage—
Yet will Measure obtain triumph where Chaos failed:
    Prophet, you, of a mental health
Only art can provide, skyed in a solar glow.

149. Finish packing and then relax

fourth asclepiadic
> /x /x x/ x/
> /x /x x/   /x x/ x/
>   /x /x x/ x/
> /x /x x/   /x x/ x/

      Finish packing and then relax?
Though to reason inclined, yet I resist that plan.
      Something wants me to read and write,
Spending time as I wish—duty obliged to wait.

      Deadline pressures I always like:
They themselves lend a rush—rapid and happy both.
      Freedom, whim with a spice of risk
Will, however, delay, grandly, the task required.

      Rebel gesture—an emblem fit,
Speaking loudly: I'm bound, yet am a creature free!
      All my years have I lived this way,
Starting when, as a boy, time I would let slip by

      Never touching the violin,
Then, sweet idleness done, knowing the lesson day
      Soon would come, I would labor hard:
Practice long and intense—urged by the *daimon*'s will.

150. Boldly sang my Berlin-spring friend

fourth asclepiadic
```
        /x /x x/ x/
/x /x x/   /x x/ x/
        /x /x x/ x/
/x /x x/   /x x/ x/
```

    Boldly sang my Berlin-spring friend
All the while I prepared Jewish and Luther hymns:
    Prefatory, the serenade
I have planned to refresh people before my talk:

    Roles that Christians and Hebrews play
In elaborate new stories Muhammad told,
    Crucial, all, to the vast Qur'an,
Illustrating the truths Allah had valued most.

    These 'twill be my arousing task
Into drama to shape, coloring vocal tones,
    Letting voices regain their life,
Each with timbre to suit feeling of sacred strength.

151. "Speak to me of the sculptured ILM"

fourth asclepiadic
/ x / x x/ x/
/ x / x x/   / x x/ x/
/ x / x x/ x/
/ x / x x/   / x x/ x/

"Speak to me of the sculptured ILM."
That's the question that I, here at the Thomas
  Church,
    Pose each day when the people come:
"Concept-wrought though it be, will it a vision
  bring?"

    Said a dancer, "A bloom unfolds:
Narrow down at the root, rising to wider view.
    Every morning I, waking, dance,
No planned motion to make, simply what comes to
  mind."

    "Seen head-on, 'tis a proud, fierce bird,
Beaked and crested and brave, master of all he
  finds."
    "Turned around, 'tis a wide-mouthed cry—
Yes, an angel of calm, feminine beauty, right?"

152. "Don't grow up—it's a trap!" A sign

fourth asclepiadic
    /x /x x/ x/
/x /x x/   /x x/ x/
    /x /x x/ x/
/x /x x/   /x x/ x/

    "Don't grow up—it's a trap!" A sign
Cried, graffitoed in black, high on a building wall.
    Next, on DRINK DEVIL pub, a door,
GATE TO HELL, would entice, warm, and inform, at once.

    On a neighbor-façade is drawn
What a drama to see! Framed by a window comes,
    Angry, into the room, a man
While his wife, in dismay, cowers beneath the sheets.

    Hanging down from the window ledge
Here's a gentleman, quite pink in his birthday suit,
    Holding on for his life, to whom
Immortality Art grants—at a painful price.

153. When he goes on a pray'r retreat

fourth asclepiadic
```
        /x /x x/ x/
/x /x x/  /x x/ x/
        /x /x x/ x/
/x /x x/  /x x/ x/
```

      When he goes on a pray'r retreat,
So the pastor explained, always he brings along
      Pen and notebook. The first few days
Very hard will it be, keeping the silence rule:

      So intent is the drive to speak,
Words he'll utter perforce, written against the will.
      Only after the wish is quelled
Can tranquillity come, granting monastic peace.

      Quiet weeks are a goal that we
Only later enjoy, trained in a strict regime.
      Meditation can then ascend,
Unobstructed the path traveled within at last.

154. Endless time of a night deprived

fourth asclepiadic
    /x /x x/ x/
/x /x x/ /x x/ x/
    /x /x x/ x/
/x /x x/ /x x/ x/

    "Endless time of a night deprived,
Now you're taken away, O my gazelle—our love
    Sad-abandoned, a broken bond!
Could you truly forget how on the roses we

    Lay enwrapt in a single shawl,
Single necklace of pearl forming a treasure warm,
    Like two boughs intertwined in joy,
Single body we seemed, molten, a single heart.

    Up above were the heaven-stars,
Gleaming kindly upon love they were made to
  share—
    Gold, with blue for a jewel cloth..."
So wrote Abd'r-Rahmán, Córdoba's caliph-king.

155. Three I laud, of Qur'anic fame

fourth asclepiadic
>/x /x x/ x/
/x /x x/ /x x/ x/
>/x /x x/ x/
/x /x x/ /x x/ x/

>Three I laud, of Qur'anic fame:
Adam, first, who could say all of the angel-names,
>Modes of Being, the Ninety-Nine,
Each one coming from God—goals we may yet fulfill;

>Abraham, whom the Lord had spared
When his father had tried, after the gods were smashed,
>Setting fire to the living youth!—
Yet when rescued by God, father he pardoned, kind;

>Joseph, third, who the brothers gave
Food—but not only *that*—also the blessèd shirt!
>This the blindness would quickly heal
Plaguing Jacob, alas!, wailing the long-lost boy.

156. "Unicorn" she would "rather be"?

fourth asclepiadic
    /x /x x/ x/
/x /x x/ /x x/ x/
    /x /x x/ x/
/x /x x/ /x x/ x/

    "Unicorn" she would "rather be"?
So the T-shirt proclaims. What does it indicate?
    Would she rather have been a man?
Her companion is old, possibly needing care:

    Aging grandmother? What demands?
Might she feel that the fates gave her a life too hard?
    She is wondrously beautiful:
Oh, how thankful I'd be, just for a hinted smile...

    Lovely, too, was the Kurd I met
Flying here to Berlin. *Book of Zerdusht*, claimed she,
    Offered spirit a freedom voice—
No commandments of men urged in a mullah's word.

157. Tones arise when the man arrives

fourth asclepiadic
>/x /x x/ x/
/x /x x/ /x x/ x/
>/x /x x/ x/
/x /x x/ /x x/ x/

>Tones arise when the man arrives:
Hark, afar, to the shawm, sackbut, and barbiton.
>Fate with freedom in sky connives:
I like water have come, wind-like will soon be gone.

>Coffee's finer than nectar-wine
Should the magian request, Angel the best to hear:
>All are Names of the Strength Divine—
Sweet to you is the one chosen to bring it near.

>Savor warmth with a coldness blent:
Every breath you inhale, taste how the levels change.
>Air autumnal, the element
Reaching treetop will stir, heighten our skiey range.

>Grant me song till the dying day.
Heart my helper remain, breathing the deep Serene:
>Life is drama, so let us play.
Prayer, player the same—Will of the Global scene.

158. New York/Pennsylvania Disaster
in the light of Al Gore's film

fourth asclepiadic
    / x / x x/ x/
/ x / x x/   / x x/ x/
    / x / x x/ x/
/ x / x x/   / x x/ x/

    Record breaking, the paper said.
Why be taken aback? Storm-borne, with falling trees,
    Floods afflicted us, much like these,
Just a year ago. Sea, waters corruption-fed,

    Heated, mean that the hurricanes
Rise more fiercely and fast. Oftener, too. Our fault!—
    Shooting venom at heaven's vault—
Warming currents of air, causing horrendous rains.

    Act of God? It's an act of *ours*.
Inconvenient indeed—facing the dreadful *Truth*.
    We're bequeathing our hapless youth
Disproportionate plagues, dwarfing their human pow'rs.

    Whirlwinds howl from an outraged cloud:
Stop defiling the sky, sapient serpent proud!

159. Bluish mauve in the sky tonight

fourth asclepiadic
    / x / x x/ x/
/ x / x x/   / x x/ x/
    / x / x x/ x/
/ x / x x/   / x x/ x/

    Bluish mauve in the sky tonight,
Wholly motionless all, helps me direct my gaze
    Where the boughs of the maple tree
Thin extend and become armlike in will to reach.

    Ever thinner they bear a strength
Borne from root to the blue, witness of wish to climb
    Toward the nourishing solar glow,
Or, in chillier time, pallor of languid moon.

    Radiating, a group, in pray'r,
Are they moving? The mind wants me to answer, Yes.
    Changing focus to view each one,
First I think, it is true! Then: you are wrong, don't lie.

    Back I go, to the writing desk,
Where the vision I gained, patient with stare intent,
    Alters, bending to sly desire:
How they tremble and sway, seeking in dream their aim!

160. Ancient Snake Worship

*after reading world-science.net on Sheila Coulson's
claim to have found a site of python veneration, 2006*

fourth asclepiadic
    / x / x x/ x/
/ x / x x/   / x x/ x/
    / x / x x/ x/
/ x / x x/   / x x/ x/

    How I'd love to believe it true:
Oldest ritual rock, seventy thousand years
    Hid, then suddenly brought to view—
Dented, twenty feet long, moving!—it so appears,

    Viewed in firelight!—the snout nearby
Sundered now from the snake's head that the cave
    contains.
    Sheila Coulson, who knew the high
Value granted the three beasts of the local plains,

    Told us, too, of the paintings near:
Cave-walls boast a giraffe, elephant—hallowed, dear.
    Python! El? and Apollo? Well...
Later, maybe, but now—rescue the snake from hell!

    Climbing sun in a shiny sky:
Let it burnish the bright snakeskin—excite the eye!

VI
Stichic Strophes: Fifth Asclepiadic and Hendecasyllabic

161. Strength and vigor we love: thus when we look, charmed, at a waterfall

fifth asclepiadic
/x /x x/ /x x/ /x x/ x/
/x /x x/ /x x/ /x x/ x/
/x /x x/ /x x/ /x x/ x/
/x /x x/ /x x/ /x x/ x/

Strength and vigor we love: thus when we look,
  charmed, at a waterfall,
Comfort comes with a rush: movement that's not ever
  required to stop
Tells the poet: to live, here is a view which is an
  emblem we
Rightly treasure—a sign, marvel you feel, now, in
  your lungs and heart.

Yes, we're going to die, yet in our life motion will
  never fail:
Loud the sound that the blood flowing will make:
  this in a curving shell
You most clearly can hear: people will say, That is
  the ocean-tone.
Amplified is the rush ear-blood has made! Physics
  and faith are one.

Grateful tune of the sphere! What do I mean? Loud
  circulation you
Hear by grace of the shell—this may as well speak of
  a circle true.

Breathing's upward and down, inward and out. Yet it depends upon

Travel round and about, never in doubt, midnight to daybreak-dawn.
Up to sixty per cent we have been lent water in body weight:
We in waterfall see pleasure that *we* feel in our high estate.

162. Hi there! Learning to use metrical forms history left behind?

fifth asclepiadic
/x /x x/ /x x/ /x x/ x/
/x /x x/ /x x/ /x x/ x/
/x /x x/ /x x/ /x x/ x/
/x /x x/ /x x/ /x x/ x/

Hi there! Learning to use metrical forms history left behind?
Know that getting the brain ready to move isn't a tricky thing.
Rather, shaping a tune made of a theme casual, random, shows
Nothing stands in the way. Practice awhile. Soon you'll have made it yours.

Merely write of your life. Anything goes. I the podiatrist
Have to visit: he'll try making my nails free of a fungus growth—
Problem common on all continents: bad, bothersome everywhere!
Also, calluses need smoothening down: cracks will infection tempt.

Hey, I'm starting to feel really at ease: fifth the asclepiad
Quickly mastered, the mood greatly improves, making the fingers dance.

Horace, thanks to your aid, traveling fast, loving
    computer skill,
I'm in Rome and New York, doubly at home, eager to
    hymn your praise!

Maybe, too, I've applied something I loved so in your
    country odes—
Verse a farmer would speak, telling of sun, wheat,
    and the newborn lambs
Filled with vernal delight. Then, as the cold comes to
    the landscape brown,
Drink your wine by the fire, happy with friends,
    humming a tranquil tune!

163. Truth I've newly acquired: this I would like, here, to impart to you

fifth asclepiadic
/x /x x/ /x x/ /x x/ x/
/x /x x/ /x x/ /x x/ x/
/x /x x/ /x x/ /x x/ x/
/x /x x/ /x x/ /x x/ x/

Truth I've newly acquired: this I would like, here, to impart to you.
Let's begin with a way, earlier learned, Hebrew can help us feel
Challenged more when we're made fully aware how in a single word
Two things endless are blent, known to be *one* thing to admire in awe.

What's *olám*? It can mean thoughts that, combined, thinking will overwhelm:
Place unbounded and time endless in range, World and Eternity.
Two unlimited things—Universe, Time—glad who inhabits both!
These we, favored, inhale, loved in the heart, merely when breathing air.

Thus I pondered before. Now I can add: what does *he-élem* mean?
Something *there* but *concealed*, veiled and obscured, not to be viewed or known.

Think *he-élem, olám.* One is the root—shared by the
  twofold thought.
Time and Universe, then, something will hide,
  something we can't perceive.

That from which there arose Time and the World?
  This will remain unkenned.
Yet I also have heard: people were all—yes!—in Its
  image made.
"Know thyself?" We can try, yet in the end, we'll in
  the depth be lost.
Space Unending and Time—also the Cause—deep in
  our nature hid.

164. Breathing in, we can feel mouth-tongue-and-throat cooled by the evening air

fifth asclepiadic
/x /x x/ /x x/ /x x/ x/
/x /x x/ /x x/ /x x/ x/
/x /x x/ /x x/ /x x/ x/
/x /x x/ /x x/ /x x/ x/

Breathing in, we can feel mouth-tongue-and-throat cooled by the evening air,
Also cooling the sweet sips of the mild coffee that wakes the brain.
Warm and colder, the mix mirrors the change made in the twilight hour:
Every night in July twenty degrees lower than day will fall.

Quiet comes to my aid, letting the taste move to the foreground-mind.
I in silence can bathe, purity gain, essence refreshed and clean.
Friend Computer a print adds to the mood: shown is a brindled cat
Resting calm on her side, savoring peace, liking a summer nap.

Reader, long have I loved writing for *you*—showing my ways to form

Word-song featuring new patterns of shape, triplets
   in vocal dance.
Tell me: how have you liked hearing the Greeks,
   Romans revived in tone?

Write me: tell me your thought. Should you approve,
   we a renascence may
Yet create when the soul, joying in hymn, raising the
   voice in pray'r,
Chants to That Which Is Hid—laughing, in tears: *You
are my Only Home.*

165. Goddess entered the room, baby asleep, silent the night and calm

fifth asclepiadic
/x /x x/ /x x/ /x x/ x/
/x /x x/ /x x/ /x x/ x/
/x /x x/ /x x/ /x x/ x/
/x /x x/ /x x/ /x x/ x/

Goddess entered the room, baby asleep, quiet the
  night and calm,
Gift serene to bestow, treasure to have, yet with a
  strange delay.
Finger dipped in the sweet honey they taste only who
  never die,
She the lips of the babe touched and a charm uttered
  that none could hear.

Sixty years would the deed sleep unrevealed, ev'n as
  the baby slept
Now who, rising refreshed, under the spell, naught of
  the gift would know.
This lay deep in the heart, even as if, hidden and
  strange to tell,
It in castle were kept, bolted and locked, guarded by
  thorn-trees 'round.

Shaken—earth and the sky, so that the man, white-
  haired and sixty-one,
Touched with lightning collapsed—days in a faint,
  finally raised alive,

Ears now filled with the tones Deity gave, hearing the Spirit-Name
Saved for coming of age, singing unsealed, free for the world to love.

166. Please, don't ask—'tis a thing wretched to know, either for me or you

fifth asclepiadic
/x /x x/ /x x/ /x x/ x/
/x /x x/ /x x/ /x x/ x/
/x /x x/ /x x/ /x x/ x/
/x /x x/ /x x/ /x x/ x/

Please, don't ask—'tis a thing wretched to know,
   either for me or you,
What the gods may intend, Leuconoé! Even in
   Babylon
Calculation will fail—simply endure, patient, what's
   handed out,
Whether winters get worse, ór if the last Jupiter
   picked for us—

Waves that rage even yet—weakening rocks deep in
   Tyrrhenian sea—
Proved enough. Be prepared, straining your wines,
   hope in our span so brief
Cutting short, while our life, jealous of time, races to
   no avail.
Seize the day, make it yours. Thén be content. Future
   you cannot trust.

Ode Eleven Book One, Horace you hear, chanted in
   New York speech.
Fifth asclepiad he, using it well, calmly commends
   to us—

Rhythm leaping about, yet with a firm beat for a solid base,
More athletic and more acrobat-skill asking than modern style.

Seize the day is a thought perfectly phrased: never abandon that!
All is number may come quickly to mind, too, from the olden world:
This, Pythagoras' tone sounding again, chimes with Horatian tune.
Meter, number, and beat—giving me strength—love, and a length of days.

167. Cruel weapons, I fear, Venus can wield, so you will soon find out
Horace IV.10

fifth asclepiadic
/x /x x/ /x x/ /x x/ x/
/x /x x/ /x x/ /x x/ x/
/x /x x/ /x x/ /x x/ x/
/x /x x/ /x x/ /x x/ x/

Cruel weapons, I fear, Venus can wield—so you will
 soon find out
When the bloom on your cheek, feature of pride, fades
 unawaitedly,
Hair worn shoulder-length now, floating in grace, then
 will have fallen down,
All the roseate health fainter in shade, feeling the
 years come on.

Satin-smooth will the dear face that we knew cede to
 a texture rough...
Ligurínus, you'll cry then with regret, noting the mirror
 view:
"Would that feelings today might, by a gift, those of
 my youth return—
Joys come back from the past, comforting-glad, mood
 of delight restore!"

Some feel time in a stream, quieting dream, bearing
 the mind to sea.

Others think it a storm, menace enorm, bidding the heart to fight.
Some just call it a clock, fearing to balk, mild in the master-sight,
Others, dim with dismay, brush it away, turn to eternity.

Time's my lady of love—rhymes with above—under, surrounding, too:
Tidal rhapsody we, avid in spree, shape with a hallelu.
Meter speeding along, we with a song hymn when the birds are gone:
Teach the sun to believe, rhythmical heave, bodies the words of dawn.

168. Don't be planting a tree, Varus I pray, soft in the Tíbur ground
Horace I.18

fifth asclepiadic
/x /x x/ /x x/ /x x/ x/
/x /x x/ /x x/ /x x/ x/
/x /x x/ /x x/ /x x/ x/
/x /x x/ /x x/ /x x/ x/

Don't be planting a tree, Varus I pray, soft in the Tíbur
  ground
Right near Cátilus' wall, till it is time, first, to be
  planting vines.
God it pleased to propose difficult tasks fit for the
  drier folk:
Biting worries, he thought, won't go away save by a
  stringent rule.

Who when mellow with wine speaks of the poor, talks
  of the army draft?
Aren't you, Bacchus our Dad, Venus the Sweet, better
  for evening chat?
Sad that people abuse, nevertheless, present of
  Bacchus kind:
Centaurs, rabid with drink, shameful defeat knew at
  the Lapith hands;

Thracians, drunken in fight, also we blame: Bacchus
  would warn them well

*Not—with greedy desire—laws to neglect, rather a
   limit set.
You, Bassareus white, never I'll shake, nor will
   disturb your rule.
Not so brazen a thief ever am I, leaf-covered holy
   things*

*Bold in daylight to snatch. High hold the drum, horn
   (Berecyntus') too!
These the lawless will aid, blinded by self, thinking
   that Glory comes,
Empty crown for to raise, highly unwise, whim with a
   mocking grin:
Secret squanderers they, lacking in faith, clearer than
   see-through glass.*

Drum and trumpet I hear, not by the drunk played
   at a revel fest—
No, a grandeur of tone wants to resound, long as the
   art we prize.
Bacchus, Venus are glad—ardor and love swelling
   the heart awake:
Lungs we widen to cry: Horace applaud! Prosper the
   bronzen song!

169. Fifth asclepiad themes—adding them up helps me to comprehend

fifth asclepiadic
/x /x x/ /x x/ /x x/ x/
/x /x x/ /x x/ /x x/ x/
/x /x x/ /x x/ /x x/ x/
/x /x x/ /x x/ /x x/ x/

Fifth asclepiad themes—adding them up helps me to comprehend
How the meter befriends one who would psalm chant to the waking dawn.
First, untrustworthy time none will foresee. Maybe for mental health
Here's our permanent gift, topping them all—*living, the day I seize.*

Next, our mirrors reveal only what soon fades in the flight of time:
Shakespeare, too, had advised never to hoard gifts that our nature gave.
Love means giving, and song bursts from the soul filled with the joy of breath,
Body, mind, and the heart made to beget, granting our Parent thanks.

Third is *mental control*, worthy of men shapen erect to stand,
When imbibing a bliss, whether of wine or of the loved embrace.

Warmth of blood is a boon while we, alert, taste of
 the passion-hour—
Yet, with gratitude formed, art will survive, paying it
 forward more.

170. Swift Wind of Welcome
friendly musical message for Mark Poliks

hendecasyllabic
/x /x x/x /x /x

Walked a man in the very dead of winter
Yet in awe 'mid the dawning open quiet
Intimation a vastly whitened landscape
Might unveil to the hardy questing hiker
Mood attuned to the wisdom of the flying
Windswept flakes with a hidden heaven spectrum
Touched by fingers of Iris when she wakened
To a world that an early exhalation
Upward into a radiant day dispelling
Thickened heaviness—which accumulated
Over many an hour of Lethe sleeping
Freed while now the increasing light had widened
So that after the gathering of power
Scattered strength in rewarding warming outflow
Health would lend to the still resilient creatures
Feeling heat as a comfort spreading thankful
After knowing impatient imprecation
Less availed than acceptance of the restful
Alteration that played the planet gamut.

171. February

hendecasyllabic
/x /x x/x /x /x

Februá, with a name that brings the chilling
Whips of winter before the wool-swathed hearer,
Mars' own mother was called. To me, austerer
Month than March though her son was keen on
  killing,

February, in Rome, earned fame with fertile
Lupercalia whips, brought out the beaters:
Young and eager to be the dire defeaters
Winter feared, they defended Venus' myrtle—

All while whipping the women. What a scandal!
So thought Rome when the popes attained their
  power.
Lupercalia—no! The final hour
Came, whip trodden below monastic sandal.

Then the Purification of the Virgin
Feast was held, that a female bud might burgeon.

172. Plato and the Flute-Girl
comment on an anecdote in Eric Voegelin,
Plato and Aristotle

hendecasyllabic
/x /x x/x /x /x

Writer wise, when he tells a legend claiming
Plato, dying, desired to hear a Thracian
Flute-girl, kind as the gracious, mild Phaeacian
Lady loved in the *Odyssey*, is aiming

Hopefully to suggest an elevating
Lesson. Plato, who heard the maiden stumble
Over rhythms that made her start to fumble,
Moved a finger to mark the beat, elating

Both himself and the girl with playful teaching.
Thracian maiden... Indeed, his own dear mother—
She'd been also a Thracian—here's another,
Kindred, beautiful. Memory was reaching

Back to birth—or a prior time? A treasure!
Number—Heavenly Form—a primal pleasure.

173. Listen, Lesbia, let us live in loving
Catullus 5

hendecasyllabic
/x /x x/x /x /x

Listen, Lesbia, let us live in loving!
Rumor spread by the stern old gossip codgers
Let's appraise at the worth of not one penny!
Sun may set and again awake in dawning:
We, however, if once our light is guttered,
Spend unmoved an eternal night in quiet.
Give me kisses a thousand, then a hundred,
Then a thousand again, another hundred,
One more thousand, and then a final hundred:
After all of the thousands we have counted,
Shake the abacus well, erase the number,
Also keeping the evil man from envy
Who's unable to tally up the kisses.

Yo, Catullus! I love that rebel spirit!
Thirteen lines—may it prove your luck is winning!
Horace told you to seize the moment—well, then,
Best keep busy: of action be the master!
Chronos, Time, is with Kronos, god defeated,
Badly, wrongly confused—they vastly differ.
True, the father of Jove is old, bent over,
Leaning closer to earth the more he's weakened.
Time, though, sprightly as Hermes at the seashore
When a lyre from a shell he made and played it,
Sings to Love with the spindrift ever-mindful:
Spry and spraying and spree are lives of mortals
Climbing high as the tide in vital triumph.

174. Young, who bothers to read obituaries?

hendecasyllabic
/x /x x/x /x /x

Young, who bothers to read obituaries?
Random fates of the folk of other nations
Than the country the reader's blest to dwell in...

As reports of the Wall Street market figures,
Or the winning and losing of a sport-team,
Stories told of the dead could not engage me.

Later, after I gained a few more decades,
Vital-mortal statistics fueled int'rest:
Where am I in the stages of Becoming?

We a story enframe where start and finish
Can't be known: 'tis an episode of weather,
Told in form of the tide, a lasting pastime.

Now, the eyes to a different level wander:
In obits, from the warm emotion people
Feel, I siblings acquire, an aunt, a cousin.

Briefly thus I awakened am to travel
Through a sample of patterns of our breathing,
Love and grief and the cycle that conjoins them.

175. Who, I wonder, would like this new-made booklet?
Catullus 1

hendecasyllabic
/x /x x/x /x /x

Who, I wonder, would like this new-made booklet?
(Pleasing, smoothed with a pumice, quite attractive...)
You, Cornelius, may—so take my present!
You have never condemned my trifles, even
After offering all our long-drawn hist'ry
(Daring, singular 'mong Italian writers):
Three big volumes—by Jupiter!—you gave us—
Wise, elaborate. Take this thing I've written,
Nondescript though it be, O Virgin, patron!
That it long may outlast our present era.

Paradox that the chanter gladly savors:
Lyric, made in the heart, not schooled and weighty,
Nor intended for academic honor,
Penned, in fact, by a stenographic servant
Writing down what a hidden speaker wanted,
Won't compete with a story big, imposing,
Yet, by virtue of grace we never merit,
Granted rather by talent well invested,
May, by aid of the Muse whom we're entreating,
Sing as long as a human heart will hearken.

176. While Septimius held his lover Acme
Catullus 45

hendecasyllabic
/x /x x/x /x /x

While Septimius held his lover Acme
Close to heart he declared: "If with abandon
I no longer can love, and prove unready
For a constant devotion though our lifetimes,
Then—as often as people perish lonely
'Mid the Lybian heat, the searing swelter
Felt in India—then will I be going
Bold, undaunted, to meet the green-eyed lion."
Love, approval to show, was sneezing leftward
As it rightward had sneezed before, in answer.

Acme, bending her head in sign of welcome,
Eyes—infatuate—of her lover kissing—
Wine-red lips, a delight for him she favored—
Said, "Septimius, life of mine, so be it.
Servants máy we remain of one great master,
Letting grander and keener passion kindle,
Burning soft in the marrow of your dear one."
Love, approval to show, was sneezing rightward
As it leftward had sneezed before, in answer.

Having so with a perfect omen started,
Thus they love and are loved in dulcet union,
Poor Septimius, lucky man, attached to
Acme—Syria, Britain both excelling.

*As for Acme, she finds her every pleasure
In Septimius only, her beloved.
Who a happier couple could imagine?
Who a passion conceive, a love more blesséd?

Shall we seek for an answer? 'Tis a challenge...
Here's my double reply: "Good health! Gesundheit!"*

177. You, of Romulus' line most gifted speaker
Catullus 49

hendecasyllabic
/x /x x/x /x /x

You, of Romulus' line most brilliant speaker,
Best of present and past, O Marcus Tully,
Future numberless orators excelling,
You Catullus, your grateful hearer, praises
Even though he's the worst of all the poets,
Ev'n as truly the worst of all the poets
As the finest are you of all defenders.

Cicero, we may guess, would find the tribute
Suspect, filled with a not quite hidden insult.
Present, future, and past alike defeated
By the man to be flattered—who'd believe it?
Friend Catullus, you tend to be sarcastic.
Like Septimius—dear, derided lover—
You have Cicero lauded, yet while sneezing.

You, Cornelius Nepos, weighty thinker,
All things knowable knowing, plus some others,
Little gain from a poet who's composing
Ten short lines that are destined for the ages.
Every value Catullus lauds he quickly
Undermines with a wild exaggeration.
Did you, Lesbia, get those myriad kisses?

178. Triple miracle rose for me awoken

hendecasyllabic
/x /x x/x /x /x

Triple miracle rose for me awoken:
Any thing in existence when there didn't
Have to burgeon an object, place, or person—
Merely being's a daily present wonder.

People walking about a rounded planet,
Each one knowing a world, an earth horizon
Changing momently, sky direction upward—
Second wonder is creaturely awareness.

Members, we, of a boundless pluriversal:
Heaven getting in breath, each heart inhaling
This, and giving it back, in conversation,
Third of wonders will lend, no end, forever.

179. Dining well is a guarantee, Fabellus
Catullus 13

hendecasyllabic
/x /x x/x /x /x

Dining well is a guarantee, Fabellus,
When you come in the next few days (god willing)
If you also will bring a nice big dinner,
Not forgetting a girlfriend who's attractive
Nor the wine and the wit providing laughter.

Charmer, keeping in mind these kindly favors,
You're assured of a grand old time. The wallet,
Sad to say, of your friend is lined with cobwebs.
In return for your gift you'll savor friendship
(Maybe something more elegant and pleasant):

I will give you an oil which to my girlfriend
All the Cupids and Venuses had granted.
Smelling this, you'll be tempted to request that
Into nothing but Nose the gods may turn you.

Here the Irony Master, god-belaureled,
Made a jest of a cordial invitation:
"Should you come and provide an entertainment—
Dinner, company, jokes, and fine imbibing,
I'll repay you for splendid contributions:
You'll a fragrance enjoy—for love essential."

180. Paradox from the game of life emerges

hendecasyllabic
/x /x x/x /x /x

Paradox from the game of life emerges.
Not adept with machines, I fell in love with
You, my friendly computer, who endowed me
Straightaway with the gift of rapid magic,
Writing lyric as fast as I could feel it,
Making speedier syntax flow more freely,
Stimulating the heart to quicker thunder,
Blest machine! who my days have quite transfigured.

Numbers never attracted me: they errors
Constantly have occasioned, worse with aging.
Lately, though, there's a number that enthralled me,
Never ceasing to help, arouse, and counsel.
Each of us with a hundred billion brain cells
Favored is. And the mighty figure, sacred,
Learned by me from the *wunderkind* computer,
Loudly tells of a godly wealth of power.

'Tween the first and the second cup of coffee,
You that came with a driving rush of insight,
Number-thought and machine, from Strength
   Unbounded,
Wisdom bearing in nighttime visitation,
Take my praise: the invigorated psalmer
Aid with grace of the other hundred billion—
This the count of the galaxies uncovered
By astronomers working with your guidance.

181. If Mary Had Borne Twins

Matt. 5:29. "And if thy right eye offend thee, pluck it out, and cast it from thee: for it is profitable for thee that one of thy members should perish, and not that thy whole body should be cast into hell. 30. And if thy right hand offend thee, cut it off, and cast it from thee: for it is profitable to thee that one of thy members should perish, and not that thy whole body should be cast into hell."
18:8. "Wherefore, if thy hand or thy foot offend thee, cut them off and cast them from thee: it is better for thee to enter into life halt or maimed, rather than having two hands or two feet to be cast into everlasting fire. 9. And if thine eye offend thee, pluck it out, and cast it from thee: it is better for thee to enter life with one eye, rather than having two eyes to be cast into hell fire."
Mark 9:47. "And if thine eye offend thee, pluck it out: it is better for thee to enter into the kingdom of God with one eye, than having two eyes to be cast into hell fire...."

hendecasyllabic
/x /x x/x /x /x

"Listen up! If your eye is getting greedy
Gouge it out! and you'll never have a problem.
Grabby hand? The solution's clear and waiting:
Hack it off! and you buy eternal freedom."

Jesus preached, and his darling sister listened.
He, so fond of Jazoola, hoped to help her.

"Moody? Brother, you tend to get depressive.
Comes the gloom, and you start to sound peculiar.

What you're claiming today is just plain wacko:
You'll be fine when the mental storm is over."

"Ah, Jazoola... You're right! It's true—no kidding:
I should talk to the womenfolk more often...."

182. "The Poet Nothing Affirmeth"

modified hendecasyllabic
x/x /x x/x /x /

The poet nothing affirms and never lies.
Akin to worms and to Hermes of the skies—
Within him, germs of our life—each wheat seed—
   rise:
He turns the terms and will stir the words—oh, wise!

Echinoderms are a seaborne starry prize;
Hellenic herms may a landmark recognize—
My lyric mirthfully sperms—a fine surprise!
The squeamish squirms, but the bright ones realize.

What's right returns and the lighter lending tries.
What's fiery burns—and it warms or scarifies.
What's lively spurns all the norms it clarifies.
What's high-wired yearns and aspiring, rending,
   sighs.

Keats' lucent urns had portrayed a great surmise.
What blue Lucernes in the Wilbur-lady eyes!

183. Hendecasyllabic Sonnet on a Ted Kooser Poetry Workshop, with Dodecasyllabic Response 3/22/06

hendecasyllabic /x /x x/x /x /x

"Put yourself in the way of luck," he offered.
Then: "Establish a little bit of order."
"Keep your work" was a point: a longtime hoarder,
He'd recycle a verse in prose. He'd proffered

Bits of jottings that grew, accumulated,
Till he spotted a unity accruing.
Serendipity suited him, not ruing
Even cancer and chemo. When he'd waited

In oncology wards where many, trying—
Simply trying to live, had made it clearer
Humbled plainness of thought would bring us nearer,
That's when fortune arrived, a gratifying

Windfall, sobering too. He thought his drinking
Hadn't helped him at all. He left me thinking.

dodecasyllabic x/ x/ x/x x/ x/x

He spoke of serendipity, radiation,
Of waiting in oncology wards, of humbling,
Of strokes of luck, despair, and of daily writing,
Of weeping willow leaves on a morning windshield,
With each a kiss if things in your life are moving,

Or if you're having family troubles, maybe
Boats filled with bones.

"Along comes Ezra Pound and a T. S. Eliot,
And they're the Hiroshima and Nagasaki
Of poetry," while Frost, in the whole big complex,
Was quite ignored, "too easy" to please the critics.
For eighty years the people have felt excluded.
A poem's not an oyster to be cracked open.

184. While the boughs of the arching willow tower

hendecasyllabic
/x /x x/x /x /x

While the boughs of the arching willow tower,
Wands bow down to the farther ground of power.
Peace achieving, the tree is contemplating
Hunger, love, and the under-solace waiting.

Rousing fount with a waterfall combining,
Sky unbounded and ground-life unconfining,
Stately plant in palatial quiet captured,
Sculpture brother of mine has mind enraptured.

Wind awaking to sway the branches riant
Leaves will breeze to demise with ease compliant,
Playful ways of the years of autumn showing:
Quick are we in our coming and our going.

Nature's art that can liberate from stricture
Sighing heart in a film will, tristful, picture.
Soul, inclining and rising, are you crying?
Flying children are dyed in hue undying.

185. What bad mind, little Ravidus the Wretched
Catullus 40

hendecasyllabic
/x /x x/x /x /x

What bad mind, little Ravidus the Wretched,
Drives you into my lyrics, headlong falling?
Who's the god you had called on, quite unwisely,
Now preparing to rouse a fight demented?

Would you furnish the food of hourly gossip?
Would you stoop to the worst for daily rumor?
Aim soon gained!—for you wished to love my lover,
Knowing well that the penalties are lasting.

Empathy is the writer brave expecting
Soon to get with a fight he calls demented,
Undeflected by fear of self-arraignment,
Thinking manly revenge an act most worthy:

'Rabid scoundrel who dared to be a rival,
Had you planned to escape our twofold anger—
Mine and also the god's? That wrath is judgment
Waking boldly the heart aflame with passion!'

186. Ah, Licinius—what a day! what pleasure!
Catullus 50

hendecasyllabic
/x /x x/x /x /x

Ah, Licinius—what a day! what pleasure!
Games we played in my little notebooks—many,
Just as if we had planned on being clever
When exchanging our witty little verses
Penned with meter experiments abundant,
All made jolly with jokes and wine so tasty.
When I left, having loved your wit delicious,
I, Licinius, charmed, my head a-flaming,
Felt so roused that I couldn't touch my supper,
Nor could sleep—little eyes remaining open.

Moving 'round on the bed—ungoverned, wildly—
Crazed, impatiently waiting for the dawn-light,
Wanting always to see you, keep conversing,
I had wearied my limbs with constant motion:
Scarce alive on the bed they lay, immobile,
While this poem I wrote for you, my joker.

Read it through—you will comprehend my sorrow:
Don't be rash, but to fond entreaty listen!
I must pray that you not reject me, comrade,
Or by Nemesis you'll be truly punished—
Harsh that goddess—be careful!—don't upset her.

What a heavenly plan: release your feeling
Through the writing of lines in vital meter,
Lyric made in a testament of friendship,
Volume shapen with mind and heart united,
Rival wit, and the flame-love higher climbing.

187. Done with shopping, and heading for the exit

hendecasyllabic
/x /x x/x /x /x

Done with shopping, and heading for the exit,
Thinking only of waiting for the taxi
Which would come, I was told, in fifteen minutes,
I'd been startled by one who, coming toward me,
Made me suddenly readjust my focus.

She my twitch of the head had surely noticed,
Quick result of the altered eye direction.
Broadly smiling, she happily acknowledged
What my body and mind at once accomplished
Paying tribute instinctive to the vision.

Dark-brown, flowing, the long hair wavy, lustred,
Face quite delicate-featured, eyes of thank-you,
She was feeling, I know, the same deep gladness
Beauty grants to the viewer and possessor,
Double present of coupled smiles delighted.

188. How in heart of my heart I want to wander!

hendecasyllabic
/x /x x/x /x /x

How in heart of my heart I want to wander!
Reached the back of beyond, then went beyonder,
Lover-passion advancing ever fonder,

Connoisseur of the theater of weather,
Heathen, sleeping on mead amid the heather,
Vision pinion-directed by a feather,

Wayward, needing to stray in every valley,
Meter-forager, bravely out to sally,
Crowded images brainwave-wise to rally,

Lone I, 'mid the alone, the holy-speaking,
Rivers under the ground with dowser seeking,
Jinns intuiting wheresoever sneaking,

Glad, with gift of the tune divinely dowered,
Depth and height would combine to be empowered
As by dew and the light the ground has flowered:

May hendecasyllabic versing aid me,
More intently to be what You have made me:
Daily bolder, although some years delayed me.

I would here, in a sabbatine conclusion,
State my aim of a manic-mantic fusion,
Striding forth from illusion to Allusion.

VII
Alcaic

189. Al-Jábir worked in front of his home one day

alcaic
x/ x/ x/x x/ x/
x/ x/ x/x x/ x/
    x/x /x /x /x
  /x x/x x/x /x

Al-Jábir wrote in front of his home one day
That in a little town by the desert lay
        When past him ran a hundred camels:
   Thundering hooves no restriction trammels.

A rancher then arriving inquired, "Did you
By any chance a herd of my camels view?"
        "I noticed nothing," came the answer,
   "Loving your labor's a task enhancer."

The rancher, wild, replied, "Yet I see the dust
Has covered you! The animals ran, I trust!?"
        Al-Jábir looks: he can't deny it.
   Algebra dwells in a realm of quiet.

190. The lady pastor told me she'd liked my talk

alcaic
x/ x/ x/x x/ x/
x/ x/ x/x x/ x/
    x/x /x /x /x
  /x x/x x/x /x

The lady pastor told me she'd liked my talk.
Said I, "The play of thought on your lively face
        And in your eyes I followed often,
    Wanting to check on your next reaction."

When yesterday she came to the Thomas Church,
Her cheerful greeting heartened me once again.
        Her eyes with gladness brimming over
    Made me so grateful I can't help smiling.

The feeling just returned with a further grace.
While noon-bells chimed, the children in courtyard played:
        Their voices loud in high rejoicing
    Birdlike and floating my heart transpórted.

191. Consider what a motherly heart can do

alcaic
x/ x/ x/x x/ x/
x/ x/ x/x x/ x/
    x/x /x /x /x
  /x x/x x/x /x

Consider what a motherly heart can do.
Asiya, Pharaoh's wife, with enraptured soul
        The new-found infant Moses welcomed:
  "Maybe we'll make him our son! I love him!"

The baby's mother soon she'd invite to court:
Asiya, Mother, Princess for him would care,
        The child whom now all three could treasure,
  Blesséd alike and in love united.

When Pharaoh's feeling hardened against the Jews
And plagues began, Asiya in outrage cried:
        "Great Lord of Moses, help me, save me,
  Take me away from the wicked tyrant!"

The King was stubborn. Yet, when confronting death
While chasing Hebrews fleeing his wrath by sea,
        "Blest God!" he cried, "Whom I've offended,
  Praised be the Lord!—I to faith surrender!"

Asiya turned the soul of a man of stone
To Kindness, Truth, and Light which had ever dwelt
        Within her heart. O Loving Mother,
  Long may I treasure the Heaven Lesson!

192. My friend was paid a fee to contribute help

alcaic
x/ x/ x/x x/ x/
x/ x/ x/x x/ x/
    x/x /x /x /x
  /x x/x x/x /x

My friend was paid a fee to contribute help
To people who'd enrolled in a lecture course
        Where those who'd long forgotten laughter
    Practiced reviving the skill—it's healthy!

The pupils faced each other among the trees
And gave each thought a laughter-promoting theme,
        Encouraged in a woodland setting
    Thus to anticipate joys long hidden.

The oddest thing my friend would discover soon
Appeared when people trying their best to laugh
        Brought forth instead an ardent weeping!
    Molten emotions had won their freedom.

193. My friend likes giving flowery compliments

alcaic
x/ x/ x/x x/ x/
x/ x/ x/x x/ x/
    x/x /x /x /x
  /x x/x x/x /x

My friend likes giving flowery compliments—
A Pakistani ultra-politeness form.
       "The people such a lecture never
   Heard as the one you have just delivered!—

No deed achieved by tones and the words alone,
But one where all the body had taken part:
       Remembering your recitation,
   They will recall the Qur'anic *drama*."

"You like exaggeration." "Indeed I do.
Exaggerating's needed in art and love.
       The Lord Himself exaggerated
   While He was making the world of creatures."

194. I have to say, my *Fat Little Wireless Book*

alcaic
x/ x/ x/x x/ x/
x/ x/ x/x x/ x/
    x/x /x /x /x
  /x x/x x/x /x

I have to say, my *Fat Little Wireless Book*
Would pleasure any person who cared to look—
    The light blue lines in fine alignment
  Pairing the pages with non-confinement.

Here's Çatalhöyük, home of the Hittite gods
That march in single file in their well-trained squads
    With Phrygian caps (of ancient glory)
  Mirroring dwarves' in the Snow White story.

I also find good notes on the sculpture made
By Ron Gonzalez, fantasies where he played
    With body parts of creatures perished
  Made into forms that the critic cherished.

My recent entries tell of Berlin and of
The Middle East calligraphies which I love,
    The Thomas Church, the celebration
  There of the Protestant Reformation.

195. A movie should be made of the varied styles

alcaic
x/ x/ x/x x/ x/
x/ x/ x/x x/ x/
    x/x /x /x /x
  /x x/x x/x /x

A movie should be made of the varied styles
That, while the plane flew many a hundred miles,
    The standing parents used while swaying
  Children to sleep who were tired of playing.

A man with jerky pattern of up-and-down
Could then have learned 'twas making the baby
  frown.
    Although the toddler was remaining
  Patient—one needed some "parent training."

A woman, rather, showed that a four-beat dance—
Two steps to right, two left—could the mood enhance
    Of any child. I saw one smiling
  Tranced by the rhythm, his mind beguiling.

196. Conduct while looking down and around you now

alcaic
x/ x/ x/x x/ x/
x/ x/ x/x x/ x/
   x/x /x /x /x
  /x x/x x/x /x

"Conduct while looking down and around you now,"
I heard the words oracular, half awake.
        In dream, was I symphonic leader?
    How to interpret the wonder-summons?

I take it as a comment on how to feel
When writing this, my book of the golden forms.
        We'll aid pro-ancient pioneering,
    Viewing the goal as a revelation.

Upon a conic section I thought I stood,
The hearers guiding lithe with a deft baton:
        Vigný beleaguered Moses beaming
    Showed as alone in a mount-ascension—

Below, the folk; above, the unbounded blue.
You're bearing no command, but a metered gift:
        Look 'round you as a heartened eagle
    Bringing a present of independence.

197. A virtuoso lives in the twofold rule

alcaic
x/ x/ x/x x/ x/
x/ x/ x/x x/ x/
    x/x /x /x /x
  /x x/x x/x /x

A virtuoso lives in the twofold rule
Of liberating strength and hermetic school.
      Virtù is passion born of power
    Helping the acrobat-acts to flower.

The veins, the neurons, ganglions, arteries,
Though brachiated, ramified, work with ease:
      They heart-heat move in systematic
    Thrilling agility acrobatic.

The ancient Greek Olympics contained a test
Of music-making. Who would perform the best?
      The well-grown statuesque athletic
    Acrobat mastered the tone-aesthetic.

Steep might and freedom seething in ocean tides
Mean falling, rising, storming, an awe resides
      In law-thewed young, in thane of thunder,
    Ever-abiding above and under.

198. If we the plan of Rilke would here fulfil

alcaic
x/ x/ x/x x/ x/
x/ x/ x/x x/ x/
    x/x /x /x /x
  /x x/x x/x /x

If we the plan of Rilke would here fulfil
And, using magic, dragon- to princess-form
        Convert, we'll need a mood well-suited:
    There, in the background a ruined castle

With blood-red battle tower we'll change to green
And Eden-grasses plant in a dream, a trance;
        While Monschau turns to Mondschau, let's to
    Beethoven—*Moonlight Sonata*—listen.

199. Third Symphony: if no one had told of war

alcaic
x/ x/ x/x x/ x/
x/ x/ x/x x/ x/
    x/x /x /x /x
  /x x/x x/x /x

Third Symphony: if no one had told of war,
Nor uttered thought of German or Japanese,
    We wouldn't be requiring guidance
  Through the Stravinskyan thinking pattern.

Unprecedented, maybe, the rhythm strength,
Whose main appeal's in balance of planned with
  strange—
    Insistent, yet accommodating,
  Every assertion with person-power.

In contrast to simplicity of motif
Are timbres rich as any an empire graced:
    Had Rimsky-Korsakov not written,
  Half of the color I feel were absent.

The sudden introduction of novel hues
In wand'rings of complexity never dreamed
    With distant relatives acquaint us,
  Quickly arrived and as soon departed.

200. Concerto—string quartet with orchestral friend

alcaic
x/ x/ x/x x/ x/
x/ x/ x/x x/ x/
    x/x /x /x /x
  /x x/x x/x /x

Concerto—string quartet with orchestral friend—
Where Handel's work by Schoenberg had been re-
    dreamed:
        To me, not even *Pulcinella*
    Better appeared in Stravinsky-treatment.

By godlike playful strength of a wayward will
Techniques beyond what Mahler and Strauss applied
        Are called upon—O ardent freedom!
    Space-time Aladdin on artful carpet.

Rubato, volume-range, and percussive pluck—
Odd interludes of neo-romantic bliss—
        Each fiddle's elfin-tone harmonic—
    Swim in a limitless pentimento.

201. Four Telemann cantatas—
I felt an ease

alcaic
x/ x/ x/x x/ x/
x/ x/ x/x x/ x/
    x/x /x /x /x
  /x x/x x/x /x

Four Telemann cantatas—I felt an ease
When thinking, these one might have performed at home
       With music-minded friends invited:
    So the "soirées" that we held in high school—

We called them that, it had such a grownup sound—
Sweet offerings post-prandial mood improve.
       The Music Master: *Cecidērunt,*
    Though *in profundum* the scale went downward,

Could not dismay, for sprightlier wit was king.
The *allerschönsten Lippen* would love deny
       Yet failed in that attempt. A lover
    Can't be rejected when love's within him.

Funereal lament for a bird that died!
We might be saddened, yet with returning spring...
       Predictable, our reassurance:
    Briefly bemused we enjoy what's tuneful.

Die Hoffnung ist mein Leben—my life is hope.
Philosophy concludes what we knew before:
       The grace of happy chymic humor
    Never will fail us for entertainment.

202. Max Reger—solo cello, a triple suite

alcaic
x/ x/ x/x x/ x/
x/ x/ x/x x/ x/
    x/x /x /x /x
  /x x/x x/x /x

Max Reger—solo cello, a triple suite,
A trinal opus: here we can watch him grow.
        But even at the start I see a
    Youthful delight in the fugal writing.

We gladly pause to ponder the marvel-deed:
A polyphonic feast for the cello? Yes!
        The man I thank who dared to tackle
    Challenge with valor—O sing the hero!

Praeludiums with pleasure the heart relax
Before the dances leap that abound in play
        And when *Andante* comes to wander
    All of the variants lead to wonder.

When Pater claimed that song is the aim of art
He prophesied what here I would fain attempt:
        Loved tones of English, mother-music,
    Wing me the speed of my cupid-arrow!

203. Works two and thirty Henry the Eighth composed

alcaic
x/ x/ x/x x/ x/
x/ x/ x/x x/ x/
    x/x /x /x /x
  /x x/x x/x /x

Works thirty-two had Henry the Eighth composed,
Melodious-toned, that might by his life be glozed.
        In faith that merit love obtayneth
    Fate he bewayles when the maid desdayneth.

He'll many tunes devote to the claim of youth
To have its will in honor and cordial truth.
        If head and heart conflict, says Harry,
    Pray to the Lord when you're forced to tarry.

Strong lyric impulse here: when the solo sings,
An obbligato part will adorn the King's:
        She's ivy-like, in love entwining
    Flexible gesture, his own divining.

This *cortegiano,* master of courtly love,
Says Youth Will Rule, though bowing to pow'rs
  above.
        A church he founded. Morals foundered?
    Music had flowered if royals floundered.

204. In every bagatelle of the Bartók set

alcaic
x/ x/ x/x x/ x/
x/ x/ x/x x/ x/
    x/x /x /x /x
  /x x/x x/x /x

In every bagatelle of the Bartók set
We're taught the deep effect of the finger-touch
        As in a calm Cathayan painting
    Stroke of the brush is a feeling-token.

Though *Microcosm* tunes in the children's book
Developed each a feeling, we here will find
        An episode, with alteration:
    Delicate subtlety, then an outbreak.

The suddenness of change, and rubato—too,
With storm-and-waning—"moody" would be the term
        I'd pick, as when in teenage troubles
    Meaning will swing between all and nothing.

205. In 3 + 3 + 2 we've a way to change

alcaic
x/ x/ x/x x/ x/
x/ x/ x/x x/ x/
    x/x /x /x /x
  /x x/x x/x /x

In 3 + 3 + 2 we've a way to change
An eight-beat measure: then to the tune we'll add
        Impassioned memorized adornments:
    Fiddle and singer and woodwinds know them.

The man has told a story, and now we'll hear
A woman's heart outpoured in defiant cry:
        The long, long notes in richened valor
    Travel through keys with connective tremblings.

Bulgaria! You've wandered a way distinct
From less inventive makers of tonal form—
        Conjoining moods of color-contrast
    Loved by the brain for the brave-crazed rhythm.

206. A silent white, as here on the page I face

alcaic
x/ x/ x/x x/ x/
x/ x/ x/x x/ x/
    x/x /x /x /x
  /x x/x x/x /x

A silent white, as here on the page I face,
Will frame in meditation the notes that each
        Evoke a dream-life hid in cloud-bank,
    Hinted in delicate floating treble.

In post-Romantic Haydn, the rondo paced
For mindful calm Buddhistic and Schubert-like
        Will dare the slowest player-breathing
    While in the height is the faintest prayer.

Duet, then, of the intimate reverie
That muted vocal tone-will is living-through…
        Another couple come to join them:
    Lyric religion and mind-game child-time.

Extreme the poise and planning of every touch
For double purpose, making the tension rise:
        Devotion-goal, responsive timing—
    Finally, bliss of the boy-whim triumph.

207. Yes, "man was ever hasty": the sermon-quote

alcaic
x/ x/ x/x x/ x/
x/ x/ x/x x/ x/
      x/x /x /x /x
   /x x/x x/x /x

Yes, "man was ever hasty": the sermon quote
That comes from Holy Writ has a portrait-note
      For me, innerved, with brain made eager,
   Music-bewhirled, as a tone-intriguer.

Composer tribute project I haven't stopped,
But—music drive too speedy—a tune upcropped
      Reluctant to await example...
   Fingers and feet give an impulse ample.

I have to dance—my heart, as a flutterer,
Commands romance: upswept we the Voice prefer
      That calls: A joyful noise be making!
   God has appeared! and the day is breaking!

The dervish-dance, the journey in pilgrim shoon
Are each a movement needing the boost of tune.
      Your Name is Poet? Tone be master:
   Servant of Art, let the heart beat faster!

208. What's therapeutic? *Therapon* had in Greek

alcaic
x/ x/ x/x x/ x/
x/ x/ x/x x/ x/
   x/x /x /x /x
 /x x/x x/x /x

What's therapeutic? *Therapon* had in Greek
The meaning of *attendant,* the one you'd seek
      In sadness. Friendship—splendid tonic
   Pleasant to drink if your ill is chronic.

When scattering my bread on the waves I raise
No pray'r it might return in the latter days,
      Yet giver-spirit, liberated,
   Strangely is moved with a mood elated.

The deepest part of love is the gleam unsought
Within a thankful eye: 'twill the man have taught
      How beauty, of itself awaking,
   Good will endue as a daylight breaking.

Dear spirit, who attend when I yearn for you,
At length you ev'n return—blessed gift—you *do!*
      What healed me in a psalmer-voicing
   Others let feel in a calm rejoicing.

209. The nineteen-nine concerto for cello proves

alcaic
x/ x/ x/x x/ x/
x/ x/ x/x x/ x/
    x/x /x /x /x
  /x x/x x/x /x

The nineteen-nine concerto for cello proves
Not grand, romantic—rather, novella-swift.
        The fated theme, our hero's name-card:
    Four-note obsession of Shostakovitch.

'Tis manic agitation, a kind of cheer
Infected by depression, the folk-motif
        Despairing, daring, through the city
    Fleeing with glee from a nightmare mindset.

More soft than mother's lullaby comes the tune
Of cello with an oboe in counterpoint:
        When clarinet takes up the crooning
    Solo will switch to an obbligato.

The song is calming, yet it is tearful, too,
Until in dream-harmonics away it drifts
        To blend with heavenly celesta:
    Overcoat-reverie, Gogol-story.

No swaggery cadenza from early time:
Soliloquy, instead, of a Hamlet-depth.

>   A sullen wrath is ugly, sulky,
> Goaded to rise by the theme returning.

Prophetic, that—for next with pogróm-like threat
The signature of doom on the sky will blaze:
>   The folk motif—an army marching.
>   Thuggish, the crowds, and their numbers matter.

210. I'm fourteen years of age and today I face

alcaic
x/ x/ x/x x/ x/
x/ x/ x/x x/ x/
    x/x /x /x /x
  /x x/x x/x /x

I'm fourteen years of age and today I face
A wonder-prospect keeping the blood-beat high:
    Auditioning with Zathureczky,
  Russo-Hungarian music master.

I need to be accepted: with tensile heart
I'm practicing the piece he will want to hear—
    Achievement gauging, plus potential:
  Here is Corelli, with *La Folía*.

Fast-forward sixty years—came a compact disc;
Folías—more!—three centuries' worth of these!
    France, Portugal, and Spain—the four-chord
  Field is a "ground" for superb "divisions":

A march, lament, or brawl of a *branle*, or jig—
No limit for Marais or Martín y Coll
    With lute and bass or treble viol,
  Crisp castanets and a frenzied feeling.

Jordi Savall explained that *folía* means
Two near-akin ideas in Portuguese:

>   "Insanity" and "wild amusement"
> Equally suit me, today, recalling
>
> The happiness brought on by the kindly smile
> Of one who'd be my mentor and spirit-guide:
> I hear him yet, the Franck sonata
> Playing, his favorite madness-grandeur.

211. With *"Alles jauchzet, lacht"* I arise to write

alcaic
x/ x/ x/x x/ x/
x/ x/ x/x x/ x/
    x/x /x /x /x
  /x x/x x/x /x

With *"Alles jauchzet, lacht"* I arise to write
While fountains, blinding, shine in the skiey light.
        The oboe and the voice are vying,
    Sportive adornment with joy allýing.

With *Singe, Gott zum Preise* the boyish dance
Will echoes of Davidian psalm enhance.
        The hill, the lamb in bliss are leaping:
    Dotted, the rhythms are fieldward sweeping.

The current-streams *der spielenden Wellen* wave:
In soothing mood they earth and the spirit lave.
        The song with instruments competing
    Offers the noontide a riant greeting.

The cadences that want to resolve but don't
Lead mind, delighted, far from its weary wont,
        Each air, that, giddy, we are lost in,
    Made like a park in the Age of Austen.

In Handel's neo-classical parks we find
Surprises planned with care and with art designed:

> They're built to suit the guided tourist:
> Views "picturesque" are of all the purest.
>
> We're startled, too, repeatedly by the sound
> *Da capo*s offer—improvisation found
> > Exuberant beyond all measure,
> > Bearing the legend *In Freedom, Pleasure.*

212. A gray and drippy morning of early June

alcaic
x/ x/ x/x x/ x/
x/ x/ x/x x/ x/
    x/x /x /x /x
  /x x/x x/x /x

A gray and drippy morning of early June
Would soon be lightened while, in a long massage,
      The muscle fiber tension devils
    Learned they'd be cudgeled away forever.

Returned, I found a treat: the computer screen
Revealed plump berries gathered from Sarah's yard.
      (The time is ripe—for Minnesota.)
    This I would mail to my friends—a present.

Next, brunch (delayed) for one who's forbidden jam:
Ezekiel toast and pesto with pine-nuts mild
      We top with fiery pickled mango,
    Sent to me here from a Hindu village.

My kitchen I with foods of a world away
Can fill: the *saag* or spinach and mustard greens,
      The *dal* of lentils, onion, eggplant—
    Save me the fare of the airplane travel.

The radio's beginning the final part
Of that Tchaikovsky symphony most admired

> By me, who loved it back in high school:
> Only the Fifth had a sudden breakthrough—

A theme in unrelentingly minor mode
Would—silenced—yield to marching in triple time
> That led the mood-swing transformation
> Turning our journey to manic gladness.

Who melancholy bore as a burden learned
That fate is molten down by the newly freed:
> A four-note bang on hammered anvil—
> Beethoven beat!—and the Fifth we *answer*.

213. King Solomon's great Canticle I revive

alcaic
x/ x/ x/x x/ x/
x/ x/ x/x x/ x/
    x/x /x /x /x
  /x x/x x/x /x

King Solomon's great Canticle I revive
So people won't forget that a body-love
        By pagans hymned in Bacchus, Venus,
    Gained in the Bible an honored standing.

And thus I newly versified all the words
That, as in fine Egyptian papyrus-tune,
        Extend romantic invitation:
    Now we can sing them in English meter.

The reading that for YouTube I plan to do
Will colloquies contain with a host of those
        Who love had known in joy or sorrow,
    Jewish and Christian, Hellenic, Muslim.

To help ensure impressions will longer last
I'll then perform, while playing the violin,
        A Yiddish folk song and to Sabbath
    Angels of peace give a hymn in Hebrew.

214. Roused by Rossi
"Odecha Ki Anitani"

alcaic
x/ x/ x/x x/ x/
x/ x/ x/x x/ x/
    x/x /x /x /x
  /x x/x x/x /x

Let's grant I have a task—even two or three—
But need to keep the sense that I yet am free:
        By prefacing or interspersing
    Writings I've chosen, in prose or versing,

I feel the whoosh of Liberty Victor surge!
From convict-mood will never delight emerge:
        Before the breaker, stand in welcome,
    Bravely alert, whether heav'n or hell come.

Awake, alive, this day that the Lord has made,
I'll cry Give Praise! till finally down I'm laid.
        Hymn, aid my impulse-elevation,
    Bidding it sing with a soul-elation.

Be rival! Temerarious, teach aright
Your younger brother: lift to a higher light
        The torch that speeds your bridegroom-racing,
    Juiced with the hues that the trees are gracing!

What some had rubble deemed, a rejected stone
With scorn to distant field by the builders thrown,
        Behold reclaimed by those enshrining
    What the divine had been long divining.

Unless the home be raised to the height of psalm
In vain the makers labor. A strength in calm
          Will rouse from underground the fountain
        Centuries buried beneath their mountain!

215. Proofreading Plus

alcaic
x/ x/ x/x x/ x/
x/ x/ x/x x/ x/
   x/x /x /x /x
  /x x/x x/x /x

'Tis hard to guess how often one has to check
Lest foolish error better impression wreck:
       To proofread well's a wise endeavor—
     Tricky, the mind from its pride to sever!

And yet, amid this difficult marvel-work
Do I become no more than a parcel clerk?
       The drive to chant a living ballad
     Cries, and my visage is livid, pallid.

I need to speak my heart, give a rest to mind—
By finicky precision I'm too confined.
       Let therefore honeyed stream be welling,
     Speedier blood-beat again compelling!

Oh sweet the feel of running athwart the page,
The race of blooming youth overtaking age:
       The word-command itself is coming
     Merely from hearing the lute-string thrumming.

I think of you, friend Háfiz, undaunted when
You scant attention gained in the world of men:
       You yet would write, and every line a
     Reader delighted—as far as China!

216. Scorpion Venom

alcaic
x/ x/ x/x x/ x/
x/ x/ x/x x/ x/
    x/x /x /x /x
  /x x/x x/x /x

Of all unlikely medicines ever tried
It's hard to think of any so closely tied
        To vital high-adventure action—
    Tales of exotic, bizarre attraction.

A high-grade brain glioma, incurable
Till now, is threatened: comes an invader, full
        Of interest in the cancer tumor.
    (That is a fact, not a folklore rumor.)

In Israel dwelt a scorpion, yellow-hued,
Whose venom sticks to cells with the ill imbued.
        The doctors' trick will be to make it
    Radioactive, inject it, take it

To where the dire glioma will sit and wait,
Inapprehensive, yet, of a parlous fate.

VIII
Sapphic, Lesser and Greater

217. Buxtehude's *Passion* you well might call it

sapphic
/x /x /x x/x /x
/x /x /x x/x /x
/x /x /x x/x /x
/x x/x

Buxtehudë's *Passion* you well might call it—
Membra Jesu Nostri the rightful title:
Feet, knees, hands, side, chest, and the heart and
   face in
                    Seven cantatas,

Holy madrigals of the sixteen eighties,
Each with prelude played by a viol consort,
Taught the grace of body-imagination,
                    Hearing, the human

Learns a Bible passage, the Introduction,
Then relates the thought to a deed of mercy,
Dwelling on the empathy of the Savior,
                    Martyr and mortal.

Ere the cloven side we in woe envision,
Solomonic word in a song will charm us:
Dove he calls to come from her hidden nest in
                    Rock-hollow, wall-crack.

Ere to heart we turn for a clement refuge,
"You my heart have wounded, O spouse, O sister,"

In his hymn King Solomon our companion
                            Begs for compassion.

Every kind of love we in Love are given
Let be shared—be sure they are brought together.
Every body part, when I pray, is praying;
                            Thanks, when I'm thankful.

218. In Mendelssohn's *Elijah* we find (scene five—

modified sapphic
x/x /x /x x/ x/
x/x /x /x x/ x/
x/x /x /x x/ x/
      /x x/x

In Mendelssohn's *Elijah* we find (scene five—
The center of the nine) that a child is told
Three times, "Go up, and gaze at the heav'n, and say,
      What do you see there?"

The first two tries no cloudlet on high would yield,
But then—the final triumph—a roaring storm!
The child-tone I to angels' would liken—sweet,
      Pure, and endearing.

When I became bar mitzvah, I too performed
To aid the service. First came the blessing-chant,
Then Torah-cantillation, the Kiddush last:
      Maybe they saved me...

A crisis might have risen: when called to give
My talk to show interpretive skill, I found
I couldn't bring myself to come out with what
      Wasn't authentic.

My father and the rabbi the lesson planned
That I'd expound: they'd argued it back and forth.

I wrote what they directed but—(Here I stand!)—
             Couldn't recite it.

I thanked the congregation for kindness lent
In giving me a beautiful place to pray
And mark the grand occasion—I meant it all,
             Then I was quiet.

I think I proved my manhood, although my voice
Had not yet changed. And no one a comment made—
Not then nor later. Maybe my chanting gave
             Adequate pleasure.

219. Schütz the *Little Sacred Concertos* tranquil

sapphic
/x /x /x x/x /x
/x /x /x x/x /x
/x /x /x x/x /x
    /x x/x

Schütz the *Little Sacred Concertos* tranquil
Respite made, an elegant gentle refuge:
This the folk worn down by the sixteen-thirties'
                      War of Religion

Found at church when hearing a psalm of David
Reconceived in chamber sonata format.
Harmonies the organ and cello helping,
                      Boyish the voices—

Only one or two, and the tones were treble
(Had their elders gone with the warring armies?)—
Chanted praise and joy of the consolation
                      David had offered.

Here is inward Protestant thought-and-worship
Moving from the madrigal to cantata:
Times of Trouble call for a calm responder,
                      Then, now, and always.

220. I, melodic memories lauding nightly

sapphic
/x /x /x x/x /x
/x /x /x x/x /x
/x /x /x x/x /x
　　　/x x/x

I, melodic memories lauding nightly,
Heard a brave command: in the present moment
Faith restore, and know in the form you're granted
　　　　　Sappho reviving.

Love assurgent, kin to the ocean surf-wave,
Rushing, pouring whirr in a world susurral,
Heart and want have, mustering, told me, Hark to
　　　　　Dark ere the daybreak.

Patient while I wait for the hymn's arrival,
Aid I've long besought for the blood-trancelation,
So to feel the tone of the carmine ardor
　　　　　Loud in the flowing.

Me, in vein and artery living ocean,
Let the tidal winds of the ancient rhythm
Rouse to hear the roar of the inward streaming,
　　　　　Shouting, resounding!

221. Rare is the greater sapphic

greater sapphic
           /x x/x /x
/x /x /x x/—/x x/x /x

                           Rare is the greater sapphic.
Yet the swing and sweep of the line ending the streaming
   couplet
                           Harmony fits well-shapen,
Bright, the wakened ear and the eye charmed with a double
   virtue.

                           Standout performer lacking,
Yet in choir the tiny motifs amplitude lend unwearied,
                           Trembling because the wind-breath
Sprouted leaves on bough had bestirred, voicing a morning
   pleasure.

                           Birds in the branches hidden,
How I long to *see* you!—but no: singly in leaves the vision
                           Comes of the heartstring quiver
Which the cloud, resoundingly soft, tenderly so enlivens.

                           You of a transformation
Tell, O Tree with body of bird tónes in a dawntime greeting,
                           Knowledge and Life united,
Psalm unsought that came and excelled all that one might
   have prayed for.

222. What would happen, Chanter, if pen attempted

lesser sapphic
/x /x /x x/x /x
/x /x /x x/x /x
/x /x /x x/x /x
    /x x/x

greater sapphic
    /x x/x /x
/x /x /x x/—/x x/x /x

    What would happen, Chanter, if pen attempted
    Turning—skillful bird in a whimsied current,
    Loving windbreath-will in a deft surrender—
               Every direction?

              Credit your wings Icaric:
Here's a gust that telling of strength born in the chosen
   herald
              Brings me, a cloud advancing
Gloried high in boreal pride, glassed in the ocean breakers.

    Now I'm dreamt by warmth in a blue suffusion,
    Drowsy-lulled, enwrapt in a gentle floating,
    Pinions kept aloft in the aided movement—
               Breathe me, O heaven!

              Weak and bereft of power,
Shifted off to northerly chill, victim of sudden windrush,
              Mercy! I beg you—help me!
Heed my pure nepheliad pray'r—Grace to the faithful
   servant!

223. Moses, David's son had they named him. (Angel

lesser sapphic
/x /x /x x/x /x
/x /x /x x/x /x
/x /x /x x/x /x
    /x x/x

greater sapphic
    /x x/x /x
/x /x /x x/—/x x/x /x

    Moses, David's son had they named him. (Angel
    Hurried then lest relatives be distracted,
    Sign and wonder lacking.) Behold emergent,
        There, from the forehead

        Calm, of the cradled baby,
Two the rays of light that extend, leftward- and rightward-
    angled!
        'Tell of the double emblem!'
Begged the wide excitable eyes, answer in love imploring.

    Heaven wasn't deaf to the wild entreaties,
    Yet delayed for decades would be the answer:
    Many years the baby must wait before he
        Heard the commandment:

    "Moses, the son of David,
Voice and Violin are the gifts God in your heart's conjoining.
        Use them together deftly:
Be they wedded—body and soul—heaven to serve united."

224. Songs you hear are not like the ones you sing

modified sapphic
/ x / x / x x/ x/
/ x / x / x x/ x/
/ x / x / x x/ x/
      / x x/ x

Songs you hear are not like the ones you sing.
High school people, wé were musicians who
Volunteered to play at the Mental Health
                    Center for seniors.

What, on violin, would the folks enjoy?
Handel's "*Largo*" maybe—a stately tune;
Haydn's calm "*Andante cantabile*"—
                    Soothing and peaceful...?

Both of these I played—and to no effect.
Comment, conversation—the talk was loud!
Then the program manager, kind, advised:
                    "Play what's *familiar.*"

So "You are my sunshine" I tried—and now
Everything was changed! In the sing-along
Many voices joined, and the day was saved.
                    I would remember:

Music made is better than music played.
Singing means you're part of the show yourself.
Effort shared, you give and receive at once,
                    Double—the pleasure.

225. Bach has brought
(*Sinfonia 9*, F Minor)

sapphic
/x /x /x x/x /x
/x /x /x x/x /x
/x /x /x x/x /x
/x x/x

Bach has brought (*Sinfonia 9*, F Minor),
While we followed melodies intertwining,
Grave *Andante* (Beethoven, Seventh) back to
                Mind from our childhood.

Gould thus culminated the thirty studies.
What we heard were mythical people speaking—
Wiser, all, than we, for a god controlled them,
                Spoke, and ensouled them.

226. Eighth of the odes of Horace

greater sapphic
/x x/x /x
/x /x /x x/—/x x/x /x

                     Eighth of the odes of Horace—
That's the only one in the rare form of the greater sapphic.
                     I have an English version
Found where now we finally learn: What are the theme and
   treatment?

                     Lydia needs reproaching:
She allured young Sýbaris—quite torn from his love for action.
                     Swimming and soldier-drilling,
Fighting, discus-throwing are all willfully shunned,
   abandoned.

                     He, though a splendid athlete,
Far withdrawn is hidden away, totally sybaritic.
                     Think of Achilles, hidden,
Fearing Trojan combat, disguised (shame!) in a maiden's
   garment.

                     Thanks to a shrewd unmasking
Which the skilled Ulysses had planned, Greeks had a chance
   to triumph
                     Since, in the Trojan conflict,
Gods made clear Achilles would bring—crucial—the secret
   weapon!

                     Lydia, kindly listen!
Passion put aside, I entreat! Those whom the gods would ruin
                     First they afflict with madness.
Play no more the lyrical flute, sapping a manly valor!

227. Béla Bartók, double delight revealing

sapphic
/x /x /x x/x /x
/x /x /x x/x /x
/x /x /x x/x /x
    /x x/x

Béla Bartók, double delight revealing,
Granted to my youth-mind a twofold insight.
I, a seventh grader, my birthday present
                       Looked at and marveled:

Forty-four Duets. In the second volume
One selection started in six-eight timing;
Two bars done—then quickly a five-eight followed;
                       Three-four, the next one.

When the piece I played with my teacher later,
How amazing: natural, every measure,
Though our alterations in timing differed!
                       How could it happen?

Tones combined were also a bit peculiar:
I would play F natural and my teacher
Sounded loud F sharp at the selfsame moment.
                       Peppery, spicy!

Tempos crazed, and yet in coordination—
Wild the crisis-liking diminished seconds—
All so perfect, beautiful, strange—I'm crying,
                       Now, as I tell it.

228. Unexpected bird in the breath-held dusk

modified sapphic
/x /x /x x/ x/
/x /x /x x/ x/
/x /x /x x/ x/
    /x x/x

Unexpected bird in the breath-held dusk
While the clouds advancing in puffy gray
Slowly grow more weighty with fecund load,
                  Thank you for chanting!

Unperturbed, the tranquil and stately song,
Alternated pairings of up and down,
Eight or seven units in every call—
                  Come for my comfort.

Day-long damp the grass when the dew is blent
Wetly with the hesitant prelude-tries
Ere the storm-shake startle with blast enorm—
                  Janual June-life.

You at evening chant me the Name I chose
Out of all the potency-gems outspread
Merchant-like in wide caravanserai,
                  Wares for the buyer.

You're the angel-wind of a mindful time
Sent to me who felt like a beggar. Why

Sad, with will and health of a sounding wave
                    Leaping within me?

Hand, by heart and vigor of manhood urged,
Tell the welcome white of the scribal screen:
Answer I with spectrum of hue, with lute
                    Plectrum to hymn you.

229. How to vanquish claims of the vast and many

sapphic
/x /x /x x/x /x
/x /x /x x/x /x
/x /x /x x/x /x
　　　　/x x/x

How to vanquish claims of the vast and many?
Not to sense the life of the heart collapsing
Faced with many millions of wills around you
　　　　　　　Now and forever?

Multitudes of writers—I feel so ant-like!
Yes, you'll be outdone—'tis a rule of nature!
Envy's hate—you shun it, and yet feel weakened!
　　　　　　　Speak!—the solution?

Hugeness both of number and strength defeat us
Till we gain control of the world of sense-life.
Giant we can see will be shrunk beside the
　　　　　　　Size of the Total.

As for power, what are the cosmic forces?
Bigger than the Bangs will appear the Freedom
We can grasp but darkly and yet more nearly
　　　　　　　Joined to the Wholeness.

Origin of mind and the world is hidden,
Depth of both Unmanifest—yet to feel it

Lets you travel far from the sweep of number
                              Past and apparent.

Let your heart breathe sky and remember always:
None who gain Totality can be lonesome.
Better, worse are nil in the Unapparent
                              Grace that impels you.

230. Hear my lyric lines for the long-haired Ella
for Sarah, Jeremy, Izzy—and Ella

sapphic
/x /x /x x/x /x
/x /x /x x/x /x
/x /x /x x/x /x
　　/x x/x

Hear my lyric lines for the long-haired Ella.
Brown, black, tan, and white, she is tranquil,
　napping.
Cats are fond of that: in Moroccan desert,
　　　　　They were the Night Ones!

All day long they'd sleep, and at eve awaken,
Soon pursuing aptly the agile rodents.
Quick, and also clean, the athletic felines
　　　　　Came unexpected.

Pious, every one, to perform ablutions,
They for careful grooming would be rewarded.
"Loving cats is part of the faith," a pupil
　　　　　Heard from the Prophet.

Chanting words that lilt in a sapphic strophe,
Calming repetition a gentle petting,
We the mood will soothe of the sleeping creature,
　　　　　Aid in her dream-life.

231. Friend Chagall, be blest, for the *Dead Man*'s living

sapphic
/x /x /x x/x /x
/x /x /x x/x /x
/x /x /x x/x /x
    /x x/x

Friend Chagall, be blest, for the *Dead Man*'s living
Which you made, returned from humiliation
After insult barked in the stifling art-school
                      Petersburg offered.

Reading Jackie Wullschlager's tome engrossing,
I was thrilled you'd left the horrendous climate,
Seeing artists, even the rich collectors,
                      Dying, despairing.

Corpse upon the street, by the Sabbath candles
Crazily surrounded, a shrieking woman
Holding up her hands in a rabid horror.
                      Higher, a housetop

Fiddler, unperturbed while the clouds fly past him,
Plays—to whom? And why? Do we need a purpose?
Aye! a poet summoned to free the spirit,
                      Sad and triumphant!

Nineteen eight: we're back in Vitebsk, the town that
Aaron Copland later recalled in music

When, with quarter-tones, an enigma-trio
>> He was creating.

Bérnard Greenhouse, Daniel Guilet (my teacher),
Plus Menáchem Pressler the magic-handed—
Jewish heroes, all, of the Beaux Arts trio,
>> Played it, as fated.

Who's the fiddler, winds on the roof enduring?
He's the one back home—a survivolinist!
Yes, the king is dead—but he's breathing, singing!
>> *Let me embrace you.*

232. Elegy for Margaux Fragoso
author of Tiger, Tiger

sapphic
/x /x /x x/x /x
/x /x /x x/x /x
/x /x /x x/x /x
    /x x/x

Grief and lamentation! A cancer battle
Bore away my friend to a death untimely.
Margaux's childhood-narrative, *Tiger, Tiger,*
              Dwells in our spirit.

Seventeen, the countries the book appeared in.
Many more translations, I'd guess, will follow.
Here we learn how crimes of abuse inflicted
              Couldn't defeat her.

Writing that was elegant, rich, and fervent
We were blest to hear in an early prelude:
Every class began, in my course on William
              Blake, with the students

Each reciting paragraph-long reactions
Written in reply to the latest reading.
Margaux's contribution would always heighten
              Feeling and insight.

More than that—unquelled is the effervescence
Out of tales of metaphor-travel rising
Yet within the memory-mind of all who
              Thus had been favored.

233. Simple, real—the joy of a second childhood

sapphic
/x /x /x x/x /x
/x /x /x x/x /x
/x /x /x x/x /x
      /x x/x

Simple, real—the joy of a second childhood:
A1C kept low may delight occasion—
Evidence we care for our health with lesser
                    Intake of sugar.

Diabetic checkups are quite rewarding:
Homework—if you did it, and all correctly,
Now will "make your day," in the current phrasing:
                    High-grade report-card.

There, as part of training, a pleasant intern
Helped in posing questions. Her name was Sarah.
I recalled the earliest education
                    Given my daughter.

(Many years the mind will at random travel.
That's the profit granted an elder poet,
Threescore years and ten—even more—recalling:
                    Snapshot recaptured.)

Little Sarah showed, on a paper placemat,
How she'd practiced writing her name that morning—

Al, my friend, observing with charmed amusement.
                        Clever, the tactic

Chosen made the challenging "S" go faster:
First the bottom curve she would draw, and later
Add the part on top, and the letter finished,
                        Others were easy.

Lesson good to learn: from the time of Caesar,
Who divided Gaul into three clear sections,
We "Divide and conquer" have made our motto:
                        Quick and efficient.

234. June concludes—my mood is attuned, letitial

sapphic
/x /x /x x/x /x
/x /x /x x/x /x
/x /x /x x/x /x
　　　/x x/x

June concludes—my mood is attuned, laetitial.
Summer one week old—it is here—official!
Days in June are rare, meaning rich and treasured,
　　　　　Specially pleased.

Ere it part, we've leisure to pose a question.
Why's it thought Junonian? One suggestion:
She had been of weddings the long-time patron:
　　　　　Better—the "matron."

She'd at times been cruel—her fight with Venus
Shows in old *Aeneid* a spleen and meanness.
Yet for ire she'd plenty of provocation—
　　　　　Jove a fixation

Had, pursuing maidens he found attractive:
He, imaginative, by overactive
Sportive life had driven his wife to madness.
　　　　　So, with the gladness

Weddings will occasion to poet dreaming,
Gentle tear will also appear beseeming.
Think "I do" and soon is the eye-dew gleaming:
　　　　　Guests, though, are beaming.

235. Glorious cat, you're brindled

greater sapphic
>/x x/x /x
/x /x /x x/—/x x/x /x

      Glorious cat, you're brindled,
Blending tones that, reddish and black, shade into brown
 and tannish;
      White as an added feature—
Lower face and neck and the paws—all of the fur-tone
 brightens.

      Portrait and landscape melded:
Tints that forest floor will adorn, hinting of winter
 snowfall
      Trace in the early springtime,
Yet with hues of earth and the leaves—warmer the days
 emerging.

      Part of your head is hidden:
Autumn-umber pillow is put right where your chosen
 colors
      Wondrous in rich abundance
With the fabric sing, and the twain harmony sweet
 engender.

      Sideways-and-back reclining,
You a deep contentment enjoy, lying on blanket, gentle:
      Cleverly well-supported,
Known by all who see you as one given a peaceful
 wisdom.

236. Thoughts on Things Greek
for Camille Goodison

sapphic
/x /x /x x/x /x
/x /x /x x/x /x
/x /x /x x/x /x
      /x x/x

Thrilling thought—to swim in the holy wordstream
Flowing down today from the living Hellas.
Drowning out the dole, the bereaving birdscream,
      Sappho will tell us

How the poets, drawn to their daily labor,
Felt the sun Olympian dawning, shining,
Filled with joy of timbrel and pipe and tabor,
      Lyre unrepining.

I returned from Grecian rejuvenescence
Purified, renewed, though alas I never
Learned the language. Yet does the heady essence
      Dwell with me ever.

Traveling may be like a waking dreaming,
      Daybreaking, gleaming.

237. Vegetarian Values

sapphic
/x /x /x x/x /x
/x /x /x x/x /x
/x /x /x x/x /x
      /x x/x

Bunny's back and scouting the dewy grasses,
New unsampled greenery to discover—
What he finds he'll try: and a human viewer
        Claims a relation.

Acorn squash with coconut filling—also
Just a little sugar from palm tree garnered—
Microwaved—and softened—the skin is mildened,
        Edible, gentle.

Next, the rich Ezekiel bread, well toasted,
Needs—no jam, indeed, but a veggie topping.
Salsa—fine! Tomatoes that any rabbit
        Knows how to cherish.

238. Sapphic Rewrite of Christine's Anni Poem

sapphic
/x /x /x x/x /x
/x /x /x x/x /x
/x /x /x x/x /x
    /x x/x

Treetop bare, the eyes will be led, so easy,
Into swimming yellow: how soon we're turning...
Think of garden snakes, how they're warmed by
   compost,
             Then, of the rabbit,

Loving ripe tomatoes of later summer
That the ground were hugging, the unavailing.
I'm at peace, no more than a pane of glass to
             Night and the northwind.

239. The Standout

sapphic
/x /x /x x/x /x
/x /x /x x/x /x
/x /x /x x/x /x
      /x x/x

"Indian" the summery visitation
Zephyr paid, delayed in a dream of Aries,
Made the lazy estival trees, yet resting,
            Tension suspended,

Loth to wake, in reverie held unmoving,
Still their will to head for a chilly season:
We, as well, are lulled, a caressing treasured,
            Cold-time forgotten.

In a cab meandering through the village,
Leaves part green but largely reduced to yellow,
Suddenly I'm jolted: an apparition
            Comes—from the Bible.

Tree prophetic, blazoned in vivid scarlet,
Streaks dark purple, floridly torching orange,
Wonder, sign, and emblem of autumn-lauding,
            Joys me—a life-thrust.

240. Sapphic Sonnet

sapphic
/x /x /x x/x /x
/x /x /x x/x /x
/x /x /x x/x /x
      /x x/x

What if we decided to write a Sapphic
Sonnet with Shakespearean standard rhyme-
  scheme:
Would traditions meld in a single time-stream,
            Trans-topographic?

Trans-historic? See how a strange idea,
Entering the mind in a playful spirit,
Odd enough that timider folk might fear it,
            Later will be a

Thing as nature-loved as a game of tennis
Or, if you would rather, a swim in summer,
Energizing, lively. More stagnant, number,
            More of a menace

Were to be reluctant when thought comes calling—
            That is appalling.

241. Choral works of Schütz and of Gabrieli
for William E. Culverhouse

sapphic
/x /x /x x/x /x
/x /x /x x/x /x
/x /x /x x/x /x
/x x/x

Choral works of Schütz and of Gabrieli
Frequently will feature a lively pattern:
"Metric modulation," today we name it—
Joy for the hearer!

Want to see a similar shifting rhythm
Now in words? I grant you the scope is smaller,
Lasting but a measure—a "foot," the poets
Oftener call it.

Two-four, two-four, three-quarter, two-four, two-four:
One odd bar—that's all—in the line I've written.
Think you like the mood? Then you'll love the
  closing:
Three-quarter two-four.

Tell me: the effect—is it wholly novel?
Might it seem a thing that I just invented?
Old it is, revered, and a form the *ancients*
Loved to distraction!

"Sapphic" they had named it, commemorating
One the Greeks deemed best of the chanting women.
She was even dubbed, in the words of Plato,
        "Tenth of the Muses."

Gabrieli, Schütz—do you hear me, patrons?
This I'll hope, invoking your potent blessing.
Ancient, newer loves I conjoin in concord:
        Bless you forever.

242. "The Coming Storm"
painting by George Inness

sapphic
/x /x /x x/x /x
/x /x /x x/x /x
/x /x /x x/x /x
     /x x/x

Clustered bunched-up leaves to the storm-wind
   bowing
Feel with trunk and branches a thrilled subjection—
Which aroused a vigorous hidden power,
         Passive and active.

Look! a single bush that, bewildered, turning
Sideways pushed by whirl of the winds that free us,
Power countervails with a root resistant,
         Proud as a hero.

Cloud-banks driving life to a thrust of wonder
Mirror, crouched in buffalo-shape, the leaf-clumps—
Waking patch of light in a fissure aiding
         Sight with precision.

IX
Experimental Rhythms with Duplets and Triplets

243. Barbaric Yawp: A Dactyl-Compromise

x/x x/ x/—/x x/x x/

I sound my barbaric yawp over the roofs of the world.
In Whitman's Hellenic line civilization is king.
The syllables gone—no prob: Grecian the spirit remains,
If slightly de-dactyled—plus: added unaccented start...

Nor ever will reader carp: strange, catalectic the end.
For this I applaud as well: firmness, unshakable will.
I like it and, unafraid, trumpet the beauty abroad.
The irony's bound to tease pupil and scholar alike.

Discipular comes the cry, tribute to mastery hurled!
Acquire what you can, say I: condor of yonderlust, fling
The dithyramb, paean, hymn, startling the morning
  refrains
Loud-sounded of cloud-spanned bird, widening lyre of a
  heart.

You, poet, in skill "denied," slyly a lessoning lend:
No matter how yawped the thought, meter's more
  deepening still,
The beat of the leaping blood, thundering maelstroming
  god:
The pilgrim will wingprint leave, painting the sky of his
  hike.

244. Étude on a Phrase by Avideh Shashaani

/xx /x /x /x
/xx /x /x /x
/xx /x /x /(x)
/xx /x /x /(x)

Beautiful, eloquent, and tender:
Present that holy life can render,
Dactyl—remainder thrice trochaic—
Best for a fest panathenaic.

Duple and triple rhythms linking
Stimulates many-metered thinking.
So will a fiddler's bow-direction
Smoothly be changed with no reflection:

Cannily skill relaxed applying,
Mind will on craft imbibed relying
Forearm and upper arm and hand
Levers at varied speeds command.

Structures in art diverse creating,
Deep is the heart immersed, elating
Him that will sing and her that reads
When the unfearing spirit heeds.

245. Choriambic Sonnet: Ruskin
meter also employed by the subject himself;
vide *Tim Hilton,* John Ruskin

/x x/ /x x/ /x x/
/x x/ /x x/ /x x/
/x x/ /x x/ /x x/
/x x/ /x x/ /x x/

Madness—the fair maid of my heart: how could it be?
Time of a dream serpent-return, year after year...
Séance: I know Ursula, Rose, both will appear,
Holy, with Joan, burned at the stake. Touch it, and see:

Twice is enough. Quickly—the flame, towering high!
Horrible rags wave in the air wildly today—
Look at the big blackening cloud stretching away
Over the hill, fibrous and foul, filling the sky.

Where is the new manuscript-book ordered, the *St. Ronan*? And who'll rightly decide whether I stay?
Cook is the Queen! Mark what you do, send them away.
Magdalen, she. Path to a new—Why did I faint?...

Turner and Blake—truly a test, finding the deep
Well of the red rose, and the sylph-casket to keep.

246. Triplets Triply Considered

Line 1: x/x x/x x/x x/x
Line 5: xx/ xx/ xx/ xx/
Line 9: /xx /xx /xx /xx

The joy of the amphibrach: what's more engaging?
We rode at a canter, surveying the land—
Refreshed and receptive—the horse with free hand
Scarce guided, ungoaded, all tension assuaging.

But the anapest hastened the pace of the ride
As the winds became brisker and summoned with song:
When we hear them go by we accelerate—long
Is the road, and it's right!—the horizon is wide.

Dactyls, relaxing the speed of tetrameters,
Tell us to look. The inviting vicinity
Gladdens. The rhythm repeats the affinity
Galloping has with expanding parameters.

Roaming, and running, and roving, we say:
Here's catalexis, we'll call it a day.

247. Trochee Begins and Lends a Triplet-Twist

Sambhogakaya—the "enjoyment body"—points to the experience that space is not really emptiness as we know it; there's energy and color and movement. It's vibrant, like a rainbow or a bubble or the reflection of your face in a mirror. It's vivid, yet nonsubstantial at the same time. Sambhogakaya refers to this energetic quality, the fact that emptiness is fluid and vivid. Sound is often an image for sambhogakaya; you can't see or capture it, but it has vibration, energy, and movement.
   —Pema Chödrön, Start Where You Are 64–65

/x x/ x/ x/ x/
/x x/ x/ x/ x/
/x x/ x/ x/ x/
/x x/ x/ x/ x/

Making enjoyment body out of space:
Rainbow and bubble, then reflected face,
Crown the impalpable with added glow;
Music may set the air in motion so.

People are speaking, each in cadenced phrase,
Questioning, answering in welcomed ways;
Solo, the trumpet sibling-kind to strings,
Pleasure, in singing, from the kindred brings.

Tafelmusík that Telemann had made
Offers no doctrine to the folk displayed

Hearing a lesson taught by whim and mood,
Dulcet caprice and blust'ring winds and rude.

Twining and fugal, wise, and iris-hued,
Mirroring gaze in brightened faces viewed.

248. My head is awhirl with competing demands

duple and triple rhythms
x/ x x/ x x/ x x/
/ x x/ — / x x/ x
x/ x x/ x x/ x x/
/ x x/ — / x x/ x

My head is awhirl with competing demands:
      What should come first? What will be second?
A rational planner the task understands:
      Work—be immersed. Follow what beckoned—

The choice doesn't matter so much as you think.
      Focus on goal. Don't be distracted.
The swimmer afloat must keep moving—or sink:
      Stay in control—traps counteracted.

The amphibrach form will a gallop induce:
      Choriamb stops. Then we advancing
Our movements will pattern while keeping them loose:
      Pauses and hops, canter enhancing.

Whatever you sing, to the world you will show
      Triplets can breathe—deeply, in freedom.
The mind gathers life when permitted to *go*!
      Folk will enwreathe poets who lead 'em.

249. A marvelous poet I'm copying here

duple and triple rhythms
x/ x x/ x x/ x x/
/ x x/ — / x x/ x
x/ x x/ x x/ x x/
/ x x/ — / x x/ x

A marvelous poet I'm copying here:
    Háfiz the name. Famous, a Persian.
Beginning a lyric he never will fear
    Crisis may claim writing-subversion.

He'll ever be sad the beloved denies
    Plea or request. Therefore he's drinking,
A ready resort when bad fortune defies
    Lover by test. Rising, not sinking,

He's ready to write, weary tulip of red,
    Remnants of ash deep in the chalice.
He'll sing about problems unsolved and be led
    Ev'n by the lash, feeling no malice.

He'll chant about love which is valid despite
    Lack of reply. Glad he rehearses
The plaint of the nightingale: praising the bright
    Blossom, he'll sigh—perfect the verses!

250. Invigorate, breeze—while we bathe in the air

duple and triple rhythms
x/ x x/ x x/ x x/
/ x x/ — / x x/ x
x/ x x/ x x/ x x/
/ x x/ — / x x/ x

Invigorate, breeze—while we bathe in the air—
    Breath in the lung, freshened emotion
Pervading with ease and a shedding of care,
    Lending the tongue poet-devotion.

You birds in a choir the beginning of light
    Heralding while hymns are awaking
The viewer and hearer at waning of night—
    Fervent your style: day is a-breaking!

You, soloist, nearer, more piercing and clear,
    Me have you sought, blessing releasing:
Loved guardian-patron of summery cheer,
    Boon have you brought, vigor unceasing.

In playing the role of the leader of birds,
    Bolder, the best, avian burden
Unlading of lesson prophetic, may words
    Hold for you, blest, poetry-guerdon!

251. The poets who either by chance or by fate

duple and triple rhythms
x/ x x/ x x/ x x/
/ x x/ — / x x/ x
x/ x x/ x x/ x x/
/ x x/ — / x x/ x

The poets who either by chance or by fate
      Happen to find, seeking a meter,
The Bidneyan strophe, what pleasures await!
      I'll be assigned, heavenly greeter,

To welcome them here, to the realm where I dwell:
      "Rest and abide! Travel not yonder—
Relax, lying back, and we'll speak for a spell:
      Talk will provide friendship yet fonder.

Symposia we in Elysium hold—
      Bards who descánt grab our attention
Whenever they tell of discoveries bold:
      Troubadour-chant, lyric invention.

The hovering chanter on mountain and vale
      Glad looking down—godly the vision,
Nepheliad-wingéd through heaven to sail—
      Laurel his crown, sings with precision."

252. Since no one had thought of a Trumpery win

duple and triple rhythms
x/ x x/ x x/ x x/
/ x x/ — / x x/ x
x/ x x/ x x/ x x/
/ x x/ — / x x/ x

Since no one had thought of a Trumpery win,
    None would begin crafting a measure.
Thus nothing they'd brought of a feasible scheme—
    Greedy folk's dream, GOP's pleasure.

So Senator Toomey this morning explained,
    Palpably pained: that is the reason
Belligerent predators cannot agree
    Though it may be prey-hunting season.

The moderates claim the extremer are mean,
    Seeming serene: twenty-two million
Of all their Obamacare aid to deprive,
    Wildly they strive, many a billion

Of dollars to give to the wealthiest few
    (Thinking askew!). Why not be nicer
And steal a bit less and continue to smile,
    Hiding your bile? (Guile, thou art Spicer....)

253. Adam and Eve would snatch a fruit

trochee line-openers for a triplet effect
/x x/ x/ x/
   x/ x/ x/
/x x/ x/ x/
   x/ x/ x/
/x x/ x/ x/
/x x/ x/ x/

Adam and Eve would snatch a fruit
     And warning fail to heed.
Radix malorum—evil's root
     Had proved so great a greed.
Youthful were they, and yet with pain
Prudence of Middle Age would gain.

Golden the mean, so Greeks would teach,
     To virtue is the key.
Moderate aims will not impeach.
     Excess, deficiency—
Both of them speak of troubled times:
Lethargy sleeps, ambition climbs.

Headed for planet death are they
     Who wisdom boon refuse.
Character's Fate, the ancients say:
     Our lives we soon may lose
Guided by greed. Turn earthward, gods,
*Adam*ant-curst, or turn to clods.

254. Building on Scriptural Rhythms

duple and triple rhythms
/x x/ x/x x/x
/x x/ x/x x/x
/x x/ x/x x/x
/x x/ x/x x/x...

Qur'an 23:96. Repel evil with that which is better....
23:109. ...Thou art best of all who show mercy.

Evil repel with that which is better:
Thou art the best of all who show mercy.
Quickly supplanting lapse with improvement,
Proving good sense in action advancing,
Kind to your heart in smiling not weeping,
Shunning regret, lest ego-absorption
Make you neglect the path of the pilgrim,
Gladly admit: while living we're moving,
Leaving behind the past and its baggage.

Thou art the best of all who show mercy:
Evil repel with that which is better.
Straight is the path of steady intention—
Pardon what's done, make room for the future.
Wanderers we, who godlike in motion
That which we plan enact in our travel.
Emulate One Who world-life imagined,
Lauding in song the power 'tis granting
Dream to create, that earth may be heaven.

255. My sleeping-waking cycle disarranged

iambic alternating with amphibrachic strophes
Line 1: x/ x/ x/ x/ x/
Line 6: x/x x/x x/x x/x

    The sleeping-waking cycle disarranged
    By odd concatenation of events
    The rhythm of my body-being changed
        Awhile, with an expanding sense
That after lengthened nap, in ample recompense,

        The future, more empty, more urgent, was crowding,
        Like swelling of waters around me, to shake
        The brain yet adrowse, to arouse, to awake:
        For Nothing's a force, and the course of its coming
        Is meant to dispel what my lethargy-clouding
        Too heavy had rendered: the heart began drumming—

And then I thought: the artful planning—how benign—
For productivity evolved the right design:
To wait until the favored hour draw nigh the dark
        Which, favored brother, uttered, Hark!
    Prepare to greet the supersolar light

        In soul and hymn: the time is right.

256. The influence, the inflow, penetrated slowly

iambic alternating with amphibrachic strophes
Line 1: x/ x/ x/ x/ x/x
Line 9: x/x x/x x/x x/

The influence, the inflow, penetrated slowly:
Things written long ago, then recently revised,
Gave rise to feelings that invite the rhyme of "holy"
And yet which I had wholly left unrealized
By daylight-mind, while yet succumbing to their vigor
In unaccustomed ways, a strategy applying
Which might suggest that I with Rilke had been vying—
By pressure felt from sly Unconscious' wily rigor.

    You're getting impatient to hear what I learned?
    The Rilke technique is delay, circumvention,
    A hesitant wrestling, a hidden intention,
    The topic, though central, refused any mention.
    Indeed, clever fox, to ensure you'll have earned
        A grasp of the hard-won sublime
        And all of its grandeur can savor,
        The writer insists on the favor
    That meaning delayed will impose, and the time
    It takes to interpret oracular rhyme.
        He'll even surmise that he needn't
    For pronouns provide any clear antecedent...

A slower, pensive tempo suits when you've the goal
Of showing in an object its unfolding role
Within the Being and Becoming it will face
It its appointed void and presence, time and space.

And yet, to ensure you're not falling asleep,
The length of the lines he won't uniform keep
    Forever, but sometimes may leap,
    And so, with a laugh or a smile,
Entice the attention, the chanter beguile.

257. Getting a Haircut

2 amphibrachs, 2 iambs in each line
x/x x/x x/ x/
x/x x/x x/ x/
x/x x/x x/ x/
x/x x/x x/ x/

"My oldest is seven, Aurora." "Dawn?
How perfect—the sunrise, the waking day.
Is that what you had in your mind?" Can't say,
I once looked it up, but the time's long gone—

And Scarlett, my second, is three." "Oh my,
Another bright red in the morning sky!
From *Gone with the Wind*? Had you *that* in mind?"
"Well, no, but I hear it a lot, I find."

"A love for what shines—for the color red!—
What beautiful names: are they like your own?"
"I'm Jessica." "Nice, but the color-tone—
Not quite so predominant, I'd have said..."
"No, Jessica's *boring*. I thought: no more
Of that!—we'll have names that will *not, not bore*!"

I glanced in the mirror, my hair now done.
The colors, undyed, would survive the test
Of boredom avoided. What sudden fun!
Hair black on the left, with the center white,
Then black—how symmetrical!—at the right.
You'd think of a bird with a rising crest.

258. Daring, Will You Dance with Me Awhile?

iambic lines with initial trochee for triplet effect
/x x/ x/ x/ x/
/x x/ x/ x/ x/
/x x/ x/ x/ x/
/x x/ x/ x/ x/

I am an unknown animal whom not
Any biologist could rightly name.
He is a beast no lasso prose might tame:
Sonnetry psalmer—ever novel thought

Flowered in feeling, paramecium
Passion, rememb'ring elephant, star quarrel,
Lion elation, tiger strife, auroral
Rapture and anger, spry chrysanthemum

Anthem, or tantrum of a whirling lizard,
Maybe a mammoth—old unquiet bones—
Riddle-striation deep in ochre-stones,
Fleeting and leaping mayflies, or a blizzard

Skrymer-besqualled when krakens heave the sea
Moving the meter-music maker, me.

259. The Nature of the Sonnet

iambic lines with initial trochee for triplet effect
/x x/ x/ x/ x/(x)
/x x/ x/ x/ x/(x)
/x x/ x/ x/ x/(x)
/x x/ x/ x/ x/(x)

Vexing verbosity will irk.
Once iteration's gone, we can,
Gardening, weed a furrow, scan,
Farmerlike, wise, the rising work.

Watched will the germination be,
Gratefully garnered. Now the meta-
phor's in the granary. So let a
Challenge from winter come. We'll see...

Credit? Insurance? Wait—a birth cer-
tificate, an identity
Card is a kind of sonnetry—
Lasting, I live! Hold back your mirth, sir.

Artist reborn is found in our
Garden of metaphoric pow'r.

260. Encountering Horace

iambic lines with initial trochee for triplet effect
/x x/ x/ x/ x/
/x x/ x/ x/ x/
/x x/ x/ x/ x/
/x x/ x/ x/ x/

Graduate school, a survey course.
Novel: a long one, called *Tom Jones*—
Plodding along the plot, the horse,
Workaday, feeling weary bones

Needing a respite. Henry Fielding—
Prosy. But now, to pleasure yielding,
Quickened, I hear, in Chapter Ten,
Something as lively now as then:

Quoted are limpid lines from Horace.
Lonely, a melancholy lover,
Cold as the winter's cloudy cover,
Sings of a laughing lady for us.

Piercing the fog, a tuneful ray!
Lord, how I laughed!—again, today.

261. Spoken by a Matriot
first asclepiadic

each line with 2 trochee-plus-iamb units for triplet effect
/, /, /x x/ /x x/ x/
/, /, /x x/ /x x/ x/
/, /, /x x/ /x x/ x/
/, /, /x x/ /x x/ x/

War! War! What is it for? Why do we send away
Joy filled boys to be killed! How can we stay so blind?
Weak, old, senile or sold, speak with a single mind:
"One—Grand—National Plan! Unity—come what may!"

Wait? No. Mate, you must go! Avarice, that's the ground:
Greed. Land. These will command, leading the bosses on,
Blithe, bright, smiling, and white. Followers cringe and fawn.
Doubt? Don't! Patriots won't! Pride is the fiend they've found.

Wild youth, childish, in truth—many of them—will hear:
"Fight! Serve! Smite, never swerve—hark to your country's call!
See? Stand! Heed the demand: tyrants will fail and fall!"
Bold, true, soldiers like *you*, comrades that hold you dear—

Fight—stride—right by your side: brother will run to shield
Blood warm brother from harm—friends, on the battlefield.

262. Overheard

lines with trochee openers for triplet effect
/x x/ x/ x/(x)
/x x/ x/ x/(x)
/x x/ x/ x/(x)
/x x/ x/ x/(x)

"Like it's—I mean it's, like"—the weeds
Conquered and all the words were gone,
Basilisk venom on the seeds,
Pale the remainder, wasted, wan.

"Gonna because I gotta... Wanna?"
Toxic the flora, torpid fauna
Waft a miasma through the wind,
Worsen my asthma. We have sinned.

Cockatrice came to stay. Immortal
Writing is dead except in tomes
Dead from neglect. Infected homes.
Issue from television's portal

Language-pandemic PCBs,
Prison-affliction, lip disease.

263. *Tremendum*
on reading Donald Capps, Men, Religion, and Melancholia

lines with trochaic openers for triplet effect
/x x/ x/ x/ x/
/x x/ x/ x/ x/
/x x/ x/ x/ x/
/x x/ x/ x/ x/

Buttoned-up *Jäcke*, blue, transpiercing eyes,
Ever devoted, seeking discipline,
Otto would, soulful, view the holy in
Mystery Tremor-Lender, crucifies

Pride for a vision *to be trembled at.*
Here is the truthful child-self portraiture:
Punished, he'll stay reluctant to demur—
Sacred the *Ipse dixit*, and that's that.

Tremor—I too enjoyed it, but I sought
Rather the shiver-thrill that Dickinson
Lauded—the hair-raise, goosebumps—puzzling fun
Coming from poetry. Arose a thought:

Heavenly *Adonaïs, Kubla Khan*
Spoke for the god and brought the trembling on.

264. Blowing your nose, more of the cough, what a routine!

lines with trochee-plus-iamb combos for triplet effect alternating with iambic hexameter lines
  /x x/ /x x/ /x x/
x/ x/ x/ x/ x/ x/x
  /x x/ /x x/ /x x/
x/ x/ x/ x/ x/ x/x

    Blowing your nose, more of the cough, what a routine!
I'd never thought of trying verses treating illness.
    Coffee required—haven't a choice—keeping awake
Has got to be the number one consideration.

    Always before, I'd have assumed such a design
Would only work when I portrayed a celebration.
    Here I will show quite the reverse proved to be true:
Expended effort comes across—then happy stillness.

    Never afraid, test the unknown, what can you lose?
Per aspera ad astra! Circle worlds, Magellan!
    Art will be long—ear, nose, and throat soon will be
        cured.
Important isn't fate alone but how you mold it.

    Staying alert? Quatrain the fourth! Soon is it done:
The final lines confirm the story as I've told it.
    Mood has been cheered, coughing displaced, worry
        forgot—
What's coming up? Stay tuned—tomorrow I'll be tellin'...

265. Half Asleep, and Later Answered

8–line iambic opener, with "answer" in anapestic quatrains
xx/ xx/ xx/ xx/
  xx/ xx/ xx/
xx/ xx/ xx/ xx/
  xx/ xx/ xx/

"O you that came to me in flying air,
Come stay a while and be my latest where.
If both the my and me you don't admire,
Shine through the two, transmutable to fire."

"It mightn't be the time for ear to wake,
So, briefly journeying, the dream-flight take,
Tired mind, and when returning let the eyes
Made free of ego pressure be more wise."

.....

Be more kind to the I—merely rhyme it with sky,
   And the me—let it rhyme with the sea.
Let encompassing You be the rhyme for the blue,
   That the color may lustier be.

Of the westfall and dawn let the red carry on
   From the flood to the blood in the heart.
Let the yellow of sun be the smile that is won
   When the mind is replying in art.

In the orange behold, solar-boldened with gold,
   What will forth in the orchard outpour.

Keep the green as our hope, so we'll headlong elope
               To the meadow and heaven adore.

Let the spectrum include both the yous partly blued:
               Dark of indigo, violet mild—
Purple hint of a musk when euterpal at dusk...
               We a folder of joys have compiled.

Seal of blindness unbind when you element find
               To alembicate striving and aim.
Be the small in the large the emotional charge
               In the soul where the Whole finds a name.

266. Latter-Day Cinderella; or, Do You Myth Me?

alternating trimeter and tetrameter lines, opening trochee option for triplet effect— first quatrain:
　/x x/ x/
x/　x/ x/ x/
　x/ x/ x/
x/　x/ x/ x/

　　Evelyn and Jeannette,
My mother and her sister, were
　　Continually set
Apart. "Which girl do you prefer?"

　　Considered uglier
My mother was, though probably
　　What disadvantaged her
Was being stout. A symmetry

　　Of feature, face well-made,
Pleasant and regular, she had.
　　My grandma felt dismayed.
Failure. It was considered bad

　　Not to be thin. Could she
Marry *at all*? Or—*suitably*?

　　Grandpa had wanted boys.
Got girls—then thought: a girl can be

Doctor, or lawyer... Joys
Foreseen consoled him readily.

    Jeannette tried law school. Bad.
Who cared? She'd find a wealthy man.
    My mother, though, was glad
To study medicine, which can

    Fire up an eager mind.
Toronto University
    Delighted her. She'd find
She had become a fine M.D.

    Profession? Family?
Jeannette planned neither, curiously.

267. Portrait of a Lady

alternating trimeter and tetrameter lines,
opening trochee option for triplet effect—
first quatrain:
  x/ x/ x/
/x x/ x/ x/
  x/ x/ x/
/x x/ x/ x/

     My father's family
Used to look up to Cousin Rose.
     Two claims to praise had she,
Priding herself on both of those.

     She played the violin—
Had a certificate to show
     Noted distinction in
Music. The only one to go

     To high school in the Old
Country, completing second year—
     In Russian!—Girl of gold!—
So promising, it would appear—

     Literate, gifted. We
Listened, and smiled admiringly.

     Briefly, what happened next:
There was a man she'd thought to marry.
     Her heart-loved hopes were hexed.
How he would dawdle, tease, and tarry...

> I'd learned the Russian tongue
> And asked her once what poetry
> > She'd loved the most when young.
> Favorite Russian writer? She
>
> > Answered with eager ease:
> "Lérmontov! Insight—deeply wise!"
> > "*Say* a line—*would* you? Please?"
> She stared at me with steady eyes.
>
> > Her Russian made me choke:
> "Life is a foolish, empty joke."

268. Passport

alternating trimeter and tetrameter lines,
opening trochee option for triplet effect—
first quatrain:
  /x x/ x/
 /x   x/ x/ x/
   x/ x/ x/
 /x   x/ x/ x/

     Nineteen thirteen, the year.
Grandma and children, racked with fear
     (Eleven, nine, six, four),
Left the Ukraine. We may deplore

     Her fate, at thirty-five:
How could she keep the kids alive
     When, in Toronto, she
Saw her poor husband horribly

     Killed when he slid and fell
Off of his peddler-horse? They tell
     How she was left alone
With little she might call her own.

     She had to marry soon.
He was well off, a crucial boon.

     True, he was older—much.
But he could buy a home and such…
     Tenants would rent. She'd cook.
Her life took on another look.

Though often she would shout—
A temper!—he would never pout—
　　Patient (my cousins say),
And merely looked the other way.

　　Passover Eve! How he
Had startled been when, suddenly,
　　She weakened. Hospital.
Aged one-O-four, and sorrowful,

　　He hanged himself. And she
Recovered fully, speedily.

269. Jinx

alternating trimeter and tetrameter lines,
opening trochee option for triplet effect—
first quatrain:
  /x x/ x/
x/ x/ x/ x/
  x/ x/ x/
x/ x/ x/ x/

    There was an eerie jinx
On transport in our family.
    It shadowed them. One thinks
Of Ḥayyim's life primarily—

    My uncle—though, again,
I never met the man, of course—
    He'd gone, like Grandpa, when
Falling that morning from his horse.

    Fire engine! Ḥayyim hung
On to the speeding shiny truck
    Which, of a sudden, flung
Him off—uncannily bad luck—

    Leaving a son, and wife.
They, too, led an uncommon life.

    Sammy was very odd,
Smit with a wildness, violence,
    As of a demon-god,
That made no human kind of sense.

> They tell me that he tried
> Strangling his mother. None could say
>   Why. But he soon was tied
> Up and sedated, whisked away.
>
>   In close confinement he
> Month after month lived quietly.
>   My cousin every year
> Visited him. To interfere
>
>   Further no soul would dare.
> And so he spent a lifetime there.

270. Idyll

alternating trimeter and tetrameter lines,
opening trochee option fo0r triplet effect—
second quatrain:
  x/ x/ x/
/x x/ x/ x/
  x/ x/ x/
x/ x/ x/ x/

     In Penetanguishene
Aunt Molly ran a candy store
     (With Sammy no more seen
And Ḥayyim dying long before).

     A factory for wool
Used to be situated in
     The town. I guess you'd pull
The fibers that they'd later spin

     If you were hired to work.
My father helped to treat the fleece
     One summer, didn't shirk
Duty but loathed the smell and grease.

     And me he'd never force
To have a job. I'd take a course

     In summer, happily.
Often, in August, we'd go see,
     Afterward, Grandma, far
Away. We'd go by Pullman car.

Delightful company!
English was difficult for her.
  Sitting there, quietly,
Was what we'd usually prefer—

  So easy to relax
While my step-grandpa, Zaydie Max,
  Would read the Yiddish news
And offer snacks I'd not refuse.

  She couldn't write her name—
But kind and clever, all the same.

271. Two Attractions

alternating trimeter and tetrameter lines,
opening trochee option for triplet effect—
second quatrain:
/x x/ x/
x/ x/ x/ x/
/x x/ x/
x/ x/ x/ x/

    Best Western, he declared,
Was where they'd be at eight A.M.
    I wrote it down. I *cared*—
Looked forward, now, to seeing them—

    Harry and Ethel—whom
I didn't think I'd ever met.
    There, in the breakfast room,
I waited, waited—couldn't let

    The morning disappear...
I'd followed orders faithfully:
    Why were they not yet here?
I asked a waitress. Well, the key

    Was knowing there were two
Best Westerns. Frantic, for a few

    Minutes I tried to nab
A taxi. Got one! Off we sped—
    Ah! there they were. The cab
Had raced. Annoyed, discomfited

> Was Uncle Harry, not
A very tranquil-tempered man.
>   Aunt Ethel, soothing, thought-
ful, helpful, smoothed his mood—her plan
>
>   Always... I'd asked my dad,
Many years back, if maybe we
>   Could go to Kingston. "Bad.
There's just the penitentiary
>
>   And Uncle Harry—why
Venture?" A twinkle in his eye.

272. Today I Am a Man

alternating trimeter and tetrameter lines,
opening trochee option for triplet effect—
first quatrain:
  x/ x/ x/
x/ x/ x/ x/
 /x x/ x/
x/ x/ x/ x/

    Bar Mitzvah time it was.
My grandma came to Bloomington—
    Tricky to do because
Her clubfoot slowed her. Once begun,

    The great adventure grew.
Indianapolis hotel—
    The Claypool. What a view!
Governor's suite! It so befell

    Those were the only rooms
Available—a busy day
    Although a rumor looms
Over the place, the papers say:

    Someone was killed a week
Before. ("A scandal—weird—unique!")
    The ceremony I
Relished. To sing the kiddush and
    In Hebrew chant the high
Whirl of Ezekiel, the grand

Ox-, lion-, eagle-, man-
Faced angel beasts about the throne
Of God: what chapter can
Compete with *that*? I was, I own,

Thrilled. To compose a talk?
The rabbi and my father aided...
Though quite inclined to balk,
I wrote what they had indicated.

I thanked the congregation
But—*skipped the speech!* "Adult" elation...

273. Holiday

alternating trimeter and tetrameter lines,
opening trochee option for triplet effect—
first quatrain:
  /x x/ x/
x/   x/ x/ x/x
  x/ x/ x/
/x x/ x/ x/x

     Midland, Ontario.
At twenty, after graduation
     From college, I would go
Visit my cousins. Jubilation!

     I'd likely get a suit
As well. My Auntie Sadie had
     A clothing store, to boot.
I loved her. I was always glad

     To see her lively boys,
Five of them. Gleaming, wide blue eyes,
     Good humor, vibrant voice,
And laughter—she would light the skies.

     My Uncle Meyer's rage
Good Sadie lightly could assuage.

     We got to see the lake,
There, at the end of Main Street, and
     I knew I'd want to take
A dip. My mother, right at hand

> Would have a doctor-book
> Or journal volume she could read
>   And never have to look
> At water—said she had a need
>
>   To be distracted, so
> She read. And I prepared to go
>   Into the waves. Fifteen
> Minutes had passed. Refreshed, and clean,
>
>   And feeling good, I spied
> My mother. Silently, she cried.

274. Train Whistle

iambic tetrameter, optional trochee
opening for triplet effect—
second quatrain:
/ x x/ x/ x/
x/ x/ x/ x/
/ x x/ x/ x/
/ x x/ x/ x/

Lived in the house for thirty years
But never thought I'd hear the freight
Train's lonely wistful wailing. Late
At night. So faint. Yet aging ears,

Even, can make it out. A print
By Edward Hopper came to mind.
Sunset. A railway station. Find,
Quiet, the elegiac hint.

I grew up in a home not on
The "wrong" side of the track, and so—
No fading wail. My daughter, though,
Hears, from her bed, that drawn-out yawn

Made by the train—the same hometown
I spent my youth in. Tracking down

The traces left by trains in my
Boyhood, I think of visiting
Cousins and Grandma. Then, the thing
Most deeply thrilling was to lie

Carried across the countryside.
Clanking and rolling of the wheels
Under my pullman bed. One feels
Headed for newness. Future's ride.

The Scots Guard, Pipers to the Queen,
Would play. It was the Exhibition,
Toronto's yearly, proud tradition—
Their own "World's Fair," the crowded scene.

My dad was questioned at Black Rock
(Your papers?). He'd re-dream that shock.

275. Fairy Tale Mood

alternating trimeter and tetrameter lines, opening trochee option for triplet effect—first quatrain:
　/x x/ x/
/x　x/ x/ x/
　/x x/ x/
/x　x/ x/ x/

　　Here is the region where
Strange are the legions of the air.
　　Fiber and fold of cloud,
Bunches or clumps, around will crowd

　　While rays jut out behind,
Outlined upon a mist. You'll find
　　Refulgencies will look
As in a Bible story book.

　　Mormon and Millerite,
Bewitched and blinded by the light,
　　Felt an especial grace
Poured out upon the holy place.

　　Virginal Vestal sky
Enrayed, inwrought with fire on high.

　　Next to the curb, a doe
Was feeding. Not a car would go
　　Near in the early morn.
Brisker, a wind was being born.

She looked aside. Soft eye
Of glossy black. I went right by.
　　The grass blades, growing long,
Were tender, edible, though strong.

　　I'd never been so near
To any young unmoving deer.
　　After the outlined rays
Here was another hymn of praise.

　　Idyllic day for me—
Random, the *Märchenpoesie*.

　　Prince Charming, whom we'd cheer
In childhood tales, would next appear.
　　Upon his shirt I saw:
CAPABLE HONEST FEARLESS. Flaw

　　He couldn't ever have—
No, he'd provide a saving salve.
　　Should any maid require
Rescue, he'd be her child-desire.

　　Or so we may suppose.
Thorns on the early morning rose
　　Dark-warningly arise—
But we'll remember sparkling eyes.

　　Mario's Pizza boy.
We saw him toss the dough. Enjoy!

276. Getting Ready to Fight

trimeter and tetrameter lines, opening trochee option for triplet effect—
second quatrain:
   x/ x/ x/
/x x/ x/ x/
   x/ x/ x/
x/ x/ x/ x/

The red assertive outbursts blurt,
     The yellow leaves compete,
The gusts have given the alert,
     The hints of hail and sleet...

     The weak ones at our feet
Speak of the whirl of early hurt,
     The strong will stay to greet
The maelstrom ready, malapert.

     Blustery calls are curt,
Followed by long ones, fiercer, fleet,
Targeted, screaming, to maltreat
     Unweaponed, or ungirt,

People unguarded on the street.
Swift winter victories are sweet.

277. Reply to Kind Acknowledgments
for Liz and Jaimee

0iambic pentameter with optional trochee opener for triplet effect—
first quatrain:
/x x/ x/ x/ x/
x/ x/ x/ x/ x/
/x x/ x/ x/ x/
x/ x/ x/ x/ x/

Few are the days when humor wouldn't aid
To spike a mood, a lotus nectar sweet.
Hermes, the lyre-inventor, ever fleet,
Loud prankster-boy, so proud of what he'd made—

He's on the Internet, and on Eudora,
Electron-light and photon-fast, with fun,
A zany game, no shame at what he's done,
More lively-sprightly than Petrarchan Laura.

The old Hellenic Muses all were female.
Mercury? No. But music, humor too,
Make him the tenth, quick-wingéd Muse, a new
Patron of all who poetize by e-mail.

Then pray, with paean, dithyramb, that he,
Wily, beguiling, smile on you and me.

278. Rolando's Diner

iambic hexameter with optional trochee opener for triplet effect—
second quatrain:
x/ x/ x/ x/ x/ x/
/x x/ x/ /x x/ x/
/x x/ x/ x/ x/ x/
/x x/ x/ x/ x/ x/

"That's what I need, I think—whatever's in that book.
To meditate, relax—I ought to take a look..."
She'd made good apple pie. Now, all hyped up, she took
A swift and lively glance. "Relaxing" was the hook.

"Remember, any thought you have—it isn't you.
Think of it as a cloud moving along the blue—
Watch it go by, float on... Identifying too
Much with a thought is bad. They're pausing, passing through."

"Say, *that* would be a help. I'm so preoccupied—
My daughter's getting married Saturday. I'm tied
Up in the plans, and what a hassle. Think how I'd
Feel—I'm so knotted up—the mother of the bride!"

"You are so lucky, what a blessing!" What a smile.
Mastery—mild. She'd caught the meditating style.

279. Detroit Airport

iambic pentameter with optional trochee opener for triplet effect—
second quatrain:
x/ x/ x/ x/ x/
/x x/ x/ x/ x/
x/ x/ x/ x/ x/
/x x/ x/ x/ x/

Two ladies are delayed along with me.
Lisa, the catastrophic damage claims
Adjudicator for insurers—she,
An eager energetic seeker, aims

To take the early morning flight at eight.
Layover in Atlanta? Long one? Fine.
In Binghamton by two—not extra late…
Kim, on the other hand, can not divine

A reason for a rush. The earliest
Flight she could get: three in the afternoon.
Four-thirty back in Bing. All's for the best.
No bank employees' picnic? Still a boon.

"God's telling me, 'Slow down.'" Two bulky books
On growth and care of puppies. Pleasant looks.

280. Two Sonnets

iambic hexameter and pentameter sonnets, each with optional trochee opener for triplet effect—
first quatrain:
/x x/ x/ x/ x/ x/
/x x/ x/ x/ x/ x/
/x x/ x/ x/ x/ x/
/x x/ x/ x/ x/ x/

Sonnet translation-and-reply: now twenty-five
Times have I done it, making dialogues with men
Writing alone, and I do also—yes, but then
Bringing myself and them in timeless time alive—

Loving to do it, and the marvel of the thing
Is that in all the world of words I'd never known
A dialogic rhyme-realm of the kind I own
As if it were a magic land and I the king.

I love to write, devise, and even lecturing.
Rivaling, too, I love—admire the clinamen,
The summing-up transumption coming in again.
I'll do another twenty-five, I love to sing.

Party for resurrected bard-guests have I thrown:
Poet nor friend who's dead need ever be alone.

Sonnet: a playing wave, a stray saltation,
The trial of a pressure by a free
Being, effectual entelechy,
Growth as a guide outvectoring vexation.

Suppose I pour what means the most to me
Into a vessel for alembication:
Wæs hal! Ves heill!—that Viking-Saxon glee
Is yet a wassail of exuberation.

Growth will begin, an organism rise
From a compounding by the principle
Whereby the acorn, seeking for the sun,

Moving a sap through channels, ramifies
Until the plumping buds feel overfull,
Not knowing what is finished, what begun.

281. Sonnet in a Meter of George Herbert

lines of variable length, optional trochee openers for triplet effect—
first quatrain:
$$/x\ x/\ x/$$
$$/x\ x/\ x/\ x/$$
$$/x\ x/\ x/\ x/\ x/$$
$$/x\ x/\ x/\ x/\ x/$$

      Double, the mindfulness:
   First, of the sonnet, learned last year;
Next, of a body vigil. None the less
Festal the flesh, though now is ever near

      A knowledge that may bless
   If mortal life have moral, clear
The vulnerable wonder; find success
If watching be responsible, if here

      With calm resolve that stress
   Directed be to effort, mere
Dull mulling be avoided. Bravely guess
What life commands: go boldly, foiling fear.

      Re-feeling Windermere,
Dare to be wakeful: seek what may endear.

282. On Reading a Memoir Essay by Andrei Guruianu

iambic pentameter with optional trochee opener for triplet effect—
first quatrain:
/x x/ x/ x/ x/
/x x/ x/ x/ x/x
x/ x/ x/ x/ x/x
/x x/ x/ x/ x/

It was a thing we knew we had to see.
Pincushion, thimble, string—plain introduction.
Seek deeper, and of course you'll raise a ruction.
Odds and—beginnings? Ends. We cannot flee.

Your father's T-shirt fit you, and you'll be
Fit to reclaim the past. A secret suction
Drew you to form a pattern 'mid the fluxion:
Not all I learn is lovely, but it's me.

The bloodstained blazer marked the wedding day,
Marring it, and the two are fast entwined.
Scar of Ulysses—there, new-agéd, find.

We are at hazard. Sailing, danger, play,
Scylla, Charybdis, risk—it's what we are,
Making and marring, borne unwarned afar.

283. Minuet of the Will-o'-the-Wisps
from Hector Berlioz, The Damnation of Faust

iambic pentameter with optional trochee opener for triplet effect—
second quatrain:
/x x/ x/ x/ x/
/x x/ x/ x/ x/
/x x/ x/ x/ x/
x/ x/ x/ x/ x/

Born of the rich corruption of the marsh,
Candle, the spirit of the dead in fire,
They lead you slogging through the swampy mire
For treasure, quicksand, precipice. The harsh

Damned or indentured sparkles from a lyre
Learn an elaborately gallant dance—
Elegant, equable, the measured prance.
But watch: the flames that climb and flicker higher—

Dampened, confounded, baffled! Cloudy chords
Mean a complete obliteration by
Cold fog. Then quiet... Look again! Up—high
On thermal currents, leaping—see?—the hordes

Piccolo pitches reaching! blinding bright!—
Glittering, fluting sprite-swarms fool the night.

284. Why Did I Laugh?
on leaving the fitness room at JCC

iambic hexameter with optional trochee opener for
triplet effect—
first quatrain:
x/ x/ x/ x/ x/ x/
/x x/ x/ x/ x/ x/
/x x/ x/ x/ x/ x/
/x x/ x/ /x x/ x/

My body felt refreshed—machines for muscle tone.
Closing the door behind, I had to laugh out loud.
Piled horizontal strokes, converging racks of cloud,
Met in a triumph sign, speaking to me alone.

I faced a single series of them, strolling home.
Stretching, extending, orange-yellow, with a swell
Of brightness in the wider center, parallel,
Paler in fading length. Between them, fur, or foam,

Lavender-gray, left places for a shade of blue
That I had seen—the ceiling of a rococó
Church in a picture book—then, varying the view,

The strips begin to blend, the orange turning rose,
Tones more intense together. Purple-gray will go
Along, while smoke of wood-fire chilly air-gust blows.

285. Introduction to Poetry

iambic hexameter with optional trochee opener for triplet effect—
first quatrain:
x/ x/ x/ x/ x/ x/
x/ x/ x/ x/ x/ x/
/x x/ x/ x/ x/ x/
x/ x/ x/ x/ x/ x/

> *How good to thank the Lord, utter a hymn of praise*
> *For lovingkindness in the morn, and trust at eve...*
> —Psalm 92.1–2

A decade—ages ten to twenty—weekly, I
Would read aloud the Friday evening service—made
Mainly of psalms, although the praise of angels played
A role, and of the Sabbath Bride, soon coming nigh

To heal the heart—in Hebrew for my family
(No temple being near) in the Sephardic way
I had been taught, the one that people speak today—
How thousandfold a blessing-destiny for me!

Rolling, a rhythm like the one I'm writing here,
Broad and magnific, every long psalmodic line,
In double-three, or -four, or mixed, a moving throng,

Thrilled me. What throat and mouth were making for the
  ear
Told of an underlying might undying. Mine
And...whose? Millenniums of music made me strong.

286. Thoughts on "A Mystical Ballad" by James Russell Lowell

iambic pentameter with optional trochee opener for triplet effect—
first quatrain:
x/ x/ x/ x/ x/
x/ x/ x/ x/ x/
/x x/ x/ x/ x/
/x x/ x/ x/ x/

A maiden fair with snowy breast that glowed
Below her golden hair, bright lunar light,
Felt, when the west wind rose, one quiet night,
Lily-aroma... Memory, a goad,

Try as it might, awoke her not. Instead,
While the soft calm inclined into the day,
Glory, an aura, 'round about her lay:
Her soul had gone, her flower witheréd.

Meanwhile a man, in mist of distant clime,
Was wholly filled with wildest oneness. He,
Brother become to all on land and sea,
Transported by a lore transcending time,

Cried, but arising, now would always know
He was a poet. Edgar Allan Poe

Had found a brother-dreamer, for when James
Lowell depicts the newly mystic bard,

He sounds a darker note, a saying hard
Yet helpful here. Despite the lucent claims

Made of a lightened clay, ethereal,
We learn the lover-heart would "curdle" when
A lily fragrance came too near!—and then,
Blood troubled by a flow'r, the mind is full

Of an awareness of the lost Lenore,
Annabel Lee—virginal mothers all.
Their lily whiteness wilted, they appal.
The seeming theme of either: Nevermore.

Cras, cras, corvina dixit. Yet again,
Dead Mother leaves deep weariness to men.

287. A New Song Rhythm

x/x xx/ xx/ xx/
/x /x /,/, /x /x /

The beauty   of the charm   of appeals   to the ear:
That is what I live for: that is why I'm here.

The feuding   of the art   of the breeze   and the fear,
Faster-coming wind-storm—amplifying drear—

The terror   of the snow   and the ice   and the wind:
Nightmare to the fearful, slowing, having sinned...

The bearer   of the glow   of delight   in the thinned
Flight-air of the tearful, over-yanged the yinned!

A seeking   of the praise   of the great   of the earth
Turns you to a coward, cowering from birth.

A speaking   of the days   that elate   sons of mirth
Yearns in you empowered, dowered and of worth.

The soppy   and the limp   and the low-   lying leaves
Fall upon the grass when lightning-blast bereaves.

The sloppy   and the primp   sadly go: crying cleaves
Autumn dawn— alas!— then dying, fasting, grieves.

The rhymer   in his home   who entrapped   yet will write—
Comfort let him feel if, sheltered in the night,

The quiet   sinking gloam   that is tapped   then despite
Summer-setting wheel-drift's molten into light.

288. First Wind of Morning
a song, versified from the prose hymn "Badeh Naseem" of Shahid Alam

iambic tetrameter with mostly trochee openers for triplet effect—
/x x/ x/ x/
/x x/ x/ x/
/x /x /x /
/x x/ x/ x/
x/ x/ x/ x/

First wind of morning, come to me!
Sunlight must take its time, I know,
Wrapped in milky heaven-glow.
Dream-trapped the air weighs heavily:
The leaves don't move, the day can't grow.

First wind of morning, don't delay:
Thirsting the poet's loath to wait.
Slow's the time when life is late.
Take, let me beg, your veil away:
Let woken soul shine roseate.

First wind of morning, early rays
Gleaming, let buds foresee their fate
That in blooms will jubilate,
Each one made free and fragrant praise
The grant of their enchanted state.

First wind of morn, from humankind
Darkness remove of nightly shade;

In the yards our light unlade—
Peace welling high and dancing find
Fulfilment, by the wind-breath swayed.

First wind of morn, who herald light,
Radiant pinions wide extend,
Gabriel, our Angel Friend,
Aid us from out the boundless height,
And grace from eyes of Maker send.

First wind of morn, your loving hands
Onto the cheeks of worried world
Lay—our care away be hurled:
Let the Unseen who understands
Reveal His Name in heav'n impearled.

289. Sonnet in Alternating Iambic Threes and Fours with a Few Initial Trochees for Triplet Effect

for Metta Sama

first quatrain:
   x/ x/ x/
/x x/ x/ x/
   x/ x/ x/
x/ x/ x/ x/

      To stray, to play around—
Hymning in rhythm, wayward sound—
      With meter most of all—
Will let us live before the fall

      (Bad early apple greed).
It isn't taking *in* we need
      But what, in letting *out*
Our feeling, we may spread about,

      Choiring of life to praise,
Gratefully glad, our length of days.
      Singing will never cease
Allowing us to feel release

      Through what we greatly give:
Thrum to a rhythm, love, and live!

290. Drunk on Lilac

alternating lines in duple and triple rhythms
x/ x/ x/ x/ x/ x/ x/
    xx/ xx/ xx/x
x/ x/ x/ x/ x/ x/ x/
    xx/ xx/ xx/x

By loving sonnets hybridized with other metered forms
    We uncover a way of becoming.
So widen five to seven. By anomalizing norms
    We are clearing the ear and ungumming

The eye, unclothing skin, unhatting heads. A nostril flares
    While the lavender currents are laving
The membranes and unstraining neural chains and raising hairs
    On the neck and the arms. With a craving

For yet unheard-of double-triple rhythmic mixtures we
    Are re-waving the brain, and we know it
When concepts pop like plump dehiscing pods, and crazily
    Scattered drops on the garden will grow it

In tendriled labyrinthine roots and rhizomes ramified,
    Reaching deep, climbing high, spreading wide.

291. Scribal Error?

iambic lines with frequent opening trochees for triplet effect—
first quatrain:
/ x / x x/ x/ x/ (x)
/ x x/ x/ x/ x/
/ x x/ x/ x/ x/
x/ x/ x/ x/ x/ (x)

Or zaru'a la-tsaddik? Or zaraḥ la-tsaddik?

"Light is sown for the righteous": if we alter
Only a letter of the alphabet,
Changing the *'ayin* simply to a *ḥet*,
Light "shines"! We've likely seen the scribe-pen falter.

How many kabbalistic plans were set,
Happily, by that "error" in the psalter,
Finding a fall, and yet a heart-exalter,
In the resplendent metaphor they met!

Light that had shone up high is now below,
Clipped in a shell, *klippáh*, a flaming seed.
Farther to seek the dark, the deep, we go:

Fallen, a force may be unfettered, freed.
Buried, it blazing upward now will burst:
Fountaining fire—how germinal a thirst!

Appendix A: Trisyllable Poems by Mikhail Lermontov

(1)
Angel

At midnight in heaven an angel flew by
    While limning a hymn to the sky.
The moon to the melody listened—in crowds
    The stars were attentive, the clouds.

He praised what is perfect, the bliss to be known
    In paradise gardens alone—
Of God the Almighty the chant, unconstrained,
    Was faithful and pure and unfeigned.

Embracing, he cradled a soul, free of fears,
    Who'd dwell in a valley of tears.
The tune, without words, he had tenderly sung
    Remained in that soul ever young.

And long in the world she would languish and cry
    With anguished desire for the sky,
The heavenly hymn unreplaced by the birth
    Of tedious plaints of the earth.

(2)
Desire

Oh, why can't I fly like that raven up there
    Sweeping over me now through the air?
How fine it would feel to soar high—out of sight!—
    With my freedom the pow'r of my flight!

The west! To the west right away I would fly
    Where the fields of my forefathers lie.
In mist-covered meadows, their fortress of stone
    Forsaken, they molder alone.

Their heraldic escutcheon, heroic reward,
    Might be viewed, and their rust-ridden sword:
With my wing wide outspread I would shake off the dust
    From the shield and the sword and the rust.

I would strike once again the Scots harp, minstrel bird!
    Loud the sound down the halls would be heard.
It would echo in one, in another would fade,
    So from one sound would many be made.

But my pray'rs are in vain, my hopes dashed with disdain,
    By a Fate that forever will reign!
For between my loved land's heather meadows and me
    Lies the vastating void of the sea!

Final scion of warriors fearless, I fade!
    Oh, the snow! I feel broken, betrayed!
Though I live here, was born here, this won't be my home!
    Over plains I, a raven, would roam!

(3)
Mermaid

A mermaid: she glides on the moon-lighted stream
    Of the river, more bright than a dream,
And the splash of her swimming, the sky-reaching spray,
    Will reflect every silvery ray.

Loud-sounding and whirling, the current will stir
    All the cloud-forms in mirroring whir.
As the mermaiden sings, craggy cliffs on the shore
    Make the melody echo the more.

The mermaid is singing: "The water-deeps hold
    Amid fast-fleeting glimmering gold
Of daylight not gone, fish in numbers untold
    Over cities of crystalline cold.

And there, pillowed gently on sand jewel-bright,
    Under shade of thick reeds of huge height,
Lies a warrior sleeping, the jealous waves' prey—
    A lord from a land far away.

We love to comb out, in the calm of the night,
    Curls smoother than silk, and the sight

Of that brow and those lips, lovely, comely to kiss—
    Oh, the blessing, the heavenly bliss!

But to all of our loving, I cannot tell why,
    He—so cold!—will decline to reply.
Not a word. He is still. When he slept on my breast
    Not a whisper, no breath broke his rest."

So murmurs the maid by the bright-shining stream.
    Unappeasable sorrow would seem
To bewilder the waves, while the currents bestir
    All the cloud-forms in mirroring whirr.

Appendix B
Three Poems Written Between First and Second Proofs

(1)
A Valentine

anapests alternating with iambs
xx/ x/ xx/ x/
xx/ x/ xx/ x/
xx/ x/ xx/ x/
xx/ x/ xx/ x/

May the days be warming your angel soul
In the morning rays and the waves that roll
Be in solace momently born and glad
To dissolve their form in the joy they've had.

May the shoreline sound, the abounding one,
With the barbiton as a heart of sun
And the blood made beat to a surfing tune
Be the surging tone of your secret rune.

(2)
Reply to a Friend

amphibrachic tetrameters regular and catalectic
x/x x/x x/x x/x
x/x x/x x/x x/x
x/x x/x x/x x/
x/x x/x x/x x/

I cherish your praise of my valentine poem:
The hymn-seeds I hear and I rapidly sow 'em
    In hope that the tune will the power convey
    Of making folk ponder, "Now, what did he say?"

First fun in the singing, then second in glozing
(While staying awake, favor-aided, from dozing),
    Toccatas on keyboard I touching with ease
    Bring forth (hear the galloping horse?) from the keys.

Cecilia the keyboard on organ so brightly
Could play that an angel, endearing and sprightly,
    Appeared with a spreading of wings in the room
    And soon with a question her pray'rs would illume:

"Dear friend, don't you find it quite strange that your playing
So dazzled the eye that my flight I found straying,
    Not knowing whereto I was headed? And here
    I thought I'd reached heaven. (*Correctly,* my dear.)"

The days of the wrestling with angels are over:
We rather would charm them. The heather and
  clover,
      The cardamom, nard, and the balm of the heart
      Elysïan meadows of music impart.

(3)
Anapestic Improvisation

alternating anapestic 3-beat and 8-beat lines
    xx/ xx/ xx/
xx/ xx/ xx/ xx/ xx/ xx/ xx/ xx/

      Is it possible merely to write
In a way to ensure that a taste may allure the encounterer
  found by a hidden delight
      Who in valley new-venturing strayed
For the reverie'd reason the blood of the season had issued a
  summons? He prostrated prayed
      And for lesson by vision prepared,
Feeling rhythm arise that, bestirred to the skies, would
  encourage him daily to sing what he dared.

Having fasted so long as the impulse had lasted he then had
  partaken when honey was placed
      On the lips that the houri had graced,
For he knew that the Lord had in treasury stored what he
  never must hoard but disperse to the folk.
      One that pleasure to wisdom can yoke
May in long-delayed stages have granted the ages what more
  than our bread will be nourishing food
      Should the sweven be heaven-endued.

Let the chanter whom happiness chose
Not be scanting his duty: pursue then the beauty a Nightingale
finds when beholding a Rose.

BOOKS OF ORIGINAL AND TRANSLATED VERSE
BY MARTIN BIDNEY

Series: East-West Bridge Builders

Volume I: *East-West Poetry:*
A Western Poet Responds to Islamic Tradition in Sonnets,
Hymns, and Songs
State University of New York Press

Volume II: J. W. von Goethe, *East-West Divan:*
The Poems, with "Notes and Essays": Goethe's
Intercultural Dialogues
(translation from the German with original
verse commentaries)
State University of New York Press

Volume III: *Poems of Wine and Tavern Romance:*
A Dialogue with the Persian Poet Hafiz
(translated from von Hammer's German versions,
with original verse commentaries)
State University of New York Press

Volume IV: *A Unifying Light: Lyrical Responses*
to the Qur'an
Dialogic Poetry Press

Volume V: *The Boundless and the Beating Heart*
Friedrich Rückert's The Wisdom of the Brahman
Books 1–4 in Verse Translation with Comment Poems
Dialogic Poetry Press

Volume VI: *God the All-Imaginer:*
Wisdom of Sufi Master Ibn Arabi in 99 Modern Sonnets
(with new translations of his Three Mystic Odes,
27 full-page calligraphies by Shahid Alam)
Dialogic Poetry Press

Volume VII: *Russia's World Traveler Poet:
Eight Collections by Nikolay Gumilev:
Romantic Flowers, Pearls, Alien Sky, Quiver, Pyre,
Porcelain Pavilion, Tent, Fire Column*
Translated with Foreword by Martin Bidney
Introduction and Illustrations by Marina Zalesski
Dialogic Poetry Press

Volume VIII: *Six Dialogic Poetry Chapbooks:
Taxi Drivers, Magritte Paintings, Gallic Ballads,
Russian Loves, Kafka Reactions, Inferno Update*
Dialogic Poetry Press

Volume IX: *A Lover's Art: The Song of Songs in Musical
English Meters, plus 180 Original Love Poems in Reply—
A Dialogue with Scripture*
Dialogic Poetry Press

Volume X: *A Hundred Villanelles, A Hundred Blogatelles*
Dialogic Poetry Press

Other Poetry Books by Martin Bidney

*Bliss in Triple Rhythm—A Toolbox for Poets: Nine Ways to
Shape a Word Song Shown in 300 Original Poems*
Dialogic Poetry Press

*A Treat Not Known Before:
German-American Poetic Dialogues in Ancient Rhythms*
Martin Bidney / Phlipp Restetzki
Dialogic Poetry Press

*Rilke's Art of Metric Melody: Form-Faithful Translations
with Dialogic Verse Replies. Volume One:
New Poems I and II*
Dialogic Poetry Press

*A Hundred Artisanal Tonal Poems with Blogs
on Facing Pages:
Slimmed-down Fourteeners, Four-beat Lines,
and Tight, Sweet Harmonies*
Dialogic Poetry Press

*Shakespair: Sonnet Replies to the 154 Sonnets
of William Shakespeare*
Dialogic Poetry Press

Alexander Pushkin, *Like a Fine Rug of Erivan:
West-East Poems*
(trilingual with audio, co-translated from Russian and
co-edited with Bidney's Introduction)
Mommsen Foundation / Global Scholarly Publications

Saul Tchernikhovsky, *Lyrical Tales and Poems
of Jewish Life*
(translated from the Russian versions of
Vladislav Khodasevich)
Keshet Press

*A Poetic Dialogue with Adam Mickiewicz:
The "Crimean Sonnets"*
(translated from the Polish, with Sonnet Preface,
Sonnet Replies, and Notes)
Bernstein-Verlag Bonn

Enrico Corsi and Francesca Gambino,
Divine Adventure: The Fantastic Travels of Dante
(English verse rendition of the prose translation
by Maria Vera Properzi-Altschuler)
Idea Publications

Literary Criticism

*Patterns of Epiphany: From Wordsworth to Tennyson,
Pater, and Barrett Browning*
Southern Illinois University Press

Blake and Goethe: Psychology, Ontology, Imagination
University of Missouri Press

[For e-books on Mickiewicz, Pushkin, and Bjerke
see martinbidney.com]

Made in the USA
Las Vegas, NV
17 September 2023